Interest in Islamic Economics

T0313311

The definition of the Islamic notion of *riba* is not offered in the *Quran* and *Interest in Islamic Economics* offers the reader various understandings of this Islamic economic concept.

With Islamic banking becoming a more influential factor in the West, an analysis of the concept of *riba* – generally perceived as interest – is long overdue. This book provides a framework for understanding *riba* by examining:

* Linguistics
* Classical judicial analysis
* The historical context
* Modern Economics

Interest in Islamic Economics includes contributions from international scholars who are prominent within their fields. This book is essential reading for academics and professionals with interests in Islamic studies, Banking and Securities, Economics, and Legal History.

Abdulkader Thomas is President and CEO of SHAPE Financial Corporation which offers Islamic financial products and solutions to International financial institutions. He also operates the Islamic finance research site www.ajif.org. He has nearly 25 years of diversified financial services experience and is a graduate of the Fletcher School of Law and Diplomacy in international trade and the University of Chicago in Arabic and Islamic studies.

Routledge Islamic Studies

Interest in Islamic Economics

Understanding *riba*

Edited by
Abdulkader Thomas

LONDON AND NEW YORK

Transferred to digital printing 2010

First published 2006
by Routledge
2 Park Square, Milton Park, Abingdon, Oxon OX14 4RN

Simultaneously published in the USA and Canada
by Routledge
270 Madison Ave, New York, NY 10016

Routledge is an imprint of the Taylor & Francis Group

Typeset in Garamond by
Newgen Imaging Systems (P) Ltd, Chennai, India

British Library Cataloguing in Publication Data
A catalogue record for this book is available from the British Library

Library of Congress Cataloging in Publication Data
A catalog record for this book has been requested

ISBN 0–415–34242–2
ISBN 978-0-415-58935-2 (pbk)

Contents

.

Contributors

Abdulkader Thomas is the publisher of the American Journal of Islamic Finance www.ajif.org and a leading practitioner of Islamic finance. As the authorized translator of the memoirs of Dr Ahmed Elnaggar he holds his primary degree in Arabic and Islamic Studies from the University of Chicago. Mr Thomas is widely published in the field of Islamic banking and finance.

M. Akram Khan is one of the pioneers of Islamic Economics and Finance. He has published widely on various aspects of Islamic economics including Routledge's *Glossary of Islamic Economics and Finance*. He was Deputy Auditor General of Pakistan until 2003 when he joined the United Nations' Office of Internal Oversight. He is currently Chief Auditor in the United Nation Mission in the Congo.

Vincent J. Cornell is Professor of History and Director of the King Fahd Center for Middle East and Islamic Studies, University of Arkansas, Fayetteville, Arkansas. He also serves as Chair of Studies in the Religious Studies Program at the University of Arkansas. Dr Cornell is a noted author and lecturer on Islamic studies. His major works include *The Realm of the Saint: Power and Authority in Moroccan Sufism* (Austin, TX: University of Texas 1998) and *The Way of Abū Madyan: Doctrinal and Poetic Works* (Cambridge: The Islamic Texts Society, 1996). Dr Cornell is one of the leading contemporary Islamic thinkers in North America.

Emad H. Khalil is a partner in the law firm of Jones Day resident in the Singapore office, where he co-chairs the Firm's Global Projects practice and the Asia Lending/Structured Finance practice. Mr Khalil has extensive experience with global Islamic financial transactions.

Iman Abdul Rahim is a professional translator based in Damascus.

Mahmoud A. El-Gamal is Professor of Economics and Statistics at Rice University, where he holds the endowed Chair in Islamic Economics, Finance, and Management. In the latter part of 2004, he served as the first Scholar-in-Residence on Islamic Finance at the US Department of Treasury. More information about him is available at http://www.ruf.rice.edu/~elgamal

Najwa Abdel Hadi is a professional Arabic instructor based in Fairfax, Virginia.

Ruba Alfattouh holds her degree in English from Brigham Young University and teaches English in Abu Dhabi.

M. Umer Chapra is one of the leading authorities on Islamic Economics. His career includes serving as an advisor to the Saudi Arabian Monetary Agency and the Islamic Development Bank. His published work includes the Islamic Foundation's *Towards a Just Monetary System* which is one of the primary resources in the field.

Sh. Wahba Al Zuhayli is the Dean of the College of *Sharia'a* at Damascus University and a member of numerous *Sharia'a* supervisory boards governing Islamic banks. His work *Fiqh As Sunnah wa Adalatiha* is one of the leading and most widely relied upon manuals of modern Islamic Jurisprudence.

Sh. Yusuf Talal DeLorenzo – Sh. DeLorenzo is a widely respected scholar of Islamic finance. He is a director of Yasaar Ltd, a *Sharia'a* advisory body, as well as the *Sharia'a* supervisory panels of financial institutions worldwide, including the Dow Jones Islamic Market Indexes. He has translated numerous classical Islamic *fiqh* works from Arabic, Persian, and Urdu into English and provided commentary thereon.

Preface

During the mid 1980s, I first researched the question of *riba* in our modern financial world. Somewhat instantly, I understood that the classical texts of *fiqh* do not use this term in the same way that some modern financiers and their regulators sometimes apply it. More confusingly, I understood with clarity that the broad Muslim public did not have a clear idea of the term. For years, English speaking Muslims were informed by an obscure footnote in the Yusuf Ali interpretation of the meaning of the *Quran* that *riba* only meant exorbitant interest or consumer interest, but not production interest. Elsewhere, Azharite scholars were determining that interest is simply a form of profit on a *mudaraba*. Some Muslims were of like mind with modern Jews and Christians who for the most part ignore the prohibition of interest in their own holy books.

These and other questions led to my direct attack on the concept of *riba* and its many angles. What does the Arabic language have to say? Hence, I went to a seven-hundred-year-old Arabic lexicon. How about the history of *riba* among the peoples of the book? For this answer, I am indebted to my old friend Mansour Al Mujahid. And the classical scholars, what has been their view? Here, I turned to a dear teacher, Sh. Wahba Al Zuhayli, and commissioned the translation of his seminal article on *riba* in his comprehensive compendium of Islamic law.

Through these elements of my research, it is clear that *riba* and interest are too often the same. Certainly, most banking transactions in the west are susceptible to *riba*. If that is the case, then why are we Muslims so confused? To secure this answer, I examined with my friend Emad H. Khalil's help the history of interpretive chicanery, sometimes government instigated, that has taken place in a key center of Islamic learning. I also benefited from the insights of noted Pakistani economist M. Akram Khan to develop a related piece on the difficulties that his country has faced routing out interest. Economists M. Umer Chapra and Mahmoud A. El-Gamal also provided useful economic analyses.

In the end, *riba* can be diagnosed and financial relations may be had free from it – even in America! In this humble endeavor, I am hopeful, God willing, to have helped readers to understand how to identify *riba* and live free from it. I dedicate this work in loving memory of my dear friend Said Zafar who encouraged me in so many ways to fight *riba* and bring *riba* free choices to his adopted and my native North America.

Acknowledgments

This book is the outcome of nearly 20 years of personal inquiry into a single word *riba* ربا upon which one's entire view of banking and finance turns, and for many of us there is an eternal reward for successfully evading transactions involving it. The word *riba* was not defined by the Prophet Muhammad, peace and blessings be upon him, during his life. The research that comprises this book includes important contributions from some scholars whose views I may not fully embrace but which shed light on this definition in a way so as to ease the burden of those who wish to understand what this word is, why it invalidates contracts, and how one might understand it.

I am deeply indebted to my dear friend and teacher Sh. Yusuf Talal DeLorenzo for preparing a thoughtful and kind Introduction allowing us to establish context for the book as a whole. Three kind ladies assisted me with translations of certain texts: Ms Ruba Alfattouh and Ms Iman Abdul Rahim provided key translations of two of the most important chapters. With the assistance of our auntie Abla Najwa Abdel Hadi, I was able to ensure that the translations conveyed the meaning in English that was most suitable for understanding this term in a modern financial context.

Years ago, I convinced Dr Vincent Cornell to begin his research into this matter. With his keen insights into comparative religions, Dr Cornell, whom many of us know as Sh. Mansour, prepared "In the Shadow of Deuteronomy," which is a very useful contextual insight into the question of interest in Christianity and Judaism.

Many of us have long relied on the work of Sh. Wahba Al Zuhayli. Although there have been efforts to translate his work into English, I was not in agreement with the substance of the most prominent translation, and Sh. Wahba was kind enough to authorize a fresh translation in which Ms Abdul Rahim assured that no external opinions were dragged in.

Understanding the *"Sharia'a* Prohibition of *Riba"* is a critical issue as many modern Muslims are unaware that governments have attempted to influence and sway Islamic scholars and jurists in the direction of allowing interest as not being part of *riba*. Emad H. Khalil was kind enough to allow me to restructure and redevelop one of his research papers in order to gain insight into this type of manipulation over an extended period in Egypt. The paper forms the basis for two chapters and is supplemented by a translation of the most recent Egyptian effort to come to the same conclusion of permitting interest. Eminent Pakistani scholar M. Akram Khan was generous enough to provide a short note on the same types of government interference in Pakistan in the past.

A key supporter of this research was the Islamic Foundation in Leicester, England. By their kind intervention, I have been permitted to include a meaningful paper putting *riba* into an economic context by the respected economist M. Umer Chapra who has taught us so much over the years through his research. I have also enjoyed the cooperation of my friend, but frequent sparring partner, Dr Mahmoud Elgamal. Although there are a number of areas relating to this very subject, his economic analysis of the divine wisdom in banning wisdom transcends all other debates.

It took me a very long time to work on this subject, I could have spent an equally long time attempting to achieve the erudition of the contributors. With their kind assistance, I have been able to bring together better than I could have otherwise dreamt of researching and writing alone. I am most pleased, however, that these contributions providing unique, detailed views give readers the ability to make an informed personal or academic decision about the meaning of this word and its role in finance.

Abdulkader Thomas
April 2005

Abbreviations

BIS   Bank of International Settlements
GDP   Gross Domestic Product
IDB   Islamic Development Bank
IFSB   Islamic Financial Services Board
IMF   International Monetary Fund
LTCM Long-Term Capital Management
OECD Organization for Economic Cooperation and Development
SBP   State Bank of Pakistan

Introduction to understanding *riba*

Sh. Yusuf Talal DeLorenzo

At one and the same time, Islam's prohibition of *riba*, arguably the most important element in its system of finance, is clear in terms of the importance accorded to it by the religion; yet, in terms of why this should be so, the matter is one that requires some contemplation. There is a degree of subtlety here that may very easily be overlooked. In recent years, a variety of Muslim reformists, modernists, economists, and even traditional scholars[1] have failed to appreciate the subtleties inherent in this prohibition. Then, based on their own flawed understanding, some have even gone so far as to declare that the prohibition that was, is no longer; because times have changed, and society has moved forward, and people are no longer in danger of being sold into slavery to repay their debts! Some of our modern reformers of Islamic thought have had the audacity to claim that "Islamic Finance" is unnecessary because the whole issue of *riba* is an artificial one, something from the depths of an Islamic past that is better forgotten. Still others, unable to ignore or deny the prohibition, would have us believe that Muslims in the modern world have been given license to transact with *riba* because today's society is not an Islamic society and Muslims may legitimately deal in *riba* with others in a non-Islamic society!

The motivation for such pronouncements has stemmed in the main from a lack of confidence on the part of these "reformers" that Islam can offer a valid alternative to the modern, conventional, interest-based system of finance. After all, they argue, the world of high finance today is a very sophisticated world indeed. So what could a system of finance that originated in the desert over a thousand years ago have to offer to such a world? And how could it possibly compete? In short, most of our "reformers" believe that Muslims cannot survive in the world today, either as societies, or as businesses, or as individuals, without dealing in interest. Finally, as the ultimate capitulation, they assert that there is simply no need for something called "Islamic Finance" because, after all, finance is finance. Of course, the irony in all of this is that these voices originate from civil servants, business professionals, and scholars in so-called third world countries that are literally awash in interest! So deep is the sea of debt servicing in which they find themselves that their national budgets are insufficient even to pay the interest on their loans. For most of these countries, the repayment of principal is such a remote possibility that it is never seriously considered![2] Then, finding themselves condemned in perpetuity to paying interest, their only response appears to be ... what? A pathetic attempt to discredit their own religious teachings?

The Prophet, upon him be peace, taught, "A time will come over people when not a one of them will remain other than consumers of interest; and even those who do not consume it will be effected by its dust."[3] Indeed, that time has come. But this does not mean that such a time, and such an all pervasive plague of *riba*, will or must remain. Generally speaking, this sort of teaching by the Prophet, upon him be peace, was meant more in the spirit of admonition than as prophecy. But even as prophecy, the pronouncement is not a final one. Yes, in the economies of the modern world, interest is all but unavoidable. Like second hand smoke, it can affect even those who are not directly involved in it. But that does not mean that Muslims should simply succumb to it. Because other social evils are prevalent, or because other prohibited things like pork and wine are widely consumed, this does not mean that Muslims should abandon their scruples and partake of all manner of iniquity because the rest of society finds it inoffensive! The spirit of the Prophet's teaching is to encourage vigilance in regard to *riba*. Moreover, *riba* is not merely a matter of personal morality. The allusion was made earlier to a degree of subtlety in regard to *riba*. This volume will undoubtedly make this clearer. However, to summarize the matter here at the outset, *riba* at the level of the individual may seem relatively harmless; at the societal level, however, the proportions of the problems inherent in *riba* are magnified many times over.

> O you who believe! Do not gorge yourselves on riba, doubling and redoubling it.
>
> (3:130)

Let us not forget that the first verses on the subject were revealed at Makkah, at a time when the believers were a small and disadvantaged minority. The earliest Muslims at Makkah in no way represented a group of capitalists. Nor is it likely, given their straitened circumstances, that they gave much thought to one day having their own government, or legal authority, or economic system. Even so, it was there that the first verses regarding *riba* were revealed.

> Whatever you give as riba so that it might bring increase through the wealth of other people will bring you no increase with Allah. But what you give as charity, seeking the countenance of Allah, [will be blessed] for those are the ones who will truly receive increase
>
> (30:38–39)

With its inimitable and characteristic economy of words, the *Quran* clearly identifies *riba* in this and in other verses as an injustice, an economic evil, an impediment to spiritual growth, and a threat to the welfare of society. Furthermore, the *Quran* does not deal with the subject of *riba* in isolation. On the contrary, much of the *Quranic* revelation is concerned with the reform of the individual and society. The *Quran* often speaks of how the Almighty will bring the wealthy low for their arrogance and disregard of the poor and needy.[4] The principle it teaches is that wealth is given by Allah as a trust, and that it is a trial for those who possess it.[5] Likewise, the wealthy are urged throughout the *Quran* to care for the economically disadvantaged, whether these are relatives, orphans, slaves, the poor, travelers, beggars, debtors, prisoners of war, the divorced, migrants, or whoever is in need. Greed and selfishness are roundly condemned as traits inimical to true belief. Throughout the *Quran*, the theme of justice, including economic justice, echoes resoundingly.[6]

But the question remains. When all of this is true, why is it that Muslims have so lost sight of the importance of this prohibition? The attempt to understand the situation of modern Muslims in regard to *riba* may well begin with a look into Islamic law and history.[7]

No legal system can remain viable without a subject, without an object for its application. In recent centuries, throughout much of the Muslim world, the only significant finance available to Muslims has been what Western commercial banks have had to offer. For whatever reasons, most of them political, conventional banking supplanted the *Sharia'a*-based system of finance. Without active commerce, the *Sharia'a* rules for transacting became no more than a subject of academic concern, like a dead language. Without renewal, without constant attention on the part of qualified jurists to changing circumstances and realities, those rules, like any other system, would atrophy and eventually lose relevance. In short, when *riba*-free finance was no more, the legal system that supported it became inoperative and, with nothing to respond to, it became unresponsive. Throughout the Muslim world, legal thought on the subject of transactions passed into a long period of stagnation and neglect.

Thus, in recent centuries, over much of the Muslim world, the *Sharia'a* of Islam was marginalized when Islam's social and economic institutions were displaced by Western models. For example, in the Indian subcontinent the British imported their own legal system leaving little more than what amounted to "marrying and burying" as the legitimate concerns of what they termed Muhammadan Law. Under those circumstances it is hardly surprising that a century or two later, when Muslims finally gained independence, their own Islamic legal institutions were woefully unprepared to deal with twentieth century realities. The same was true of Islamic political, educational, and economic institutions. Thus, during the decades and even centuries in which Islam's institutions were marginalized by colonial and other powers, it is not surprising that Islamic jurisprudence, with no place to apply its dynamic of *ijtihad*, was relegated to a long confinement in exclusively academic settings. In order for it to break out of the confines of academia it required a real subject, a practical and living application, and practitioners who were not only conversant with the classical discipline but who, in addition, were cognizant and appreciative of the changes the world had undergone in the intervening centuries.

At the same time, however, the economic system of the world, along with its reliance on *riba*, thrived and, as an adjunct to its connection in real terms with society, continued to develop. The industrial revolution brought about profound changes in economics and law, as did the rise of consumerism, and developments in technology. While all of this was taking place, finance and banking evolved, and so did the legal, business, and regulatory environments in which these flourished. Thus, by the time Muslims began once again to think in terms of Islamic models of finance, just after the end of the Second World War, the world had changed, business had changed, and *riba* was everywhere.

It was perhaps the wealth generated by oil that provided the real impetus for the revival of Islamic jurisprudence on the subject of finance and commercial law. In the decades of the 1950s and 1960s, at a time when newly independent Muslim states were attempting to come to terms with their cultural and religious identities, a handful of Muslim thinkers began speculating on the theoretical foundations of an Islamic economic system, often as an afterthought to their musings about an ideal Islamic state. The state banks of a few Muslim countries held conferences to discuss the subject, a few scholars published papers in journals and, in general, the interest in the subject was academic.[8] But with the wealth from oil, the petrodollars of the 1970s, a number of banks and investment houses were established with the clear mandate to operate in accordance with *Sharia'a*. This is what marks the beginnings of modern Islamic Finance.

At the time, to be candid, there was little that was clear in regard to banking operations conducted in accordance with the *Sharia'a*; in fact, the two, *Sharia'a* and banking, seemed particularly unsuited to any sort of collaboration. Indeed, throughout the Muslim world, the common understanding was that there was nothing lawful about banks. Even employment in banks was shunned in religious circles.

It was then that the new Islamic banks called upon scholars of the *Sharia'a* for answers. In those early days, there were not many scholars with knowledge of finance and banking. The handful of scholars that had published on related subjects were without practical experience, having had no exposure whatsoever to modern banking, investment funds, and capital markets. In many cases, the scholars were brought in by the banks on the basis of their reputations alone, reputations as authors and authorities on Islamic subjects in general; not as experts or authors of works on finance![9] Thus, as in any fledgling industry, there was a period of adjustment and learning. The process was a rewarding one, however, and though there were difficulties, a good deal of progress was achieved. It is possible, and not unfair, to characterize the jurisprudence of this early period, perhaps the first two decades, as the jurisprudence of revival and recovery. During this period, scholars looked to the past and reestablished meaningful connections between the *Sharia'a* and the practical world of modern commerce and trade. In this undertaking they turned to the vast body of legal literature created by earlier generations, to the rules of commerce in the legal handbooks and glosses, and to the digests of case law or fatwa literature. In many cases, the sources they referred were of their own particular legal schools of thought *madhahib*, though there appears to have been, early in this process, a general understanding among most scholars that consideration would have to be given to the opinions and methodologies of at least the four major legal schools.

At this time, too, perhaps owing to the extraordinary demands placed upon individual scholars hired as advisors, and partially in order to bring in a wider range of legal opinion representing each of the four major schools of classical legal thought, as well as regional and cultural trends, Islamic banks began to establish *Sharia'a* supervisory boards, often with as many as 6 or 8 members.

Then, throughout the formative period of the 1970s and 1980s, *Sharia'a* deliberations on issues related to modern banking were carried out collectively by formally constituted *Sharia'a* boards. Papers were written and discussed, both internally among *Sharia'a* supervisory boards and externally at conferences and seminars. The most important factor in everything that took place at the time, however, was that the jurisprudence had a real subject with which to deal and interact. The deliberations of *Sharia'a* boards were more than speculation, or theoretical musings, or academic exercises. Real issues were involved and, perhaps more importantly, real peoples' money. For, from the day the Islamic banks opened for business they have attracted deposits from average Muslim consumers, in addition to their high net worth and institutional clientele. For Muslims, Islamic Finance has come as a godsend, allowing them the opportunity to invest and transact in ways that leave their consciences clear. This has come as a great relief to Muslims the world over, even if our "reformers" continue to show disdain for the whole process.

Certainly, a part of their disdain is attributable to the mistakes and missteps taken by the industry in the early days. In Egypt, for example, a financial scandal in a high profile Islamic bank gave already hostile regulators the opening they needed to suppress Islamic banking and finance in that country before these really had a chance to establish themselves. In Pakistan, a country of very capable and sophisticated bankers as well, the attempt on the part of the government of General Zia ul-Haq in the early 1980s to "Islamize" the banking system overnight, by means of marshal law fiat, brought about patently cosmetic changes that were ridiculed by bankers and the general public. Obviously, neither of these situations did much to further the cause of Islamic Finance; on the contrary, the result was a serious loss of credibility for the industry in two key Islamic countries.

Even so, given the inherent depth and breadth of classical Islamic commercial law, modern jurists found a veritable ocean of practical and theoretical jurisprudence from which to draw upon while confronting the challenges of the modern marketplace. Then, while it might be possible to characterize the first few decades of modern Islamic Finance as a period of revival, from the 1950s to the mid-1990s, the last decade might better be understood as a period of significant innovation. Using the nominate contracts for trade and exchange as their building blocks, modern Muslim jurists have provided *Sharia'a*-compliant solutions to an ever-expanding spectrum of needs and profiles.

Near the end of the decade of the 1980s, the situation began to change. By this time, Islamic Banking and Finance had grown far beyond the expectations of even the most fervent among its early supporters. In fact, Islamic Finance was becoming recognized as something of a growth industry; and a number of multinational banks and asset management companies were taking an interest in its development. Internally too, within the industry itself, significant developments were afoot. One of the major reasons for these developments was the progress made by Muslim jurisprudents in understanding the modern businesses of commerce and finance and in applying *Sharia'a* principles and precepts to them. Another reason was the facility developed by *Sharia'a* boards with the nominate contracts, such that they began to feel comfortable with novel configurations. Other reasons for development were the growing discourse on Islamic Finance in the English language and the entry of global asset managers. Finally, the academic discourse on the subject had achieved the equivalent of critical mass and many issues were moving toward consensus, the all important *ijma'* or general acceptance of the juristic community considered a binding adjudicator (or indicator, *dalil*) in Islamic law.

Undoubtedly, big players with their human and capital resources did much to spur the development of Islamic Finance. Though their influence on the jurisprudence of Islamic Finance has been subtle, the multinationals and global asset managers helped the jurisprudence of Islamic Finance to move into a significant new stage of creativity. Certainly a part of this involved the growing facility of *Sharia'a* scholars with English. To a degree, these two factors went hand in hand. Clearly it is true in any profession that it is one thing to acquire experience, and quite another to have exposure to the top echelons of that profession. As *Sharia'a* scholars began working closely with international bankers and Wall Street insiders, with some of the most knowledgeable and talented individuals in the business, it was then that the exchange of ideas began in earnest. In some cases, a single member of a *Sharia'a* board would take part in such exchanges and then report back, formally or figuratively, to his peers on the board. Exchanges of this nature provided *Sharia'a* scholars with valuable, and often key, insights into business procedures and practices that might otherwise have remained obscure and therefore suspect. Nor was this process of exchange a one way street. On the contrary, as their own understanding of modern business concepts and practices increased, *Sharia'a* scholars were emboldened to make comments of their own, often pointing out parallels that exist between fundamental *Sharia'a* concepts of transacting and modern commercial law and then moving on to extrapolate shared concepts and to consider their possible applications in modern situations. Through such exchanges many scholars acquired an insiders' grasp for the context of modern commerce. Clearly, such exposure added perspective and depth to the deliberations of *Sharia'a* boards on the jurisprudence of modern Islamic Finance. Finally, while it may be difficult if not impossible to quantify or point directly to such intangibles, it is equally as difficult to deny their influence.

The most important factor in the transition from the jurisprudence of recovery and revival to a more proactive and participatory jurisprudence of transformation and adaptation was the reconfiguration of the nominate contracts or, perhaps more exactly, the concept that the nominate contracts may be thought of as building blocks that may be constituted and creatively reconstituted for the achievement of all manner of objectives. From the very beginnings of the Islamic banks in the 1970s it was apparent that a certain degree of adaptation was required for the successful application of the nominate contracts in modern finance. For example, in order to make the *murabaha* contract effective in the business of inventory or short term trade financing, it was necessary to depart somewhat from the classical model by combining a promise to buy on the part of a client with the actual purchase by the bank of goods from third party suppliers. Then, in addition to the actual *murabaha* contract, a further transaction is appended: the promise to purchase that is made by the client or prospective buyer.[10] This arrangement, however innocent in appearance, actually brought up a host of issues for the early *Sharia'a* boards. Nonetheless, as the needs of modern trade were such that a *Sharia'a*-compliant alternative to trade financing by means of conventional, interest-based financing was required, the classical *murabaha* was transformed into the modern *Murabaha li'l-Amir bi'sh-Shira*, *murabaha* with an order to purchase that has now become commonplace in Islamic banking.

Following the success of this experience, *Sharia'a* boards went on to engineer and approve a host of hybrid nominates, using a single nominate like *murabaha* in different configurations like parallel *murabaha*, reverse *murabaha*, back to back *murabaha*, and reverse parallel *murabaha* contracts, or using a plurality of nominate contracts in combination with one another. In this way, the nominate mainstays of classical Islamic commercial law, *musharaka, ijara, salam, istisna'a, mudaraba*, and others have been transformed and adapted in a variety of ways to modern needs and circumstances. In some cases, these were applied to bring about interest-free alternatives to conventional mortgages for the financing of homes;[11] in other cases, these became key elements in investment funds, project finance and, most recently, in *sukuk*.[12] In fact, the contracts for the financing of homes by one US company have recently been securitized and converted to *sukuk* issued by Freddie Mac with all the qualities of US government-secured paper. It would be interesting, as a case study from a purely academic perspective, to follow and analyze the transformation and adaptation of all the different nominates applied in that one instrument, as it includes the creative application of many disparate elements.

As alluded to earlier, one of the factors in the development of a modern jurisprudence of Islamic Finance has been the ability of scholars to communicate their ideas among themselves and, through debate and discussion with colleagues and peers and, to an extent, through demonstrating by means of actual business applications, to bring about general agreement and approval throughout the scholarly community. The importance of this point, of this process itself, cannot be over emphasized because the concept of *ijma'* as a legal indicator, *dalil*, carries very nearly the same authority as the revelational sources[13] themselves. Then, whatever questions, reservations, or doubts the critics of modern scholarship on this subject may have, the fact that *Sharia'a* boards and fiqh academies have been able to achieve consensus on so many key issues suffices to establish the legitimacy of modern Islamic Finance and, what is more important from a practical perspective, sets the stage for the establishment of industry standards which may, in turn, provide the impetus for real industry growth. Through the efforts of the various academies, especially those with international and regional representation, like the Organization of the Islamic Conference Fiqh Academy, and through the regular exchanges by scholars at seminars and conferences, particularly those like the annual Albaraka seminars in Jeddah, a serious process has been ongoing since the 1970s. Finally, with the establishment of the Auditing and Accounting Organization for Islamic Financial Institutions in the early 1980s, the process for bringing scholarly attention to focus on particular issues was streamlined, with the result that consensus could be brought about through an institution, and then regular standards for a wide spectrum of *Sharia'a*-related issues could be approved and implemented. Finally, the newly established Islamic Financial Services Board (IFSB) ensures that the efforts of *Sharia'a* scholars for the achievement of consensus and standardization will find a place in legal and regulatory systems worldwide.

In the brief span of a few decades, *Sharia'a* scholars across the world have worked together and with others to bring about the revival of one of Islam's most important institutions, its finance. In the process, Islamic jurisprudence has undergone significant development. Moreover, the revival of Islamic commercial energies has led to an expansion of cooperation and mutually beneficial exchanges between Muslims and other peoples of the world. All of this has come about as a result of the attempt by modern Muslims to deal with the problem of *riba*. Today Islamic Finance is an industry with huge growth potential. Perhaps its greatest challenge, however, is an internal one: to make modern Muslims aware of the problem of *riba* and to assure them that viable alternatives to the financial products and services that they currently depend upon are available to them, or soon will be, *in sha' Allah*.

As the readers of this book will soon discover for themselves, the issue, while certainly complex, is not beyond reason or comprehension. The author deserves our thanks for his admirable presentation of the complexities attending the revelation, interpretation, and application of the prohibition of *riba*. In fact, Abdulkader Thomas has begun in a modest but effective way to emerge as one of Islamic Finance's most effective voices. In recent years, he has published a *Guide to Understanding Islamic Home Finance*, scholarly chapters in books, and a definitive book on the subject of Islamic bond equivalents (*sukuk*). In addition, he has spoken eloquently about Islamic Finance at numerous forums and conferences worldwide; and he has proven himself an effective teacher at seminars arranged for financial professionals. On the internet, his efforts, too, have been legion. In addition to maintaining a website for *The American Journal of Islamic Finance* at www.ajif.org, he is a regular contributor to ongoing web discussions and is ever prepared to clarify, assist with, or even speak out in defense of, issues of current relevance in the field. As a practitioner, he has been responsible for many key innovations in Islamic Finance, and consumers in the United States and elsewhere have benefited from his work in bringing Islamic financial products and services to market. Given the nature of the challenge outlined in the preceding paragraph, the work of the author will become increasingly more valuable in the months and years to come.

Wa billahi al-tawfiq!

Notes

1 The author will discuss the opinions and reasoning of some of these scholars in this volume.
2 Last year I had the opportunity to address an interfaith conference on North South Economic Inequalities and was the only speaker to point a finger at interest as the culprit, even though each of our faiths, the three Abrahamic faiths, is in possession of scripture that clearly prohibits interest. Afterwards several delegates admitted to me that, even though they were vaguely aware of the scriptural teachings on interest, they had never thought of interest in the context of a real factor in the perpetuation of economic inequality!
3 This hadith was related by Abu Hurayrah and was included in the collection of Ibn Majah, *Kitab al-Sunan* (2269). The commentator, al-Sindhi, writing in the eighteenth century of the Common Era, when much of the Muslim world had been colonized by European powers, explained that the hadith pointed to another of the Prophet's miracles because he had foretold the future. Then, in an exclamation of pious dismay, he wrote, "This refers to our own times. Verily we belong to Allah, and unto Allah is our return!"
4 *Quran* 17:16, 23:64, 28:58, 28:81, 57:24.
5 Ibid., 2:155, 3:186, 8:28.
6 Ibid., 17:35, 6:152, 26:181–183.

7 Much of the material in the paragraphs that follow is taken from my paper for the London Conference in May of 2004 held by the IFSB. The paper was titled, "Shariah Boards and Modern Islamic Finance: From the Jurisprudence of Revival and Recovery to the Jurisprudence of Transformation and Adaptation."

8 It is interesting to note that as early as 1953, the State Bank of Pakistan had hired an Egyptian economist with Islamic credentials as a consultant tasked with helping to bring about reform in the banking system. It is even more revealing to note that very little was accomplished at the time and that the expert later proposed bending the rules of *Sharia'a* to allow for lending at a premium, for which he suggested the name *'aqd al-tamwil* (financing contract)!

9 Dr Muhammad Abd al-Ghaffar al-Sharif, *The Shariah Supervision of Islamic Banks*, paper presented at the First Conference of Shariah Supervisory Boards for Islamic Financial Institutions, organized by AAOIFI in Bahrain, October, 2001.

10 In fact there are two promises inherent to this transaction; the promise of the client to buy from the bank, and the promise of the bank to sell to the client. The entire matter became the subject of much discussion by the scholars at the First Conference of Islamic Banks at Dubai in 1979. Their collective fatwa approving this arrangement was a significant milestone in the jurisprudence of modern Islamic finance.

11 Brief descriptions of how all three of these nominates have been adapted to form the basis of different home financing programs may be found in Abdulkader Thomas and Virginia Morris, *Guide to Understanding Islamic Home Finance* (New York: Lightbulb Press, 2002).

12 See, Abdulkader Thomas and Nathif J. Adam, *Islamic Bonds: Your Guide to Issuing, Structuring and Investing in Sukuk* (London: Euromoney Books, 2004).

13 These, of course, are the texts of the *Quran* and the *Sunnah*.

1 Riba in Lisan Al Arab*

Translated by Ruba Alfattouh, Abdulkader Thomas, and Najwa Abdel Hadi

Riba

The grammatical declination of the noun *riba* is *yarbu-rubuwwan-riba'n*. *Raba* (the past simple verb) means: increased and grew. The inflectional *arbaytuhu* (first person pronoun and objective included) means, "I increased it." In the Holy *Quran*, "*yurbe* the charities" means, "increase the charities." From here, the forbidden *riba* was taken. God the Great said, "The *riba* you perpetrate (*leyarbuwa*) to augment people's money does not *yarbu* (grow) with God." Abu Ishaq said, "*yarbu* means that man pays something in order to be compensated for more than he paid." In most interpretations, this is not forbidden. But, there is no reward for the one who increased what he took. He said, "*riba* is of two kinds: one is forbidden. Every loan that is returned with an increase, or for which a profit is gained, is forbidden. The permissible *riba* is to donate money, asking God for more than the money you gave away, or to give it as a gift so that you would be given even more."

With respect to pronunciation, Al Fara' said, "In the previous *Quranic* verse, the letter was read *leyarbuwa* with the *y* sound and the short *a* vowel sound after *w*. Also 'Asem and Al-A'mash read it this way. The people of Hijaz read it as (*letarbw*) with the *t* letter and as a nominative case. He said, "Both are correct." Those who read *letarbw*, the verb is for the people addressed. The clue for this subjunctive grammatical case is dropping the final consonant with the vowel *a* after it, as you should have pronounced *tarbuwanna* in the nominative case. When it is read *leyarbuwa*, the sentence means to increase the money you gave in order to get more. This is *rubuwwa* or increase. And the third does not increase with God. The *zakat* that you give seeking no return increases by multiplication.

The man *arba*. *Arba* is an inflectional case of *riba, yurbe*. *Al-rrubya* is derived from *riba*, and is lightened in articulation. In the saying or *hadith* of the Prophet, in the reconciliation of Najran people, "There is no *rubbayya*, or blood on them." Abu 'Ubayd said, "That's how it was narrated, by doubling the letters *b* and *y*." Al-Fura' said, "But, it is *rubya* lightened, by which the Prophet meant *riba* which they had in the pre-Islamic age, and the blood for which they were owed." He also said, "Analogy of *rubbayya* of *riba* is *hubbayya* of *ihtiba'*." The unwritten speech of the Arabs indicated that they spoke with the *y* sound saying *rubya* and *hubya*, and did not say *rubwa* and *hubwa*. The word's root is the letter *w*. The meaning of the Prophet's saying is that what they inherited from ancestors from the pre-Islamic age, or what they committed of a crime was dropped. Every drop of blood for which they were owed, and every *riba* they were responsible for were dropped, except their capital, which was given back to them. The word *riba* was repeatedly mentioned in the *hadith*. The root means increase from the money *raba* (past simple): increased and raised. The name *riba* is grammatically defective because it ends with the vowel *a*. In the canonical law of Islam, *riba* is the increase on the original amount of money without a sales contract. It has many rules in *fiqh*, Islamic jurisprudence.

The word mentioned in the *hadith* was *rubbayya* with the *b* and *y* letters doubled. Ibn Al-Athir said, "It is not known in the language." Al-Zamakhshari said, "Comparing it's declination method with *fu' 'uwla* of *fi'l*, it would be *rubbayya* of *riba*. As *f'l* is the first stem of the Arabic verb." The same analogy applies to *Al-ssurrayya* of *sarw* taken from *asra* (same pattern with *arba*). *Asra* the man's maids means to free them.

In the narration of Tahfa, "He who refrains will have to pay *Al-rribwa*," meaning that he who refrains from paying *zakat* will have to increase his religious duty as a punishment. It is narrated, "He who admits the *jizya* tax on non-Muslims under Muslim rule has to pay *al-rribwa*," which means that one who does not join Islam because of *zakat*, has to pay *jizya* which is more than he would have paid in *zakat* if he were a Muslim.

To *arba* over fifty and so forth means to increase. In the narration of Al-Ansar on the day of Uhud, "If you hit them at a day like this one, we will *nurbiyanna* the punishment with utmost cruelty on them." This means that we will increase and double. Al-Jawhari: *riba* in trade, and the man *arba*. In the *hadith*, "He who collected, had *arba* (increase)." In the *hadith* on charity, "It *tarbw* in the palm of the Merciful until it becomes greater than the mountain."

The stem of a plant *raba* and so forth *rubuwwan*, water was poured on it, so it puffed up. God the Great in describing the earth, said, "It has shaken and *rabat*." It is said that it meant that the earth has become greater and got inflated. Some read it "*raba't*." When read as *rabat* it is taken from *raba, yarbw*: meaning that, if added to any of the sides, it increases. He who read *raba't* with the glottal sound ('), it meant, that the earth raised in height. Somebody cursed somebody else, and *arba* in his cursing, that is, he added to it.

God the Great said, "He took them in a spell that was *rabeya*." This means that it was a spell that surpassed other spells. Al-Jawhari said, "it means exceeding (increasing), as when you say *arbayt* when you take more than you give."

Al-rrabw and *al-rrabwah* mean to be overweening and self conceited. Ibn Al-A'rabi recited:

> Without haughtiness and dazzling display and *rabwa*
> As if you two were chocked-full with saliva.

Meaning that you will not have mastery over it until after haughtiness on your tiptoes and after you are taken by *rabw* (conceit).

AL-RRABWU: The lofty spirit. *raba, yarbw, rabwan*. He was taken by *rabw*, we searched for the hunting until *tarabayna*, meaning until we were overwhelmed.

In the narration of Aisha, may God be pleased with her, the Prophet said to her, "why do I see you *hashiya* and *rabeya*." He meant by *rabeya*: taken by *al-rrabw* or the breathlessness, and that is the panting and quick breathing which the one who walks and moves fast has, and so is the *hashiya*. The horse *raba* is said when the horse becomes inflated out of running or fear. Bishr Bin Abi Khazem said:

> As if the rustling of his nostrils, if he
> suppressed *al-rrabwa*, a false bellows.

Al-Lihyani said *Al-rriba*, and its grammatical dual is *ribwan* and *ribyan*. Its root is the letter *w*. The dual was made with the *y* sound, only for easing the pronunciation toward the *i* sound in *ribyan*. The money *raba*, increased by *riba*. *Al-murbi* is the one who deals with *riba*. *Al-rrabw*, *Al-rrabwatu*, *Al-rrubwatu*, *Al-rribwa*, *Al-rrabawa*, *Al-rrubawa*, *Al-rribawa*, *Al-rrabiya*, *Al-rrabatu*: all that raised above the earth and *raba*. Al-Muthaqqab Al-'Abdi said:

> They ascended *rabawatan* and descended and disappeared
> And so they did not return to rising for sometime

Ibn Al-A'rabi recited:

> The 'Ashannaq (a name of a horse) misses being tamed
> Even if he covers the (*madeed*) extended *rabat*.

The *madeed* or extended, could be an attribute of 'Ashannaq, and it could be an attribute to *rabat*. But in the latter case, its noun pattern is *fa'eel* for *madeed*, and it stands for *maf'oola* for *mamdooda*. It could be inferred from the meaning as if he is saying *al-rrabwa al-madeeda*. If so, it would be an active participle and a passive participle.

The man *arba* if he lived on, or attended to a *rabiya* or a hill. Ibn Ahmar said describing a cow, for which the wolf frequently comes and goes after its young one:

> She *turbi* (rises) to him, so he is glad by its appearance one time, and some other time he tries to neglect him, so she becomes troubled.

In the *hadith*, "*Alferdaws* is the *rabwa* of heaven." This means the more exalted, or higher, level of heaven. Ibn Durayd, "Somebody has *raba'un* over somebody else." *Raba'un* with the short vowel for the *a* sound after *r* and lengthening the last *a* after the letter *b*. It means power or might. In the Holy *Quran*, "Comparable to a heaven with a *rabwatin*."

Note

* Translated and abridged from Mukarram, Imam Abi Fadl Jamaluddin Muhammad bin, *Lisan Al Arab* (Beirut: Dar Saadr, n.d.), p. 304. It is further abridged from the original translation, which appeared in *The American Journal of Islamic Finance* and is meant to cover only the definitional aspects relating to increase. Most elements relating to flora and fauna as well as poetry have been excised from the end of the entry where they originally appeared.

2 In the Shadow of Deuteronomy

Approaches to interest and usury in Judaism and Christianity

*Vincent J. Cornell**

The fundamental ruling on usury for both Judaism and medieval Christianity is a Biblical statement found in the book of Deuteronomy, which reads, "You must not lend on interest (*neshekh*) to your brother, whether the loan be of money or food or anything else that may earn interest" (23:19–20).[1] This passage is supported by another in Exodus, "If you lend money to any of my (i.e. Yahweh's) people, to any poor man among you, you must not play the usurer with him: you must not demand interest (*neshekh*) from him" (22:24–25),[2] as well as one from Leviticus, "If your brother who is living with you falls on evil days and is unable to support himself with you, you must support him as you would a stranger or a guest, and he must continue to live with you. Do not make him work for you, do not take interest (*tarbit*[3]) from him; fear God, and let your brother live with you. You are not to lend him money at interest (*neshekh*), or give him food to make a profit out of it" (25:35–37).[4]

In Judaism, three conclusions have traditionally been drawn from these commandments. First, although the prohibitions on taking interest in the books of Exodus and Leviticus seem to be motivated primarily by the "social welfare" considerations of Israelite society and concern for the needs of the disadvantaged, the statement in Deuteronomy has been regarded as unequivocal by all subsequent commentators and is seen to apply in practice to money lending in general. In this respect, therefore, the concepts of usury and interest must be considered functionally equivalent, as implied in the translation of the Biblical passages quoted previously.

The second conclusion to be drawn from pre-modern Jewish scholarship is that the Biblical prohibition of usury is confined only to the "brotherhood" of the people of Israel themselves and need not be applied to non-Jewish (Gentile) populations. This point of view is based on another passage from Deuteronomy, which follows directly after that given earlier, "You may demand interest on a loan of a foreigner (*nokri*), but you must not demand interest from your brother (*l'ahika*), so that Yahweh your God may bless you in all your giving in the land you are to enter and make your own" (23:21–22).[5] This so-called "Deuteronomic double standard,"[6] which was rejected as a matter of principle (although maintained in practice) by the medieval Christian Church, is seen by historians of religion to have formed a cornerstone of the kinship-oriented morality of early Israelite tribesmen. It affirms the solidarity of the clan (*mispaha*) by excluding the *nokri*, or foreigner, from the privileges and obligations of the community. The only persons exempted from this conceptual segregation of "in-group" and "out-group" domains are the protected sojourner (*ger*) and resident stranger (*toshab*), who are protected from usury by being counted as symbolic "kin" in several Biblical passages.[7] Later commentators, however, were to restrict these protected categories to include only the full proselyte or convert to Judaism (the medieval meaning of *ger*) and the "incomplete proselyte" (*ger toshab*) living within Israelite society, who although he has renounced idolatry in the presence of three devout Hebrew witnesses is still unable to maintain the Jewish food prohibitions.[8]

The third point to be noted from the Biblical passages reproduced in this section is a clear distinction, expressed terminologically, between two types of usury. The commandment against usury in Deuteronomy uses the Hebrew word, *neshekh*, which literally means a "bite," like that of a snake. According to at least one commentator, this term is used because the victim of a snakebite does not at first feel the bite, but only notices it when the serpent's venom has spread throughout his body. In the same manner, one who borrows money at interest does not feel the initial loss incurred by his loan but feels the full "bite" too late, when the accrued interest reaches an unbearable sum.[9] The text of Leviticus 25:37, on the other hand, uses *neshekh* in conjunction with another term, *tarbit* (also rendered as *ribbit* and *marbit* in later texts), for the taking of interest. Although both terms are recognized as being similar in meaning, Talmudic scholars are in wide disagreement about their exact connotations. To the Andalusian scholar Maimonides (fl. twelfth century CE), *neshekh* refers to accumulating interest, while *tarbit* is a fixed rate of interest that never increases.[10] The Jewish Publication Society's translation of Leviticus (1962), on the other hand, regards *neshekh* as "advance interest," deducted in advance, whereas *tarbit* is "accrued interest," deducted at the time of payment.[11] The Mishnah, however, regards *neshekh* as "interest" obtained in a currency transaction, whereas *tarbit* refers to an "increase" in kind, derived from the lending of produce (Baba Mesia, 5:1).[12] Whatever the case, it is clear that according to Jewish law the Biblical prohibitions of *tarbit* and *neshekh* are not meant to refer only to the restricted category of excessive interest, which is "usury" in the modern sense of the term, but rather are applicable to all interest-bearing transactions, no matter how minimal the interest charged in them may be.

According to the *Encyclopedia Judaica*, the prohibition of interest in the Bible and later Judaic texts rests on two grounds: first, that those who are prosperous ought to help the indigent, if not by gifts, then at least by extending them free loans; second, since excessive interest was considered to lie at the root of social ruin, all interest should be banned, regardless of type.[13] Despite this blanket condemnation, however, actual violations of the ban on interest were not seen by Jewish scholars as criminal offenses and hence were not subject to penal sanctions. Instead, the taking of interest was regarded as a purely moral transgression, whose avoidance would be positively rewarded by God's beneficence.[14] Only in the Book of Ezekiel can one find a Biblical passage mentioning usury as a transgression punishable by extreme measures:

> Where one man engages in filthy practices with his neighbor's wife, another defiles himself with his daughter-in-law, another violates his sister, his own father's daughter; where people take bribes for shedding blood; you charge usury and interest, you rob your neighbor by extortion, you forget all about me – it is

the Lord Yahweh who speaks ... I mean to disperse you throughout the nations, to scatter you in foreign countries, and take your foulness from you ... And so you will learn that I am Yahwah.

$$(22:12, 15–16)^{15}$$

Elsewhere in the Bible, the taker of interest is simply described as a "wicked man" (Proverbs, 28:5, 8),[16] whereas the one "who does not ask interest on loans" is a man who has the right to "enter Yahweh's tent" and live on his "holy mountain" (Psalms 15:1–5).[17]

Given the moral rather than the penal nature of the sin of usury in Jewish law, it stands to reason that any formal sanction imposed for this transgression be relatively mild in nature. Originally, rabbinical courts appear to have been empowered to fine a creditor for taking interest by rejecting his claim for the repayment of his invested capital. Eventually, however, the rule evolved that the act of taking interest did not affect a creditor's right to have his capital repaid. By the late medieval period, the sanctions imposed on usurers were to become almost entirely symbolic, although still effective if one's reputation was at stake: those who charged interest from other Jews were routinely disqualified from acting as witnesses and were not administered oaths – a prohibition that extended even to the borrower who agreed to a usurious loan. In certain texts, moneylenders who take interest from their brethren are also likened to deniers of God and apostates, who have no share in the world to come.[18]

In the Talmudic period, the concept of usury was expanded beyond the paradigms set forth in the Torah and other books of the Old Testament to include any type of business that gave even the slightest hint of interest. This so-called "dust of interest" (*avak ribbit*) became the main subject of discussions on usury contained in the Mishnah and later commentarial works, whose authors often subjected the question of the propriety or impropriety of transactions involving lending to strict standards of mutuality and functional equivalence. In the book, "Baba Mesia," of the Mishnah, for example, the following rulings on the "dust" of interest can be found[19]:

1   A person may not lend wheat at a low value and then claim it back at a higher value in order to purchase another commodity (5:1).
2   The use of a subterfuge (*ha'aramah*) to avoid the interest prohibition is not allowed, such as when one lends money to a person and then lives in the debtor's house for free (5:2).
3   A "futures market" or speculation on the price of commodities is prohibited, since it entails buying something that does not yet exist at a price not mutually agreed upon at the time of transaction (5:7).
4   "Iron-terms" partnerships, in which the lender is protected from any future loss by the debtor's agreement to pay the full value of his investment, are prohibited as well, since the contract violates the principle of mutuality (5:6).

Indeed, questions of mutuality and equity became so important to Talmudic scholars that certain of them, such as Hillel, went so far as to say, "A woman should not lend a loaf of bread to her girlfriend unless she states its value in money," and "A man may say to his fellow, 'Weed with me and I'll weed with you' or 'Hoe with me and I'll hoe with you', but he may not say to him, 'Weed with me and I'll hoe with you' or 'Hoe with me and I'll weed with you' " (5:9–10).[20]

An authoritative post-Talmudic view of usury in Judaism was put forth in the twelfth century CE by Maimonides (Ar. Musa ibn Maymun), whose career spanned the apogee of the Almohad dynasty in the Islamic West. Following the example of earlier scholars such as Hillel, who were noted for their piety and fear of God's commandments, Maimonides was primarily concerned with elucidating those "shades of usury" whose repayment could not be obtained through the courts but which undermined the sense of brotherhood that cemented Jewish society together.[21] Further systematizing the conclusions of Talmudic scholars, Maimonides conceived a fourfold division of usury, which included:

1   Biblically prohibited usury
2   Shade of usury
3   Verbal usury
4   Evasion of the laws of usury.

In practice, this meant that Maimonides included under the usury prohibition all interest-bearing transactions, non-economic gratuities in the form of "verbal usury," and a variety of other transactions in the form of sales, leases, and wages which could be considered "usurious" because they failed to express the principle of equivalence between what is given by the creditor and repaid by the debtor.[22]

In general, Maimonides shows little concern for the theoretical aspects of usury and instead condemns the taking of interest as a simple case of one Jew's exploitation of another: "Why is (usury) called *neshekh*? Because (the lender) bites (*noshekh*) and afflicts his neighbor and eats his flesh."[23] In particular, he ignores the pseudo-Aristotelian conception of the "sterility" of money so important to medieval Christian scholastics and merely restates the Talmudic principle that, "it is forbidden to lease dinars, since this is not like leasing a vessel which is being actually returned, whereas these dinars are spent and others are returned. That is why there is a 'shade of usury' in the payment of rent for them."[24] This sense of the consumptiveness (what Christian writers called "fungibility") of money is precisely why Maimonides insisted that a moneylender forego interest-derived income and instead offer gratuitous loans to his coreligionist as a matter of charity.

According to Salo Baron, Maimonides' emphasis on the charitable aspects of the Deuteronomic prohibition of usury had the dual effect of facilitating a more lenient interpretation of the prohibition, both in cases where the borrower did not really require charitable credit (such as in productive loans) and where the lender belonged to a class of persons (such as orphaned minors and scholars) who required special protection. Assuming, for example, that revenue from money lending offered the best livelihood for persons who devoted their lives exclusively to study, he denied the usurious character of credit transactions among scholars, considering the profit thus obtained to be a "gift" given as compensation to one's creditor.[25] More important to the present discussion, however, were those evasions of usury considered legally valid by Maimonides. These included:

1   The *contractus mohatrae*, which involved the arrangement of a sale below the present market price, with immediate delivery, and instantaneous resale at a future, higher market price with future delivery.
2   A type of "purchase of rents," which involved the leasing to the debtor of a field taken over by the creditor as security for his loan, the rental of which secures the stipulated income.
3   Extending to a neighbor a loan of a certain sum of money in the form of merchandise according to its supposed market value and acquiring elsewhere the same amount of merchandise at wholesale prices.
4   Acquiring deeds with a discount, by means of which a merchant could sell merchandise on credit, at a price yielding him a substantial profit, and obtain cash from the banker by discounting the bill given to him by the purchaser.[26]

In addition, Maimonides greatly encouraged the lending of money at interest to non-Jews, interpreting the Deuteronomic permission of this practice as a positive commandment.[27] Needless to say, in a pluralistic society such as Islamic Spain, where Jews comprised a small minority of the population in most localities, such a commandment to "lend to Gentiles" greatly facilitated the expansion of extensive Jewish financial networks.

The most common Jewish evasion of the usury prohibition in the medieval era was the *'iska* (Lat. *contractus trinus*), recognized but not fully approved of by Maimonides, which consisted of a particular type of "silent partnership" somewhat similar to, but not identical with, the Islamic *mudaraba*. In such a transaction a deed known as a *shetar 'iska* would be drawn up in front of two witnesses. This deed stipulated that the lender would supply a certain amount of money to finance a joint venture; the borrower alone, however, would manage the business and undertake to guarantee the lender's investment against all loss. The borrower would also guarantee the lender a fixed amount of minimum profit to be paid after a certain amount of time. To evade Mishnaic prohibitions concerning the "dust of usury," the borrower would be paid a nominal salary by the lender and the contract would stipulate (fictitiously) that both parties would share in any losses that accrued from the joint venture. In order to render this loss-sharing agreement null and void in practice, a further provision would be made that such a loss could only be proven by stipulated and mostly unobtainable evidence. In the course of time, this form of legalizing interest became so well established that, in order to comply with the strictures of Jewish law, all that was required to avoid the usury prohibition was to add the Hebrew phrase, *al-pi hetter 'iska*, to any interest-bearing contract.[28]

The evasion of the prohibition of interest-bearing transactions in medieval Judaism by means of the *'iska* contract foreshadows later attempts in medieval and early-modern Christianity to avoid the inconvenient commandments of Deuteronomy and Leviticus by redefining the concept of usury altogether. Indeed, from the very beginning Christian doctrines, whether Catholic or Protestant, concerning the issue of usury were fraught with inconsistencies and contradictions. In the first place, although the commandments forbidding usury in the Old Testament were accepted in principle by early Christian theologians, such as St Ambrose of Milan (d. 397), who rejected as outmoded the "Deuteronomic double standard" which permitted the charging of usury to Gentiles,[29] the New Testament itself contained little that was relevant to this question. Most commonly quoted in support of the usury prohibition was a passage from Luke 6:34–35, which states, "And if you lend to those from whom you hope to receive, what thanks can you expect? Even sinners lend to sinners to get back the same amount. Instead, love your enemies and do good, and lend without any hope of return. You will have a great reward, and you will be sons of the Most High, for he himself is kind to the ungrateful and the wicked."[30]

Despite moral objections to usury by a handful of influential Church fathers, among the canons of the first eight general councils of the Christian Church only one canon referring to usury can be found; this is the seventeenth canon of the first general council at Nicaea (325 AD), which forbids the practice of usury only to clerics.[31] *Usura* (profits from monetary loans, as opposed to *turpe lucrum*, "filthy lucre," which meant immoral profits from the sale of goods) was only forbidden to Christians in general after 800 AD, when decrees promulgated by provincial councils of the Latin Church expanded the Nicaean prohibition to include the laity. It was during this period, in the year 806 AD, that the first medieval definition of usury was introduced: Usury exists "where more is asked (*usura*) than is given (*mutuum*)."[32] A relatively typical example of the equivocal attitude toward usury that was common during the Carolingian period can be found in a treatise entitled Enarratio super Deuteronomium, written by the scholar Rabanus Maurus (d. 856). According to this author, the "brother" mentioned in the Deuteronomic prohibition refers to every Latin Christian, whereas the "alien" refers only to infidels and criminals. To such people one is allowed to lend money at usury as a recompense for preaching the Word and demanding repentance from sin. Implicit in this model is an attempt to limit the troublesome distinction between ethnic and religious communities in Deuteronomy 23:21 and replace it with a new dichotomy between two types of money: to take usury for the loan of "metallic money" is forbidden by Rabanus, while asking usury for proselytization and other forms of "spiritual sustenance" is permissible.[33]

The advent of the Crusades and the introduction of feudal Latin Christians to the sophisticated monetary economy of the Middle East soon prompted a reopening of the usury issue in the Latin Church as well as a profound reorientation in the nature of arguments concerning the practice of money lending. Whereas early scholars, such as Ambrose and Rabanus Maurus, continued to maintain an attenuated form of the "Deuteronomic double standard" in their opinions, contemporary attitudes were now directed toward denying such distinctions in favor of a more universalistic conception of the "brotherhood" of man under the widespread umbrella of the Catholic Church. Not surprisingly, much of this new interest in the morality of monetary transactions was prompted by economic concerns. First of all, it was realized that the text of Deuteronomy, if it were not superseded in some respects, permitted Jewish moneylenders to exercise an advantage over Christian merchants by allowing them to advance money at interest to Crusaders heading for the Holy Land. In the eyes of some Popes, especially Innocent III (1198–1216), the effective propagation of the

Crusades necessitated a severe restriction on the activities of all moneylenders, Christian as well as Jewish, clerical as well as secular.[34] It was not long before these specific concerns were replaced by more generalized fears of a radical challenge to the feudal order in Western Europe through the introduction of alien economic practices. Peter Lombard (d. 1160/1164), for example, ignores Deuteronomy altogether in his writings and lumps usury together with fraud, rape, and theft as an "illicit usurpation of another's thing."[35] His near contemporary, the Parisian exegete Peter Cantor (d. 1197), launches an even more telling diatribe against the "detestable usurers" who are now "the bosom companions of princes and prelates, who surrender to the blandishments of the money bags and promote their sons to the highest post in Church and State." These Christian usurers, to avoid sanctions, even go so far as to hide their faith and pretend to be Jews, in which guise they are protected by local princes who falsely say about them, "These are our Jews."[36]

It must be pointed out, however, that the "universalistic" economic ideology of the Latin Church during the period of the Crusades was never meant to apply to Muslims and Jews. As early as the fourth century, St Ambrose had already affirmed the permissibility of usury as a financial weapon that could be used against the enemies of Christ:

> From him, it says (in Deuteronomy), demand usury, whom you rightly desire to harm, against whom weapons are lawfully carried. Upon him usury is legally imposed. On him whom you cannot easily conquer in war, you can quickly take vengeance with the hundredth. From him exact usury whom it would not be a crime to kill. He fights without a weapon who demands usury: He who revenges himself upon an enemy, who is an interest collector from his foe, fights without a sword. Therefore, where there is the right of war, there is also the right of usury.[37]

Nearly eight centuries later, around the year 1140, Ambrose's view of usury as an economic weapon of war was reaffirmed and made applicable to Muslims, who were called "modern Canaanites" by commentators on the *Decretum* (*c*.1141) of the Bolognese monk Gratian.[38] Even more explicit were the statements of Rolandus Bandinelli, who became Pope Alexander III in 1159. According to Bandinelli, laymen may exact usury from heretics, infidels, and anyone who openly attacks the Church. Through the affliction of usury, Saracens and other enemies who are too strong to be defeated by force of arms might be recalled to the unity of the Church, and if not, would be compelled under the pressure of usury either to yield to the Church or at least not to disturb it.[39] In the era of Innocent III, Bernard of Pavia (d. 1213) also confirmed the legitimacy of taxing Saracens with usury, while Huguccio (fl. 1188) and Johannes Teutonicus (fl. 1216) legitimized the taking of usury from an enemy, "whether pagan, Saracen, Jew, heretic, or Christian, when one has the right to wage war against him."[40]

In general, opponents of usury in the medieval Catholic Church tended to view the taking of interest as sin against justice. Many clerics in the twelfth and thirteenth centuries were acutely aware that the commercial revolution then raging throughout the Mediterranean world weakened rather than strengthened the economic security of the Christian masses. Particularly troublesome was the existence of a pernicious double standard in the lending of money that penalized the poor and favored the rich. Distress borrowing, which entitled contracting an emergency loan secured by land or personal possessions, often carried a weekly interest penalty that amounted to as much as 43 percent per annum. Commercial borrowing or production loans, on the other hand, which usually involved the granting of investment capital by Italian banking firms, carried annual rates as low as 7–15 percent.[41] Church officials thus found themselves torn between the need to behave "rationally" in order to support the fiscal needs of Christian states and fill their own coffers and their responsibility to act "morally" by protecting their "flock" – the common people who were broken and reduced to penury under the wheels of unregulated commerce.

By the thirteenth century, the need to reconcile these conflicting interests led to the Church's acquiescence to numerous evasions of the usury prohibition. By mid-century, no fewer than thirteen such exceptions were regarded as "acceptable loans" by the commentator Hostiensis:

1   *Feuda*: When a fief is returned to the lender as security for a loan, the lender may take the proceeds of the fief without deducting them from the capital loaned.
2   *Fide-jussor*: A guarantor who is forced to contract a loan at interest because of his obligation may demand payment of interest from the party guaranteed.
3   *Pro dote*: If a dowry cannot be produced and land is offered as security, the husband may take the fruits of the land until the dowry is paid.
4   *Stipenda cleri*: If a layman holding a benefice belonging to the Church gives it back to the Church as security for a debt, the income derived from the benifice does not diminish the debt.
5   *Venditio fructus*: The sale of the revenues from a piece of land is made equivalent to a rent charge and thus constitutes a contract of sale.
6   *Cui velle juri nocer*: Usury may be demanded of an enemy.
7   *Vendens sub dubio*: If the future price of a commodity is in doubt, sale of the commodity for credit terms is allowed at a price higher than the prevailing price.
8   *Pretium post tempora solvens*: Allows payment of damages when the debtor fails to pay on the agreed date.
9   *Poena nec in fraudem* (also known as *poena conventionalis*): A penalty clause may be written in a loan contract to provide compensation for the lender if the debtor fails to pay on the agreed date.
10 *Lex commisoria*: A lending contract based on a legal fiction that allows an ostensible "seller" to recover his property within a fixed term, while the ostensible "buyer" retains his profits from the period of use.
11 *Gratis dans*: A lending contract in which the excess in repayment of a loan is defined as a "gift" by the debtor.
12 *Socii pompa*: When an article is lent to another for purposes of show, the lender may take payment for providing the article, because the article is not "consumed."
13 *Labor*: A creditor may take compensation for his "work" in servicing a loan.[42]

In the following two centuries, further exceptions continued to erode the Catholic Church's official condemnation of usury. These included:

1   The permissibility of investing in a *societas* or partnership (no matter how broadly based) on the grounds that there is no transfer of ownership by the investor and that the investor shares in the risk.
2   *Periculum sortis*: An "insurance charge" tacked onto a loan to secure the creditor from lack of repayment due to the disability or death of the borrower.
3   *Montes pietatis*, or Church-owned pawnshops, which practiced distress lending at nominal rates of interest.[43]

The most flagrant evaders of the usury prohibition were the Italian merchant bankers who lent large amounts of money to both political and merchant princes and in return were reimbursed for their efforts by demanding "discretionary gifts" (called *discreziones* – an extension of the *gratis dans* listed in this section) of between 7 and 10 percent.[44] Such evasions, needless to say, went far beyond the long-accepted *commenda* partnership or the common subterfuge of hiding interest-bearing loans in bills of exchange.

By the time of the German Reformation in the early sixteenth century, the ethics of the counting house had fully replaced those of the cloister in European intellectual circles. New moral and political questions posed by the creation of an economic system based on international trade, mercantilism, and a "proto-capitalist" monetary economy now caused the Deuteronomic and medieval prohibitions against usury to be seen as impediments to commerce and the formation of capital for further investment. One of the first religious figures to acknowledge these new "realities" was Martin Luther, who undermined the normative authority of the book of Deuteronomy by stating that a Christian was no longer under any obligation to follow long-dead Mosaic ordinances. Even the Gospels, he maintained, were not intended to take the place of civil law or supplant existing authorities.[45] Although he was originally opposed to usury as a form of social injustice, Luther's instinctive antipathy toward the anarchic doctrines of peasant revolutionaries as well as his pragmatic support of the political and economic interests of local German princes caused him to reevaluate his previous opinions and claim, in 1525, that considerations of "public interest" superseded the teachings of the Gospels in questions having to do with the regulation of money lending.[46] In letters to Prince Johann Friedrich of Saxony and the city council of Danzig, he attempted to enlarge the sphere of private conscience against the strict claim of canon law by maintaining that the burden of guilt should rest only "on the consciences of those who take unjust interest" and that a rate of interest not exceeding 4 or 5 percent might be morally justifiable. Most importantly, Luther went on to claim, also in his memorandum to Danzig, that in evangelical religion each person has a right to exercise his individual "Christian liberty" in the matter of making loans at interest.[47]

Writing in support of Luther, the Swiss Protestant Zwingli (d. 1531) echoed the attitudes of his German contemporary and claimed that usury is justifiable because all of the world's affairs cannot be governed by Divine Justice. Once the principle of private property has been established, he said, it becomes theft for a person to withhold rents or interest charges that are due to one's creditor, in accordance with Paul of Tarsus' dictum to "render to all their dues" (Romans, 13:7).[48] Zwingli's cynical view of human society and early-modern political systems (an attitude shared by Luther as well) rested on a fundamental belief in the immorality of man and a jaundiced view of human society as the theater of human aggressions. In such an amoral environment, the prophetic commandments of the Old Testament and the Gospels can only be reduced, in practicality, to a utopian ethic that has little chance of being maintained in the "real" world. It is an unfortunate paradox that Luther's and Zwingli's pessimistic attitudes concerning mankind's ability to merit God's grace made it easier for profane man to exercise the very lack of social responsibility that so disturbed their sense of morality.[49]

What was to become the final and authoritative word on Deuteronomy in Protestant Christianity was pronounced only a single generation later by John Calvin, who in 1545 declared as unlawful only the excessive, "biting" usury that is taken by moneylenders from the defenseless poor. As far as other forms of usury are concerned, they are to be limited only by the dictates of conscience, a rigorous application of the Golden Rule ("Do unto others as you would have them do unto you"). and the necessities of public utility: "The law of Moses is political, and does not obligate us beyond what equity and the reason of humanity suggest. Surely, it should be desirable if usuries were driven from the whole world, indeed that the work be unknown. But since that is impossible, we must make concession to the common utility."[50] In a feat of intellectual gymnastics that defies all apparent logic, Calvin puts a final nail in Deuteronomy's coffin by audaciously claiming that since "the wall of partition" between Jew and Gentile has now broken down, Jews and Christians are now free to take usury from each other, rather than both being forbidden to do so.[51]

In the writings of John Calvin, the classic Judeo-Christian discussion of usury comes full circle. From the exclusivist brotherhood of the Children of Israel, who are forbidden in Deuteronomy to take usury from each other, and the idealistic "universal brotherhood" of the medieval Catholic Church, which attempted, albeit unsuccessfully, to apply the usury prohibition to all individuals living in Christian domains, one now arrives at the "universal brotherhood"[52] of Reformation Protestantism, which sets the text of Deuteronomy on its head by making all mankind fair game for the moneylender and the merchant banker. It is important to recognize, however, that the progressive erosion of the prohibition on usury in the Judeo-Christian tradition was by no means a simple case of moral weakness or intellectual bankruptcy. Instead, it must be seen as the outcome of successive conflicts between a number of classic religio-ethical oppositions or antitheses: the material world versus the hereafter; the ideal versus the "real"; collective responsibility versus individual conscience; social justice versus public utility; and, in a socioeconomic sense, the values of relatively small-scale, agrarian and trading societies versus the efficiency needs and highly materialistic value system of the modern world economy. None of these issues are simple, and each must be examined in detail by Islamic scholars who are fully trained in law, moral theology, and modern economics if twentieth- and twenty-first-century (fifteenth century AH) Muslims are to seriously come to grips with them. By no means is it intended to imply that the abandonment of scriptural commandments and the redefinition of usury by the Protestant Christian West should be taken as authoritative by present-day Muslim thinkers. It is imperative, however, that all Muslim intellectuals be aware of the Judeo-Christian example in order to fully appreciate the difficulty of the problem that is to be faced.

Notes

* Also known as Mansur Mujahid, Vincent Cornell first presented this paper to the Second International Conference on Islamic Economics, Republic of Trinidad and Tobago (sponsored by the International Association of Islamic Banks and Muslim Co-Operative Credit Union, Ltd), March 17, 1990. Dr Cornell is presently Professor of History and Director of the King Fahd Center for Middle East and Islamic Studies at the University of Arkansas. This chapter is updated from an article which appeared "In the Shadow of Deuteronomy: Approaches to Interest and Usury in Judaism and Christianity," *al-Nahda* (10), 1–2, Kuala Lumpur, Malaysia, 1991, 39–43. It is published with that journal's permission.

1 Alexander Jones (ed.), *The Jerusalem Bible* (New York: Bantam Double Dell Publishing Group, Inc., 1968), p. 212. Hereafter, all Biblical quotations will be taken from this edition.

2 Ibid., p. 84. Biblical scholars consider this statement of the usury prohibition to be a commandment given by God to the Prophet Moses (Pbuh).

3 Editor's Note: The Hebrew root of this word is the same as the Arabic root *rbw*, "to increase."

4 Ibid., p. 136.

5 Ibid., p. 212.

6 For a discussion of this concept see Benjamin Nelson, *The Idea of Usury* (Chicago, IL and London: University of Chicago Press, 1969), pp. 3–28.

7 Op. cit., see, for example, Leviticus 29:33–34: "If a stranger lives with you in your land, do not molest him. You must count him as one of your own countrymen and love him as yourself – for you were once strangers yourselves in Egypt. I am Yahweh your God" p. 128.

8 Nelson, op. cit., p. 20, n. 2.

9 Edward Zipperstein, *Business Ethics in Jewish Law* (New York, Ktav Publishing House Inc., 1983), p. 40. This *responsum* is taken from Cohen, Abraham (ed.), *The Soncino Chumash*. (London: The Soncino Press, 1956), p. 485.

10 *Encyclopedia Judaica*, vol. 16 (Jerusalem: The Macmillan Company, 1906), p. 28.

11 Zipperstein, op. cit., p. 40.

12 Jacob Neusner (tr.), *The Mishnah: A New Translation* (New Haven, CT and London: Yale University Press, 1989), pp. 540–1.

13 *Encyclopedia Judaica*, op. cit., p. 28.

14 If ranked on the scale of the "Five Values" (*al-ahkam al-khamsa*) of Islamic *fiqh*, the Jewish attitude in regard to interest and usury would thus fall somewhere between *madmum* and *makruh*.

15 *Jerusalem Bible*, op. cit., p. 1196.

16 Ibid., p. 847, "The wicked do not know what justice means . . . He who increases his wealth by usury and interest amasses it for someone else who will bestow it on the poor." Note that these statements are contained in the section of Proverbs regarded by Biblical scholars as that which most likely represents the actual teachings of the Prophet Solomon (Pbuh).

17 Ibid., p. 685. This psalm is attributed to the Prophet David (Pbuh) himself:

> Yahweh, who has the right to enter your tent, or to live on your holy mountain? The man whose way of life is blameless, who always does what is right, who

speaks the truth from his heart, whose tongue is not used for slander, who does not wrong to his fellow, casts no discredit on his neighbor, looks with contempt on the reprobate, but honors those who fear Yahweh, who stands by his pledge at any cost, does not ask interest on loans, and cannot be bribed to victimize the innocent. If a man does all this, nothing can ever shake him.

18 *Encyclopedia Judaica*, op. cit., p. 31.
19 Neusner, op. cit., pp. 541–3.
20 Ibid., p. 543.
21 Salo W. Baron, "The Economic Views of Maimonides," in Salo W. Baron (ed.) *Essays On Maimonides* (New York: Columbia University Press, 1941), p. 209.
22 Ibid., pp. 210–11.
23 Ibid., p. 211.
24 Ibid.
25 Ibid., pp. 212–13.
26 Ibid., pp. 214–16.
27 Ibid., p. 226.
28 Ibid., pp. 217–19. See also, *Encyclopedia Judaica*, op. cit., p. 32.
29 Nelson, op. cit., p. 4. Ambrose felt that the "foreigner" mentioned in Deuteronomy referred only to ancient enemies of Israel who no longer existed.
30 *Jerusalem Bible* (New Testament), op. cit., p. 80. Christian writers of the Patristic period were often influenced by a classical Greek and Roman philosophical tradition that was hostile to commerce as being "associated with fraud and avarice, catering to luxury, and a potential source of moral corruption and deterioration of manners by virtue of the contacts involved with barbarian merchants and customs." Jacob Viner, *Religious Thought and Economic Society*, Jacques Melitz and Donald Winch, eds. (Durham, NC: Duke University Press, 1978), p. 35.
31 J. Gilchrist, *The Church and Economic Activity in the Middle Ages* (London: Macmillan and Co., 1969), p. 63. The restriction of the Nicaean usury prohibition to clerics alone was probably due to a desire on the part of Church fathers not to contravene the tenets of Roman law, which permitted the practice of lending money at interest.
32 Ibid. Note that in classical Roman law, unlike the case in medieval Christianity, *mutuum* also referred to loans made for profit. In the agriculturally based, largely barter economy of early medieval Europe, where credit demands were low and loans were made for consumption purposes out of "idle" funds or surpluses, the question of usury was not a compelling issue.
33 Nelson, op. cit., pp. 4–5.
34 Ibid., p. 7. This question was first discussed under Pope Eugenius III in 1145.
35 Ibid., pp. 9–10.
36 Ibid., pp. 10–11.
37 Ambrose, *De Tobia*, 15:51, quoted in Ibid., p. 4.
38 Gratian's *Decretum*, which condemned not only usury, but all other forms of investment and commercial partnership, such as the *commendus* and the *societas* as well, was highly influential in the subsequent development of the rigorist approach to usury, which became increasingly common in the Catholic church after 1350. See Gilchrist, op. cit., pp. 53, 64–5.
39 Nelson, op. cit., pp. 6, 14–15.
40 Ibid., pp. 15–16.
41 Gilchrist, op. cit. pp. 63–5.
42 Ibid., p. 67. Note that the type of speculation entailed in (7) in the list is prohibited in Talmudic law, while (10), (11), and (13) would fall under Maimonides' category of "shades of usury."
43 Viner, op. cit., pp. 92–7.
44 Gilchrist, op. cit., pp. 74–5.

45 Nelson, op. cit., pp. 29–30.

46 Ibid., p. 45. Note that Luther's conception of "pubic interest" is similar to the *maslaha* of Maliki Islamic jurisprudence.

47 Ibid., pp. 48–9.

48 Ibid., pp. 65–6. In the *Jerusalem Bible* this passage is rendered as, "Pay every government official what he has a right to ask – whether it be direct tax or indirect, fear or honor" (*New Testament*, p. 210). It is interesting that Zwingli neglected to mention the following passage in this selection, "Avoid getting into debt, except the debt of mutual love."

49 Ibid., p. 67. It fairness to Luther and Zwingli, it is necessary to point out that their attitudes were influenced by the threat to social order posed by the Anabaptist utopians, who advocated a boycott of many contemporary financial practices and thus were seen as a menace to the economic stability of German principalities.

50 *Opera*, X. I, col., quoted in ibid., p. 77.

51 Ibid., pp. 78–9.

52 This term, coined by Nelson in ibid., is central theme in his study of the "transvaluation of values" that lay at the foundation of Max Weber's *The Protestant Ethic and the Spirit of Capitalism*.

3   The juridical meaning of *riba*

*Sh. Wahba Al Zuhayli**

*Translated by Iman Abdul Rahim and
Abdulkader Thomas*

The definition of *riba*, and the textual evidence for its impermissibility

Lexically, *riba* means increase. Allah Most High says, "But when We pour down rain on it, it is stirred (to life), it swells *(rabat)*" (Hajj 22:5), meaning: it increases and grows. He, Most Praised, also says, "lest one party should be more numerous *(arba)* than another" (Naml 16:92), meaning: more numerous. It is said "So-and-so exceeded *(arba)* so-and-so," meaning: has more than he.[1]

In *Sharia'a*, *riba* (interest) means an increase in things specified by the Revealed Law, this particular definition being that of the Hanbali School. *Riba* is defined in the Hanafi work *Kanz al-Daqi'iq* as a surplus of commodity without counter-value in a commutative transaction of property for property. The intent of such a transaction is a surplus *of* commodities, even if only legally; thus, the definition includes both credit *riba* and invalid sales, since postponement in either of the indemnities is a legal surplus without perceivable material recompense, the delay usually being given an increase in compensation.[2]

Riba is forbidden by the *Quran*, the *Sunna*, and the consensus of the jurists.

As for the *Quran*, Allah Most High says:

- "but Allah has permitted trade and forbidden *riba*" (Baqara 2:275).[3]
- "Those who devour *riba* will not stand except as stands one whom Satan by his touch has driven to madness" (Baqara 2:275).
- "O you who believe! Fear Allah and give up what remains of your demand for *riba*, if you are indeed believers. If you do it not, take notice of a war from Allah and His Messenger; but if you turn back, you shall have your capital sums; deal not unjustly, and you shall not be dealt with unjustly" (Baqara 2:278–279).

Riba was made forbidden in the eighth or ninth year after the Hegira or flight from Makka.

As for the *Sunna*:

- The saying of the Prophet (peace and blessings of Allah be upon him), "Avoid the seven grave sins" – and of them he mentioned devouring *riba*.[4]

- Ibn Mas'ud (may Allah be pleased with him) relates, "The Messenger of Allah (peace and blessings of Allah be upon him) cursed the devourer of *riba*, his constituent, the one who acts as a witness to it, and one who acts as a notary to it."[5]
- Hakim relates on the authority of Ibn Mas'ud that the Prophet (peace and blessings of Allah be upon him) said, "*Riba* is of seventy three kinds, the lightest in seriousness of which is as bad as one's marrying his own mother; for the Muslim who practices *riba* goes mad."[6]

Other such *hadith*s will follow in the section dealing with the legal causes for the impermissibility of *riba*.

Riba is also forbidden by the scholarly consensus of the entire Muslim nation. Mawardi relates, "It has even been said that it is not permissible according to the law of any revealed religion," as can be understood from His Most High's saying, "they took *riba*, while they had been forbidden therefrom" (Nisa' 4:161), that is, as in the previously revealed scriptures.[7]

The *riba*, which is forbidden in Islam, is of two types:

1 Credit *riba*, which was the only type known by the pre-Islamic Arabs. This type is taken against a delay in settlement of a due debt, regardless whether the debt be that of a goods sold or a loan.
2 Surplus *riba*, is the sale of similar items with a disparity in amount in the six canonically-forbidden categories of goods: gold, silver, wheat, barley, salt, and dry dates. This type of *riba* is forbidden in order that it does not become a pretext for committing forbidden acts, that is, in order to prevent it being used as a pretext to committing credit *riba*, such that a person sells gold, for example, on credit, then pays back in silver more than the equivalent of what he had taken in gold.

This first type, which is the *riba* of the pre-Islamic period, is forbidden by the explicit text of the *Quran*. As for the second type, its impermissibility is established in the *Sunna* by analogy of the first type, since it too includes an increase without counter-value. A third type, namely the selling of disparate kinds on credit, is also forbidden by the *Sunna*; it likewise is considered a form of *riba*, since the delay of payment in one of the counter-values requires an increase. Similar to it in meaning is the loan that yields a profit, because it is an exchange of a thing for itself.[8]

The legal ruling of *riba*, regardless of whether credit or surplus *riba*, is impermissibility (*haram*), the transaction being invalid (*batil*) according to the majority of scholars, such that no legal consequence results from the transaction; and imperfect (*fasid*) according to the Hanafi scholars.

The types of *riba*

According to the majority of jurists, there are two types of *ribawi* sales: surplus *riba* and credit *riba*.[9]

The Hanafi jurists have defined surplus *riba*,[10] which is a sale, as an increase of capital assets above the legal standards (being volume or weight) in an exchange of like kinds.

Notice that our definition does not include the phrase "which was stipulated in the sale contract," as does that of Kasani, the phrase being unnecessary since the transaction is *ribawi* whether the increase is stipulated or not, in both sales and loans. What is meant by "capital assets" is that which is taken into consideration when determining a surplus or increase is the *quantity or amount*, not its value.

Furthermore, by using the qualifying phrase "legal standard," we have excluded those things, which are measured by length or counted, for there is no *riba* in such things.

Likewise, there is no *riba* in non-fungibles, such as in certain types of animals, carpets, rugs, furniture, lands, trees, and houses; in such things, an increase is not forbidden, and it is permissible to take a large quantity/amount in return for a lesser quantity/amount of the same kind. This is because non-fungibles are not measurable, that is, are not subject during their exchange to a unified criterion or weight. Rather, *riba* is specific to those objects that are measured by volume or weighed. Thus, it is permissible to buy five cubits of a specific cloth for six of the same, or an egg for two, or a sheep for two, on condition that the exchanges take place at the time of the contract; if the payment of either is deferred, the sale is not permissible, for it is sufficient that the objects be of like kind in order to effect the prohibition of credit *riba*, that is, the deferring of the payment of either of the two exchanged goods.

Another way of defining surplus *riba* is the sale of a *ribawi* commodity for its like kind with an increase in either of the exchanged goods.

In summary, the exchange of *ribawi* commodities makes it obligatory that like goods are exchanged in equal amounts. Equality, in the opinion of Abu Yusuf, is legally determined according to the customary standard of measurement of each particular category of commodities. Thus, that which, according to custom, is measured by weight, such as oil and ghee, must be exchanged in equal weighed amounts; and that which, according to custom, is measured by volume must be exchanged in equal dry-weight amounts.

As for the forbiddance of *riba* in the two intrinsic monies (i.e. gold and silver or that which substitutes for them of other circulating currencies), there is no difference between that which is minted, and raw ores which have not been minted. It is for this reason that the jurists have said regarding the dirham: its ore and coin are equal. However, Ibn al-Qayyim holds the sale of gold and silver jewelry which are permissible to use, such as rings and other women's jewelry, for more than their equivalent weight in gold or silver, is valid, in consideration of the workmanship involved and people's need for such.[11]

As for credit *riba*,[12] which is a sale, it has been defined by the Hanafi scholars as the preference of immediate payment over postponement, and preference of assets over debts in the two measured commodities, and the two weighed commodities when of disparate kinds,[13] or in those commodities which are neither of the two commodities nor the two weighed commodities when of like kind.[14] In other words, credit *riba* is the exchange by sale of one kind for another of like kind or for a different kind along with an excess in the volume or the weight against the delay of payment; for example, as the sale of a *sa'* of wheat for 1 *sa'*[15] and a half to be paid after two months; or 1 *sa'* of wheat for 2 *sa*s of barley to be paid after three months; or without excess, such as the sale of one pound of dry dates paid immediately against a pound of dry dates to be paid after a delayed period. All of these are examples of the commodities of different or like kinds that are measured by volume or weighed when of disparate or like kind. An example for that which is not measured nor weighed when of like kind is the sale of an apple for two apples, or a quince for two, to be paid after one month.[16] In all of these examples, credit *riba* occurs due to their inclusion of an increase in one of the two exchanged goods without any counter-value. The impermissibility of exchanging equal amounts is due to the resulting increase in value, as neither of the contracting parties would usually accept to postpone the receiving of the payment save if there were some benefit by increase in the value thereby.[1⁻] Normally, what is immediately possessed is of greater worth than what is possessed only after a delay in payment, just as an asset is better than a debt, since the debtor may prove unable to repay the debt or may violate the agreement and return something other than what was agreed upon.

Some of the scholars, such as Ibn 'Abbas, Usama ibn Zayd ibn Arqam, Zubayr, and Ibn Jubayr, were of the opinion that the only type of forbidden *riba* is "credit *riba*," due to the saying of the Prophet (peace and blessings of Allah be upon him) reported by Bukhari and Muslim on the authority of Usama, "There is no *riba* except in credit." Their argument, however, is refuted by the *hadith*s which clearly establish the impermissibility of excess *riba*; thus, Jabir ibn Zayd relates that Ibn 'Abbas went back on his opinion; and thereafter, a scholarly consensus was established by the scholars of the Followers[18] (*tabi'in*) on the impermissibility of both types of *riba*, any debate thereby being ended. In this light, the explanation of the previous *hadith* is that the Prophet (peace and blessings of Allah be upon him) was asked about the exchange of wheat for barley, and gold for silver, with a delay in payment, to which the Prophet (peace and blessings of Allah be upon him), replied, "There is no *riba* except in credit," as an answer to what had already been mentioned in the question. Thus, either the narrator of the *hadith* heard only the answer of the Messenger of Allah (peace and blessings of Allah be upon him) and did not hear the question that had preceded the answer, or failed to relate it,[19] or what was intended by his saying "there is no *riba*" was that credit *riba* is the greater of the types *riba*, much more significant in danger, more frequently occurring, and more severe in punishment than the other. Such a usage is similar to the Arabs' saying, "there is no scholar in this land except so-and-so," for in reality there are many scholars other than him, but what was meant thereby was the negation of any scholar so complete in knowledge, not the negation of knowledge altogether.

Riba, according to the Shafi'i scholars, is of three kinds:

- *Surplus* riba[20]: which is a sale with an increase in one of the two counter-values over the other; that is, pure excess, with no delay of payment. This type of *riba* occurs only in two counter-values which are of exact like kind, such as a bucket of wheat for one and half buckets of wheat, and a gram of gold for a gram and a half. This type of *riba* is forbidden by unanimity of the scholars.

- Riba *of possession*: which is a sale with delay in taking possession of either or both of the counter-values; that is, that the sale of two different kinds, such as wheat and barley, be finalized without either of them being possessed in the same session of the contract. This type of *riba* is included in the definition of credit *riba* provided by the Hanafi scholars, in their saying "the preference of assets over debts," and is a branch off of the condition that exchanges occur in both of the *ribawi* monies.

- *Credit* riba: which is a sale with delay in payment; that is, a sale on credit, the payment being due on a future date, with an increase at the time the payment is due, without settling the price against the delay. In other words, the increase is in one of the two counter-values with no counter-value against it, this increase being against the delay in payment.

According to the Shafi'i scholars, both *riba* of possession and credit *riba* occur only when the two counter-values are of disparate kinds. The distinction between these two types is that *riba* of possession occurs in the case of delay of possession, while credit *riba* occurs in the case of delay of the date of payment, by explicit mention of the delay, even if it is a short period, in the contract. In other words, the Shafi'i scholars limit credit *riba* to the case of a sale which is accompanied by a stipulated delay in payment, while *riba* of possession occurs in the case of an immediately effected sale, with a delay in possession. The Shafi'i scholar, al-Mutawalli, added another category, namely *riba* in a loan in which the occurrence of some benefit is stipulated; Zirkishi, however, states that this type may be annexed to surplus *riba*.[21]

In summary, credit *riba* is the delay of a due debt against an increase of its original amount (this being the *riba* of the pre-Islamic period), or the delay of collecting one of the two counter-values in the sale of *ribawi* commodities of like kind. As for surplus *riba*, it is the increase in one of the two counter-values over the other in the immediate exchange of *ribawi* commodities for like kind. If, however, a merchant says, "the price of this commodity, if paid immediately, is Five liras; if payment is delayed until such-and-such month, the price is six liras," then this type of delayed sale is permissible, since there is no trace of *riba* in it, as the two counter-values are of different kinds, though some scholars of the Zaydi Madhhab forbid it due to what they perceive as the occurrence of *riba* therein.

Pretexts to committing *riba*, and its ambiguous circumstances, Ibn Kathir says:

> Truly, *muzara'a*, which is sharecropping, has been forbidden; likewise *muzabana*, which is purchasing ripe dates that are yet on the palms for dates that have already fallen onto the ground; and also *muhaqala*, which is selling grains that are still in their spikes for grains which have already been harvested; all of these have been forbidden, and others like them, in order to avoid the essence of *riba*, because it is not possible to know if two things are equal before desiccation. It is for this reason that the jurists have said, "Not knowing if two objects are equal is equivalent to surplus." Hence, they forbade certain matters in order to make narrow the paths and means that lead to *riba*.[22]

The jurists' schools of thought as to the legal cause of riba's *impermissibility*

Scholars agree upon the impermissibility of surplus *riba* in seven canonically forbidden categories: gold, silver, wheat, barley, dry dates, raisins, and salt. In these categories, surplus is forbidden when exchanging like kinds. However, in other than these categories, the scholars are in disagreement:

The Dhahiri Madhhab holds that surplus is impermissible only in these types.

Another group holds that it is forbidden in every measured or weighed good if traded for its like kind; this is the most correct position of the school of Imam Ahmad and the opinion of Imam Abu Hanifa.

Another opinion holds that the impermissibility is particular to the two currencies and foodstuff, even if they are not measured nor weighed; this is the opinion of the Shafi'i scholars and one narrated opinion from Imam Ahmad. Their definition of foodstuff is everything that is taken into the stomach for survival, enjoyment, or as medication.

Another group limits *ribawi* goods only to foodstuff that is measured or weighed; this is the opinion of Sa'id ibn Musayyib, a narrated opinion of Ahmad, and one of the opinions of Imam Shafi'i.

The last party holds that *ribawi* goods are particular to foodstuff and that which ameliorates it, this being the opinion of Imam Malik. Ibn al-Qayyim considers this the strongest of opinions.[23]

We shall now discuss the most important of these legal opinions.

The Hanafi School

The Hanafis state that the legal cause for the impermissibility of surplus *riba*, or that precept by which *ribawi* commodities are known, is volume or weight plus the oneness of kind. If these two conditions are both met, both selling with a surplus or on credit are forbidden.[24] In other words, the legal cause in the four commodities mentioned in the *hadith* (wheat, barley, dry dates, and salt) is the combination of volume and like kind and in gold and silver, the legal cause is the combination of weight and the like. Thus, *riba* does not occur except when the two qualities are combined, namely the amount and the kind, that is, the amount specified by the *Sharia'a* as being measured or weighed[25] and the like kind. An example of this is the sale of gold for gold if one of the counter-values exceeds the other, for the excess in this case is *riba*, because each of the counter-values is a weighed good, this being what is meant by "amount." According to this, *riba* occurs only in fungible commodities (namely, measured or weighed goods). As for non-fungible commodities, such as animals, houses, carpets, jewelry, and pearls, *riba* does not occur therein, and it is thus permissible to trade a large number or amount for a small number or amount of the same, such as one sheep for two, because the non-fungibles (i.e. those things in which all of its particulars are the same in size and amount) cannot be measured nor weighed.

The source of this is the authentic *hadith* related by Abu Sa'id al-Khudari and 'Ubada ibn al- Samit (may Allah be well pleased with them) that the Prophet (peace and blessings of Allah be upon him) said,

> Gold for gold[26] in equal amounts, hand in hand, and any surplus is *riba*; silver
> for silver, in equal amounts, hand in hand, and any surplus is *riba*; wheat for
> wheat, in equal amounts, hand in hand, and any surplus is *riba*; barley for barley,
> in equal amounts, hand in hand, and any surplus is *riba*; dry dates for dry dates,
> in equal amounts, hand in hand, and any surplus is *riba*; salt for salt, in equal
> amounts, hand in hand, and any surplus is *riba*.

Consequently, surplus *riba* is specific to fungible, like commodities which are measured
or weighed, not those measured by length or counted, for there is no *riba* therein. As
for non-fungibles, such as individual animals, carpets, lands, houses, and trees, no
surplus *riba* occurs therein, because they are not fungibles (i.e. those things in which
all of its particulars are the same in size and amount), and thus it is permissible to
give a large amount of one of them in exchange for a lesser amount of the same kind,
such as one sheep for two particular sheep, because surplus *riba* is the excess of one of
two things of the same kind over the other in size or amount, and those commodities
which are sold according to value are not fungible goods.[27]

The wisdom behind the impermissibility of *riba* is to protect people from fraud
and harm caused by possibly thinking that one of the two kinds is more significant
than the other. The principle reason for the impermissibility is to prevent any
pretext for committing forbidden acts because if people sell one dirham for two, and
they do so only for the disparity between the two kinds: either in quality, type of
mintage, weight or lightness, etc., by means of immediate profit in one, they
achieve a delayed profit, which is the essence of credit *riba*. In other words, the
impermissibility of surplus *riba* when the counter-values are of disparate kinds, such
as the sale of wheat for barley, is forbidden by way of preventing pretexts for committing forbidden acts, so that the disparity of amount when the types are disparate
is not taken as a pretext and means to credit *riba*, such that a person takes a loan of
gold due on a particular date, and then returns the loan in an amount of silver that
exceeds the equivalent of the gold taken, in proportion to the amount of *riba*
desired. Thus, the judicious *Sharia'a* has established a simple criterion which the
majority of people can use to evaluate the disparate categories of commodities, without needing to delve into the distinctions between the different particular types in
any one category.

It is possible that the wisdom behind the impermissibility may not be preventing
the pretexts for committing forbidden acts, such as taking a lot of something of low
quality for a little of that which is high quality, in which the excess of the low quality is for the quality of the high quality; nevertheless, it is still forbidden, because of
the considerable extent of fraud involved which makes it impossible to know which
one of them is more unjust.[28]

Surplus *riba*, such as a man trading two bushels of wheat for one bushel, such that
each exchanges his goods for that of the other, does not occur frequently in transactions.

The minimal amount which effects surplus *riba*: In food, the amount which effects
surplus *riba* is at minimum half a *sa'*,[29] as no consideration is given in *Sharia'a* to less

than that amount;[30] thus, if it is less than half a *sa'*, a disparity in the amounts exchanged is permissible. For example, it is permissible to buy one handful of wheat for two handfuls,[31] or one apple for two, provided that payment is immediate. Thus, until the amount reaches half a *sa'* – as there is no standard which indicates equality – no surplus or excess is effected.

As for those commodities which are weighed, the minimal amount is less than a grain[32] of gold or silver.

However, the validity of the sale is conditional upon specifying the two counter-values, such that if one or both were unspecified, the sale is invalid according to all scholars.[33]

The kind of legal cause: Thus, *riba* is effected in everything in which this legal cause is actualized (namely, the equality of the amount plus likeness of kind), regardless of whether the subject of the transaction is foodstuff or otherwise. Thus, everything which is sold by volume, such as corn, rice, sesame, fenugreek, and plaster, is legally compared to wheat and barley, the two commodities mentioned in the *hadith* of surplus *riba*, so long as it is sold by volume. Likewise, everything which is sold by weight, such as lead, copper, and iron is legally compared to gold and silver.

There is no surplus *riba* for those commodities, which are not sold by volume or weight, namely commodities which are non-fungibles, being counted or measured by length. Thus, it is permissible to sell one egg for two, and a span of cloth for two of the same type, on condition that they are exchanged in the same session of the contract.

Criterion of ribawi *commodities*: Attention should be paid to what the Lawgiver has explicitly delineated as measured by volume, namely wheat, barley, dry dates, and salt; or weighed, namely gold and silver. The categorization of these commodities is permanent, even if the general public no longer uses that form of measurement for a particular commodity as it had in the past. This is the opinion of the majority of Hanafi scholars, the Shafi'i scholars, and the Hanbali scholars, due to the saying of the Prophet (peace and blessings of Allah be upon him), "The volume is that of the people of Medina, and weight that of the people of Mecca."[34] Thus, it is not permissible to sell wheat for wheat in equal weight, nor gold for gold, or silver for silver, in equal volume, because the explicit text of the *hadith* is a stronger proof than that of custom, and that which is stronger abandoned for that which is weaker.

We had mentioned that Abu Yusuf was of the opinion that the true criterion *ribawi* commodities mentioned in the source-text and others is custom, the criterion thus changing with the changing of the customs. His opinion is the strongest, because the *hadith* establishing the necessity of equality in exchange in *ribawi* commodities, whether of volume or weight, is based upon the criterion which was the prevailing custom during the time of the Prophet (peace and blessings of Allah be upon him), and the establishing of the legal cause of the criterion by means of the source-text can be perceived by consideration of the dominant custom. This position is further strengthened by the opinion of the Malikis which states, "If the customs of peoples differ in regards to volumes and weight, what is of consideration is the custom of the land in which the sale was contracted; as for those commodities in which there is no explicit source-text from the Lawgiver, the criterion is the practice of the people and their customs of interaction in the markets."[35]

High quality and low quality: It should also be noted that a *ribawi* commodity of high quality and that of low quality are of equal worth in regards to the criterion of *riba*. Thus, it is not permissible to sell any *ribawi* commodity for its like except for an equal amount because the quality of a good is not given consideration if it is one of the *ribawi* commodities, due to the maxim of Islamic Law, "That which is of high quality and low quality are the same."[36] The wisdom of this is that the trading of a thing of high quality with the bad will lead to the violation of what the Lawgiver decreed of forbidding disparity during the exchange of *ribawi* goods. People usually do not exchange one thing for another unless they are equal in all respects; rather, they exchange a kind for its like only if there is disparity between the two. Thus, if it was made permissible that one may trade a commodity for its like due to what it possesses of high quality, surplus *riba* would not be forbidden. The trade of something of high quality for low quality is forbidden, in order to block off any legal obscurities that may lead to *riba* and to seal off any paths that could be taken as pretexts for committing forbidden acts.[37] Based thereupon, the Maliki scholars have forbidden the sale of *muratala*, which is the sale of gold currency for that of its same description by weight, if there is a difference between the gold of the two in regards to the quality being high or low.

The legal cause for the impermissibility of credit riba: The legal cause for the impermissibility of credit *riba*, which was the type of *riba* known during the pre-Islamic period, is either of the two principal factors of the legal cause of the impermissibility of surplus *riba*: namely, either the volume or weight being equal, or being of like kind.[38] An example of such is one's buying a *sa'* of wheat in the winter for one and a half *sa'*s to be paid in the summer; in this scenario, the extra half *sa'*, which is an increase in the cost, has no counter-value, but is only set against the delay of the debt's collection. This is why it is called credit *riba*; that is, delay in paying one of the two counter-values. The increase in one of the two counter-values is against the delay of payment, regardless of whether they are of similar or of different amounts. If, in the pre-Islamic period, a man gave a loan to his brother, and the debt later became due, he would give him a choice: "either pay now, or increase the due amount"; thus, he would either repay the debt, or postpone payment and add onto the due principal, this obviously being harmful to the one in debt, as the debt may eventually consume all of his wealth.

On this basis: If the scenario is that only the amount is equal, such as in a sale of wheat for barley, or the scenario is that of a sale of like kinds, such as one apple for two, or barley for barley, postponement of payment is forbidden.[39] If the two counter-values are equal, even if he sells salt for an equivalent amount of salt on credit, this transaction is invalid, due to the oneness of the type. Such ruling, for the impermissibility of surplus *riba* is effected by the fulfillment of the two conditions while the impermissibility of credit *riba* is effected by the fulfillment of just one of the two conditions.

Since the oneness of kind is a sufficient condition to effect the impermissibility of credit *riba*, the amount being exchanged is not taken into consideration (in our example, the extra half *sa'* or more). Thus it is forbidden to sell one handful of wheat for two handfuls, or one apple for two, or one watermelon for two, etc. if payment is on credit due to the oneness of kind: this being in contrast to surplus *riba*, as we have shown.

The wisdom of the impermissibility: In general, the impermissibility of credit *riba* is due to the harm that it places on those people who are forced by need, and because it eliminates mercy and kindness between people; likewise *riba* negates the virtues of cooperation and mutual support in this life, and assists in the strong exploiting of the weak due to his being in need, as well as causing great harm to people. Thus, if money became a locus of *ribawi* trade, such as normal goods, regardless of whether the excess is due immediately or is on credit, the entire criterion for judging the value of money, which is supposed to be meticulously definite and accurate, and not subject to wild increases and decreases, would be thrown off kilter. Likewise, if credit *riba* was permissible in the selling of foodstuff by selling something for its like kind on credit, many people would rush to this type of transaction, filled with greed for quick profit, resulting in some foodstuff becoming rare, thus causing great harm to the availability of food supplies.[40]

The riba *of the banks*: The process of today's banks, in which money is lent on credit, with annual or monthly interest rates of 7, 5, or 2.5 percent, is likewise the forbidden and unjust consumption of people's wealth. For truly, the harm of *riba* is realized therein, and it takes the same ruling of impermissibility as that of *riba*, and the same sinfulness as that of *riba*,[41] for it *is* credit *riba*, as proven by the saying of Allah Most High, "but if you turn back, you shall have your capital sums." Conventionally, the word "interest" today is only used to indicate the interest on money due to delay in payment, this being the very same credit *riba* known by the people of the pre-Islamic period. As for surplus *riba*, today it is very rare. This clarifies that what is intended by the previously mentioned *hadith* "verily, *riba* is in credit," is to warn of the danger and harm of *riba*, and to point out how frequently it occurs, as we have illustrated.

Similar and different kinds: As we have shown, it is forbidden to sell a commodity for its like kind with a discrepancy between the exchanged amounts. It is permissible, according to Hanafi scholars, to sell disparate kinds with a discrepancy of amount, except for birds' meat. Thus, it is permissible to sell a kind of meat for its like with a discrepancy of amount, such as that of a thrush and that of a sparrow, because the meat is not a *ribawi* commodity, since it is neither bought by volume nor weight; the exception to this rule is the meat of chickens and geese, because these are usually sold by weight, and are therefore forbidden to be sold for disparate amounts.

The standard of disparity, according to the Hanafis, is set according to the difference in origin, such as the vinegar of dry dates and the vinegar of grapes, or the meat of cow or the meat of lamb or according to the difference in utility, such as the mohair of a goat and the wool of a sheep, for each one is used for different purposes according to industry or by a change in quality/attribute, such as the bread made of wheat, because bread is sold by individual count or weight, while wheat is sold by volume. Hence, the meat and milk of camels, cows, and sheep are considered to be of disparate kinds, the exchange of which for disparate amounts therefore being permitted; likewise, wheat, barley, corn, etc. are all considered to be of disparate kinds; bread made from white flour and bread made from wheat are likewise disparate; fat and meat are disparate; olive oil and olives are of disparate kinds; olive oil which is obtained by boiling the olives and oil obtained by pressing are also disparate; all because the intended purposes of each of them are different, and so on, in accordance with the delineated criterion.[42]

The proof of the Hanafi School: The Hanafi scholars support their position that the legal cause of *riba* is that the commodity be measured by volume or weight, by stating that equality or similarity in the two counter-values is a condition for the validity of a sale. *Riba* is forbidden because there is a surplus in one of the counter-values above the other with no equivalent counter-value for the surplus. All of this may be found in commodities not explicitly delineated in the previous *hadith*, such as plaster, iron, and their like. Equality or likeness between two things is in accordance to form and content; thus, equality of amount (being by volume or weight) establishes the similarity in form, whereas the type of commodity establishes the equality of content. This is because similarity in commodities means approximation of value, such that one *qafiz* resembles another *qafiz*,[43] and one dinar another; thus, any surplus over the first is a surplus in the amount of the commodity, it being possible to avoid such excess during a commutative transaction, and is thus considered *riba*. This is an element which is not specific to foodstuff and currencies, but is rather found in everything that is measured by volume and sold for its like, or weighed and traded for its like.[44]

In other words, what is intended by "wheat" in the aforementioned *hadith* is any commodity of value, because only a sale of an object of value is valid, and the value of such a commodity is not known except by being measured by volume; thus, its attribute of "being measured by volume" is established according to the source-text. Hence, it is as if the Prophet (peace and blessing of Allah be upon him) said, "Gold, which is weighed, for gold; and wheat, which is measured by volume, for wheat." If, therefore, what is required in order to be free from *riba* is equality in the traded commodities, then, accordingly, equality in the volume or weight is the means to being free from that which is forbidden; and since a handful of a dry-measured commodity, or a single apple, cannot be exchanged in exact amounts, then it is not possible for them to be included in the category of *ribawi* commodities,[45] that is, surplus *riba*, though they do enter into the sphere of credit *riba*, and are considered *ribawi* commodities in that regard.

It should be noted, however, that all types of wheat, regardless of their qualities or land of production, are of one kind; likewise, all types of barley and its flour, dry dates, salt, grapes, raisins, gold, and silver. Thus, it is forbidden to sell any commodity which is measured by volume or weighed from these categories for their like with any disparity of amount, even if they are of the same type or quality.[46]

The Maliki School

The Maliki scholars, according to the dominant opinion of the school, hold that the legal cause of the impermissibility of increase in gold and silver is the fact that they are valued currencies (i.e. the quality of having intrinsic monetary value); as for foodstuff, the legal cause is different in each of credit *riba* or surplus *riba*.

The legal cause of the impermissibility of credit *riba* is mere edibility, not for the sake of medical treatment, regardless whether it is nutritious and storable, only nutritious, or neither, examples of which are different kinds of vegetables such as cucumber, watermelon, lemon, lettuce, carrot, and taro, and different kinds of fresh fruits such as apples and bananas.

As for the legal cause of the impermissibility of surplus *riba*, there are two causes: that it be nutritious and storable; that is, that a person usually receives nutrition therefrom, such that his constitution be strengthened thereby, such that if he limited himself to eating only that food type, he would live without need of anything else, and without his constitution being weakened thereby. Included therein are all sorts of grains, dry dates, raisins, meats, milk, and milk products. Likewise included in the meaning of "being nutritious" are those things that ameliorate those foods, such as salt and its likes of spices, vinegar, onion, garlic, and oil.

The meaning of "suitable for storing" is that it does not spoil due to being stored for a period of time, with no particular time limit being established according to the soundest opinion of the Maliki School; rather, the limit is delineated according to the customary length of time for that particular food product. Thus, the authoritative source for what specifies this is custom, not some arbitrary specification of six months or one year, as some scholars had held.

The proof of the Malikis is that since the ruling of *riba*'s impermissibility is logically perceivable, being that people not cheat and deceive one another, and that their wealth be preserved, it then necessarily begets that this be in the staples of survival: namely, nutritious foods, such as wheat, rice, corn, vetch, dates, raisins, eggs, and the seven legumes (which are lentils, cowpeas, chickpeas, lupines, broad beans, chickling vetch, and peas).[47]

As for the similarity and disparity in kind, attention should be paid to the fact that Imam Malik considers wheat, barley, and rye (which is a sort of peel-less barley) as one kind. He also considers corn, millet, and rice as one kind, and all sorts of legumes including broad beans, lentils, chickpeas, and the like, as one kind. Therefore, it is not allowed to sell an amount of wheat for a disparate amount of barley, whereas it is allowed in wheat and corn. As for meats, Imam Malik divided them into three categories: first, meat of quadrupeds; second, meat of birds; third, meat of fish.[48]

The Shafi'i School

The Shafi'i scholars hold that the legal cause in gold and silver is their being intrinsic currencies, or having monetary value; that is, that they are what are used as payment for goods, regardless whether the gold and silver be minted or not (meaning, raw gold or raw silver). The cost of any handiwork done on the gold or silver is of no consideration, and has no effect on their value, such that if a man pays some dinars for golden jewelry, the value of which exceeds the value of these dinars, then equality of amount in like commodities is what is considered, not the value thereof. The legal cause being monetary value is limited only to gold and silver, and is not that of other coins and other types of currencies and objects of value, even if such currencies and objects are what are used to assess the value of objects. All this is because those vessels, raw ores, and jewelry which are made of gold or silver are what are used in *riba*, and are not what are used to evaluate the cost of goods; this is also the proof that if currencies (other than gold and silver) come into circulation, there is no *riba* therein.

As for the legal cause in the four remaining categories, it is edibility. Edibles are of three sorts:

The first sort includes that which is meant to be eaten as nourishment, like wheat and barley; that is, eaten most of the time. Such foods include broad beans, rice, corn, chickpeas, lupines, and other such edibles from the category of grains, on which *zakat* is obligatory.

The second sort includes that which is eaten for enjoyment. The *hadith* explicitly includes dates and other similar foods, such as raisins and figs, therein.

The third sort includes that which is used to ameliorate food and to rectify the body, that is, as medical treatment. The *hadith* explicitly includes salt, and other similar foods that also classically provided health benefits, such as *sanamaki*, *sakmonia*, ginger, and homogenous drugs such as dry seed, therein.

On this basis, there is no differentiation between what ameliorates food and what rectifies the body, because food preserves health, while medications restore it. Thus, edibles include everything that is meant to be eaten (i.e. mostly as a food) whether for nourishment, enjoyment, or treatment. Thus, the legal cause for the impermissibility of *riba* according *to* the Shafi'i scholars is edibility and monetary value. As for those things which are nonedible, such as plaster and iron, it is permissible to sell one for its like kind for a disparate amount, as trade objects, because these materials are not considered currencies or of intrinsic monetary value.

The proof of the Shafi'i scholars for this position is the following: if a legal ruling includes in its wording a derivative noun, this indicates that the meaning from which the noun is derived is itself the legal cause of the ruling; for example, in His Most Praised's saying, "The male thief and the female thief cut off their hand," it is understood that theft is the legal cause for the cutting of the hand. If one agrees to this principle, the *hadith of* Sa'id ibn Abdallah in which he states, "I used to hear the Prophet of Allah (peace and blessings *of* Allah be upon him) say, 'Food-stuff for food-stuff, for equal amounts' "[49] falls under the rubric of this principle; *for* the *hadith* makes clear that edibility is the legal cause for the legal ruling, since "foodstuff" (Arabic: *ta'aim*) is derived from "to feed" (Arabic: *ta'm*), which includes all edibles (Arabic: *mat'umat*); it is a suitable description, because it tells of the extreme importance of the four kinds explicitly mentioned in the *hadith*, since food is indispensable for the continuation of life. Likewise, monetary value is a suitable meaning, because it too tells of the extreme importance of people's need for the two intrinsic currencies (gold and silver) or that which takes their place: coins or other paper currencies.

As for the condition of "amount" as stated by the Hanafi scholars, it does not tell of any importance in these things.

Hence, three conditions are necessary to validate the sale of food for food and money for money, in the case of their being of like kind, such as wheat for wheat, and silver for silver (regardless whether they are minted coins or not, such as jewelry and raw ores). First, *immediacy of payment*, such that the sales contract does not stipulate any deferment of payment. Second, that the two counter-values be of *exact similitude* according to the criterion of the *Sharia'a*, namely that it be measured by volume if it is a dry-measurable good, or weighed if it is a good that is weighed, according to the customs of the people of Hijaz during the period of the Messenger (peace and blessings be upon him); in what is other than that, according to the customs of the land in which the transaction was contracted. Third, *immediate collection*, that is, the actual of each of the counter-values by each of the contracting parties, before leaving the place of the session of the contract. This last condition, namely *immediate collection*, is a condition beyond what the Hanafi scholars had stipulated of equality in specifying the two counter-values, regardless whether in the case of similar or different kinds, due to the saying of the Prophet (peace and blessings of Allah be upon him), "hand in hand" in both cases.

Selling commodities of two different kinds for disparate amounts, such as wheat for barley, is permissible on condition of immediacy of payment and that collection of the counter-value occur before the conclusion of the session of the contract. Muslim reports that the Prophet (peace and blessings of Allah be upon him) said, "Gold for gold, silver for silver, wheat for wheat, barley for barley, dry dates for dry dates, salt for salt; in equal amounts, the same for the same, hand in hand; and if the types are different, sell however so you may wish, so long as it be hand in hand," that is, immediate collection; this *hadith* being the source of the condition of immediacy is taken. If food is sold for another commodity, such as coins or cloth, or non-food is sold for non-food, neither of the counter-values being one of the two intrinsic monies, such as an animal for an animal, none of the aforementioned three conditions are stipulated, that is, there is no *riba* therein. The reason that there is no *riba* in any animal is that live animals are not considered food; it is also supported by the *hadith* in which Ibn 'Umar (may Allah be well pleased with him) bought a camel for two camels upon the command of the Prophet (peace and blessings of Allah be upon him).[50]

Similar and disparate kinds: Every two things which have a special name due to their essences being the same, such as two types of dry dates, or two types of figs, are considered to be one type according to the Shafi'i scholars; likewise, commodities of similar origin, such as flour taken from two kinds of wheat. As for commodities which are different in their natural names, such as wheat, barley, dry dates, and raisin, they are considered to be disparate types. In the same way, this applies to all commodities of different sources, such as flour of different sources, vinegar, fat, meat, and yogurt of different sources.

Hence, each of the following pairs is considered to be two disparate types: flour of wheat and flour of barley, dry date vinegar and grape vinegar, cow meat and sheep meat, fat of nuts and fat of almonds, yogurt from cow milk and yogurt from sheep milk, domestic cows and wild cows. Thus, it is permissible to sell them for disparate amounts. This also applies to the different kinds of birds' eggs, as well as the inner organs of animals such as the liver, spleen, heart, stomach, and lungs, even if they belong to the same animal, due to the differences of their names and qualities.

We may also include herein the fat of the back, belly, lung, head, and limbs as disparate types; likewise, watermelon, muskmelon, cucumber, and Egyptian cucumber are disparate types. As for birds, different types of sparrows are considered one type, the various species of duck are one type, and the species of doves are also one type, according to the correct position in the Shafi'i School.[51]

The Hanbali School

There are three narrations in this school as to the legal cause of *riba*. The most famous narration is similar to that of the Hanafi School, namely volume or weight plus like kind being the legal cause of *riba*. Thus, *riba* occurs with every commodity which is measured by volume or by weight if exchanged for like kind, whether it is a foodstuff or not, such as grains, glasswort, flowers, cotton, linen, wool, henna, safflower, iron, copper, etc. As for transaction of foodstuff which are not measured by volume *or* by weight, there is no *riba* possible therein. This opinion is based upon the saying of the Prophet (peace and blessings of Allah be upon him) related by Ibn 'Umar, "Do not sell a dinar for two, nor a dirham for two, nor *sa'* for two, for verily I fear that you will fall into *riba*." A man then stood and said, "O'Messenger *of* Allah, what do you say of a man who sells a horse for two horses, and a highbred camel for two ordinary camels?" The Prophet (peace and blessings *of* Allah be upon him) replied, "There is no harm therein, so long as it is hand in hand."[52] Anas likewise relates from the Prophet (peace and blessings of Allah be upon him), "that which is weighed in like amounts, if it is of one kind; and that which is measured by volume, likewise; if, however, the types are different, there is no harm therein."[53]

Nevertheless, the Hanbali scholars, in contradistinction to the Hanafis, hold that surplus *riba* is forbidden in all commodities which are measured by volume or weighed for their like kind – even if it be a small amount, such as one dry date for two, or even what is less than a grain of either of the two intrinsic monies (gold or silver) – though not in water, and likewise not in what is not customarily weighed, due to its being produced from other than gold or silver, such as those objects made out of copper, iron, cotton, etc.

The second narration is the same as the position of the Shafi'i School.

The third narration states that the legal cause for the impermissibility of *riba* in things other than gold and silver is edibility, if they are measured by volume or weighed, such that there is no *riba* in foodstuff which are not measured by volume or weighed, such as apples, pomegranates, plums, watermelons, pears, quince, cucumbers, nuts, and eggs. This also applies to dealing with non-edibles such as saffron, flowers, iron, lead, etc. This is the opinion of Sa'id ibn Musayyib, as we have mentioned previously,[54] the textual proof of which is the Prophet's saying (peace and blessings of Allah be upon him), "There is no *riba* except in what is measured by volume or weighed of food and drink."[55]

Similar and disparate kinds: In this matter, the Hanbali School is similar to the Shafi'i. They hold[56] that all kinds that share a special natural name are considered one kind, such as different types of dry dates. Moreover, it is forbidden to exchange two disparate amounts of commodities that are of the same kind, due to the saying of the Prophet (peace and blessings of Allah be upon him), "dates for dates, in equal amounts," in which he took the equality of type of the dry date into consideration, then said, "but if the categories are disparate, sell however so you wish"; and according to another version, "but if the types are different," and in another, "if their kinds are different."

If the commodities, which share the same name, are of two different geneses, they are considered to be two different kinds. In other words, materials of the same origin are considered to be of one kind, even if the purposes for which they are used are different, this being in contrast to the position of the Hanafis.

Hence, all types of dry dates are of one kind, because they all share the same specific name. Likewise, the oil taken from roses, violets, quicksilver, and the fat from the jasmine plant, if they are all taken from one source, namely oil or sesame oil, are of one type.[57] Similarly, flours, bread, vinegars, fats, meats, yogurts, cheeses, ghee, and juices: all of them are disparate types due to their different origins. Barley flour and wheat flour, olive oil and cotton oil, fats of fish, sesame oil and the seeds...all are considered different types.

The Dhahiri School

The Dhahiri scholars, and Abu Bakr ibn al-Tayyib, hold that there is no legal reason for the impermissibility of *riba* and that it is specified by the explicitly mentioned source-texts alone.[58] Their position is due to their denial of analogical reasoning (*qiyas*) as a principle of jurisprudence, and their opinion that *riba* only occurs in those six things which the Lawgiver has delineated, and all else remains in its original state of permissibility.

In summary, the legal cause for the impermissibility of exchanging different amounts of edibles is, according to the Hanafi and Hanbali Schools, volume and weight; according to Imam Malik, its qualities being nutritious and storable; for Imam Shafi'i, the mere fact that it is edible.

In other than the two intrinsic currencies and foodstuff, according to the Malikis and Shafi'is, and other than that which is measured by volume or weighed, according to the Hanafis and Hanbalis, the permissibility of increase is due to the fact that it does not affect what is necessary for the well-being of peoples' lives, regardless whether in their nutrition or their economic well-being, because their desire for profits does not lead to any great damage in their well-being.

The preponderant legal opinion

The great Maliki scholar, Ibn Rushd, states:

> If one contemplates the meanings and effective conclusions of each school, it becomes apparent – and Allah knows best – that the legal cause of the Hanafi school is the foremost of all the causes proposed. It is clear from the *Sharia'a* that the intention behind the impermissibility of *riba* is the enormous amount of unjust harm which accrues therefrom, since justice in financial transactions occurs

when commodities are exchanged for an exact equivalent. However, since exactly equal exchange is a rare thing when trading commodities which are of different essences, the dinar and dirham are used in order to evaluate their value (meaning, estimate their value). Furthermore, justice and equality in trading commodities of different essences (meaning, things not measured by volume or by weight, such as cloth) occur when their value is proportionate to one another, meaning that the proportionate value of one of the two counter-values in relation to its kind is equal to the proportionate value of the other counter-value in relation to its kind. Hence commutative transactions of countable commodities necessitate a difference of the products one to another when sold; while justice in those objects measured by volume or weight is by equality of amount in the volume or weight.[59]

However, the weakness of this opinion is that it greatly expands the scope of *riba* by way of personal legal reasoning (*ijtihad*) which is neither supported by reason (*'aql*) not by transmitted narrations (*naql*).

Ibn al-Qayyim gave preponderance to the position of Imam Malik in that the legal cause of the impermissibility of *riba* is that the object be nutritious and storable, save in gold and silver. As for the legal cause of these two commodities, he holds it is due to their intrinsic monetary value, as is the position of the Shafi'i School. For example, if iron and copper are considered to be *ribawi* commodities, then it would not be permissible to sell them or credit for immediate payment of dirhams; for if *ribawi* commodities are traded for other than their own type, then exchange for disparate amounts is permissible therein, though delay of payment is not.

Furthermore, to make weight the legal cause is also inappropriate, as opposed to making intrinsic monetary value the legal cause, because dirhams and dinars are *equivalent values* for salable goods, and value is the measure by which a commodity's worth is estimated. Thus, it is necessary that such a measure be accurate, exact and stable in order that people's interactions do not become a source of ruination, disagreement does not spread, and harm does not become severe, in which case dirhams and dinars would be of absolutely no use in trade.[60]

Professor Sanhuri gave preference to the Shafi'i School as to the legal cause of *riba*, by means of assessing the issue from a social and economical vantage point, and in so doing he penetrated into the essence of the matter, comprehending the most essential aspects of the issue. As for the Hanafi position, it is a very logical opinion, which is, however, only closer to the truth in its appearance and form rather than it is in its true comprehension of the essence of the matter.[61]

The principle forms of riba: Ibn Rushd writes that the principal forms of *riba* are five: delay against an increase in the amount owed; surplus; postponement; lowering the amount of the debt against an acceleration of payment; and the sale of food before it is possible to collect. We have already defined these types save for two, which we shall now explain:

- "Delay against an increase in the amount owed": This is forbidden by agreement of all scholars. Its scenario is that a creditor who is owed an amount postpone the due date in return for an increase in the amount due at that date. This is the *riba* known during the pre-Islamic period. It is forbidden regardless whether the debt is of foodstuff or intrinsic monies, and regardless whether it is a loan, sale, or any other kind of transaction. Instead of doing so, the creditor may sell a good on credit to the debtor until a specified date, the price including whatever extra amount he wishes to charge above his cash price.

–   The scenario for this is that a man is indebted to another, but the debt is not yet due. The creditor, in order to accelerate the payment, offers to reduce the amount owed.

•   "Lowering the amount of the debt against an acceleration in payment": All four Imams also consider this to be forbidden, because by cutting back a debt in order to accelerate the payment thereof, one is effectively increasing the debt, because by doing so one has given a monetary value to time, this value being the reduced amount of the debt.

–   A similar scenario is if one accelerates payment of a part of the debt, and delays the other part to another due date, such that the debtor pays part of the debt in gold or silver, and the other part in goods.[62] All of what has just been mentioned, however, is permissible according to all the scholars on condition that the due date of the debt have passed; likewise, it is permissible to settle the delayed debt before the due day by payment in goods, even if their value is less than the value of the debt.[63]

The practical results of the jurists' disagreement as to the legal cause of the impermissibility of *riba*

There are numerous practical differences resulting from the disagreement between the Hanafis and Shafi'is as to the legal cause of *riba*'s impermissibility, some of which are related to surplus *riba*, others to credit *riba*.

Surplus riba

In relation to surplus *riba*, the differences are apparent in the following:

1   *The sale of edibles* for an amount of its like kind that cannot be measured by volume nor weighed, such as the sale of a handful of wheat for two handfuls, one watermelon for two, one apple for two, one egg for two, one nut for two or more, etc. This is permissible in the Hanafi School, because the legal cause of impermissibility is not effected thereby, namely, amount. In relation to commodities which are measured by volume, the *Sharia'a* does not recognize any measure for amounts less than half a *sa'*; as for weighed commodities, namely gold and silver, the *Sharia'a* does not recognize a weight for amounts less than a grain, because such an amount is essentially of no value.[64]

All of this is not permissible in the Shafi'i School, due to the existence of the legal cause according to their position, namely edibility, since the defining principle of what is forbidden in this school is the sale of two foodstuffs for one another, their textual evidence for this being the *hadith*, "Food for food, in equal amounts." Equality of amount between two edible commodities eliminates the impermissibility; so long as equality, however, is not established, the transaction remains impermissible, because this is the defining principle according to their school. Thus, a handful for two and other such scenarios are not permissible.

The legal cause being amount, according to the Hanafis, necessitates the qualification of the previous *hadith* "Wheat for wheat, in equal amounts..."[65] such that it is permissible in their school to sell a handful for two, etc.

2 *The sale of measured or weighed non-edibles for like commodities*; that is, the sale of something non-edible measured by volume for its like kind, or something non-edible which is weighed for its like kind, such as the sale of a *qafiz* of plaster for two *qafiz*es of plaster, or a pound of iron for two of the same, etc.

This is all impermissible according to the Hanafi School, due to the existence of the legal cause, namely measurement by volume plus like kind (in the case of the sale of plaster), or weight plus like kind (in the case of the sale of iron).[66]

This is permitted, however, according to the Shafi'i School, because the legal cause of *riba* is fulfilled, namely, that the commodity be edible or of intrinsic monetary value. However, both the Hanafi and the Shafi'i Schools agree that it is not permissible to sell one *qafiz*[67] of rice for two, as volume plus like kind is impermissible according to the Hanafis, and edibility plus like kind is impermissible according to the Shafi'is.

Likewise, they also agree that the sale of one pound of saffron[68] for two, or one pound of sugar for two, is not permissible, because the Hanafis forbid weight plus like kind, and the Shafi'is forbid edibility plus like kind.

The jurists are in disagreement concerning some aspects related to realization of the condition of "like kind", the following being loci of the disagreement:

1 *The sale of flour for its like, or flour for grain*: The Hanafis hold that it is not permissible to sell flour made from a certain type of grain for that grain itself, regardless whether they are equal in amount or not, because true equality between them is not possible, for example, in the sale of wheat flour for wheat, corn flour for corn, etc.

However, the sale of flour made from a certain type of grain for some other type of grain is permissible so long as payment is immediate, because the kinds are disparate, for example, in the sale of wheat flour for barley.

As for selling flour of a certain type for flour of the same, it is permissible on condition that both are equal in volume and fineness or coarseness.

It is also permissible to sell bread for wheat or flour, or vice versa, for disparate or equal amounts. This is because the process of baking bread has made it a commodity different from wheat, so much so that it is no longer a commodity measured by volume; and as wheat and flour are both measured by volume, the bread and the flour are no longer similar, neither in amount nor kind. Therefore, it is permissible to exchange one for the other, even if on credit, as immediate payment is not a condition, so long as the exact specifications are delineated.[69]

The Malikis hold that the sale of grains for flour is not valid, one for the other, unless for equal amounts with no excess of one over the other. Thus, it is permissible for a person to sell wheat for flour made therefrom, so long as they are equal in weight.

If the types are different, such as if a person sells corn flour for wheat grain, it is permissible, even if the amounts are disparate, so long as collection occurs in the same session of the contract.

Likewise, the sale of bread for wheat is permissible, because the baking of the bread has made it into a different commodity.

As for the sale of flour for similar flour, it is unequivocally forbidden.[70]

The Shafi'is hold that it is not permissible to sell flour for its like (such as wheat flour for wheat flour), because there is no certain similarity between the two, due to the possible difference in fineness or coarseness between them, this difference leading to a disparity in volume between them.

Likewise, it is not permissible to sell wheat flour for wheat, nor either of them for bread, though it is permissible to sell bread for bread, or flour for flour, if the two kinds are disparate for example, in the sale of wheat bread for barley bread, or wheat flour for corn flour, as these are disparate kinds.[71]

The Hanbali School holds that it is unequivocally invalid to sell flour for the grain from which it is made, because equality is a condition in the sale of a commodity for its like. Likewise, it is not permissible to sell bread for the grains from which it is made, nor bread for the flour from which it is made.

As for the selling of flour for flour of like kind, it is permissible if sold by volume, as is similarly stated by the Hanafis, on condition that both are equal in fineness.[72]

In summary, there are two opinions regarding the sale of flour for its like: one which permits it, being the position of the Hanafis and Hanbalis, and one which does not permit it, namely that of the Malikis and Shafi'is.

2   *The sale of an animal for meat*: Abu Hanifa and Abu Yusuf hold that it is permissible to sell an animal whose meat is eaten for the meat of the same kind, because it is a sale of a weighed commodity for a commodity that is not weighed. All possible scenarios of such a sale are valid on the condition that the counter-values are both specified.[73]

The three remaining Imams, other than those of the Hanafis, hold that it is not permissible to sell an animal whose meat is eaten for the meat of the same kind, such as a slaughtered sheep for a live sheep which is intended to be eaten,[74] due to the *hadith* related by Sa'id ibn Musayyib in which the Prophet of Allah (peace and blessings of Allah be upon him) forbade the sale of an animal for like meat;[75] likewise, it has been related that the Prophet (peace and blessings of Allah be upon him) forbade the sale of a live animal for one that is dead.[76] These jurists also give by way of evidence that meat is a *ribawi* commodity, [in this scenario] being sold for its original source of which it is part and parcel; thus, it is not permissible, just as the sale of sesame for its oil is not permissible, due to the lack of knowledge as to whether the two amounts are truly equal, and thus it is legally assumed that the amounts are truly disparate.[77]

Credit riba

The following are some of the consequences of the disagreement between the Shafi'is and Hanafis as to the legal cause of credit *riba*:

First, some differences which return to the principal disagreement over the legal cause of *riba*. The legal cause of *riba*, as previously mentioned, is the quality of being measured by volume or weighed according to the Hanafis, and edibility according to the Shafi'is.

The scholars agree that it is not allowed to sell one *qafiz* of wheat for one *qafiz* of barley on credit, or to sell for a debt of an unspecified commodity that will be paid when the debt is due.[78] The impermissibility is due to the existence of the legal cause, namely either of the two conditions of the legal cause of surplus *riba*, in that case being measurement by volume according to the Hanafis, and edibility according to the Shafi'is.

The consequences of their disagreement appear in the following two cases:

1   *In the sale of non-edible commodities*: The Hanafi School does not permit the sale of one *qafiz* of plaster for one *qafiz* of limestone[79] with a delay in payment, whether by means of a loan, or a debt of an unspecified commodity to be paid when the debt is due, due to their both being measured by volume. According to the Shafi'i School, it is permissible, as the commodities are not edibles.

Likewise, the forward sale of one pound of iron for two is not permissible according to the Hanafis due to their being weighed commodities, while the Shafi'is hold that it is permissible due to their not being edibles or intrinsic monies.

The two schools agree that it is not permissible to sell one pound of sugar for one pound of saffron on credit, because one of the legal causes of surplus *riba* is fulfilled thereby, namely, their both being weighable according to the Hanafis, and their being edibles according to the Shafi'is.

However, the scholars agree that the forward sale of dirhams or dinars for saffron, cotton or iron is permissible, because the legal cause of forbidding *riba* is not fulfilled thereby, namely, equality of amounts or likeness of kind. Likeness of kind is clearly not fulfilled; as for the equality of amounts, it likewise is not fulfilled, because the weight of the counter-value is different from that of the object of sale, for dirhams are weighed by *mithqal*, while cotton, iron, and saffron are weighed by steel yard; thus, oneness of measurement is not achieved, the legal cause is likewise not fulfilled, and thus, there is no *riba* therein.

It is not permissible, by consensus of the scholars, for a person to purchase in advance the remnants of melted[80] silver for a similar piece of gold, or gold dust for a piece of melted silver, or jewelry of either of them for either gold or silver; the impermissibility is due to the existence of [the stipulation of] equal weight according to the Hanafis, since these commodities are weighed by *mithqal*,[81] and due to the existence of intrinsic monetary value according to the Shafi'is, because gold and silver are the bases of prices.

2   *In the sale of edible commodities for like and for disparate amounts*: It is permissible to make an advanced purchase of wheat for oil, according to the Hanafi scholars,

because one of them is measured by volume, and the other by weight; thus, they are of disparate amounts. According to the Shafi'is, it is not permissible, due to the edible nature of each.[82]

Second, some differences which return to their disagreement as to what constitutes a "type," and whether this is a sufficient legal cause.

We have already mentioned that, according to the Hanafi scholars, similarity of type is a sufficient legal cause for the impermissibility of credit *riba*, as they consider volume or weight plus a like kind as the legal cause for the impermissibility of *riba*. Each of the legal causes of impermissibility has two features, the legal cause not being sufficient without both of them being fulfilled; thus, each of them alone bears a similitude to being a legal cause in and of itself, and that which bears a similitude to a legal cause effects the similitude of a legal ruling, that is, similarity of type is a essential element (*rukn*) of the legal cause, not merely a condition thereof.

According to Imam Shafi'i, similarity of kind alone is not a sufficient legal cause for the impermissibility of credit *riba*, because the type of commodity is merely the locus of the impermissibility, or a mere condition for the impermissibility of *riba*, and the ruling may be based upon the condition, just as stoning is related to the chastity of a woman, the reason of this being that the legal cause is a name for a description suitable for the ruling, such that legal cause of a ruling is that cause which is suitable for what is intended from that ruling, being in this case edibility, as man continues to live thereby, and intrinsic monetary value, as it is through it that people's interests are maintained. As for kind, it has no effect in either of these matters, and is therefore considered a condition.[83]

The following results from this difference:

The scholars agree that it is not permissible to give nuts as advance payment for nuts, nor eggs for eggs, apples for apples, or a handful for a handful, due to similarity in kind according to the Hanafis, and due to their being edibles according to the Shafi'is.

Likewise, it is not permissible to give a Harawi cloth as advance payment for another Harawi cloth, due to the likeness of kind according to the Hanafi School. The Shafi'is hold it to be permissible, as for them likeness of kinds is not sufficient cause to forbid *riba*.

The scholars agree that it is permissible to forward purchase a Harawi cloth for a Marawi cloth, due to their not be like in kind according to the Hanafis, and due to the lack of edibility or intrinsic monetary value according to the Shafi'is.

It is impermissible to forward purchase currencies for other currencies according to the Hanafis, due to likeness of kind, and likewise according to the Shafi'is due to their being of monetary value.

The reasons that likeness of kind is sufficient to forbid *riba*, according to the Hanafis, such as in the sale of an animal for another on credit, that is, on deferred payment, is that the sale contract necessitates equality between the two counter-values, while there can be no equality between that which is paid immediately and that which is paid on credit, because an asset which is in possession is better than a debt, as the value of the collected money is more than that of the delayed. This meaning exists in those commodities with are edible and those of intrinsic monetary value, that is, money, just as they exist in others. This is confirmed by the saying of the Prophet (peace and blessings of Allah be upon him), "There is no *riba* except in credit," and his saying (peace and blessings of Allah be upon him), "Verily, *riba* is in credit";[84] the source-text is unequivocal, not distinguishing between that which is edible, that which is of intrinsic monetary value, and otherwise. Thus, it is obligatory to hold that *riba* is truly realized in these commodities with no qualification,[85] due to the fulfillment of the legal cause therein, namely, oneness of type.

Imam Malik holds that it is not permissible to sell an animal for another on credit, that is, on deferred payment, if the utility of those animals are similar, such as dairy sheep for another on credit, the impermissibility being in order to prevent any means to committing forbidden acts. It is permissible, however, for those commodities the utilities of which are different, such as the sale of a highbred camel for two load-camels.[86]

However, the Shafi' holds that there is no *riba* in anything other that gold, silver, foodstuff, and drink. Therefore, it is permissible to sell any such commodity for its like on credit and for disparate amounts. Furthermore, it is permissible to end the session of the contract without collection of the goods, due to what was related by Abdallah ibn 'Amr ibn al-'As, that "the Prophet (peace and blessings of Allah be upon him) ordered me to prepare an army, and at the time we were running out of camels. Hence, he ordered me to collect a charity of young female camels, and so I did, taking one such female camel instead of the two camels which are usually given as charity."[87]

Likewise, it was narrated that Ali (may Allah honor him) once sold a camel for twenty on credit,[88] and he sold Ibn Umar (may Allah be well pleased with them both) one for four[89] there being many other narrations to the same effect.[90]

The most authentic of the four narrations regarding the position of Imam Ahmad[91] is that which is equivalent to the position of Imam Shafi'i, that is, to allow the sale of two animals of like kind or of disparate kind, at equal or disparate amounts. The Imams agree that selling an animal for another at disparate amounts is permissible on condition that payment is not delayed, but rather immediate at the session of the contract.

Conclusion

Credit *riba* which was known during the pre-Islamic period is intrinsically forbidden, in order to prevent great harm from befalling either of the contracting parties, as a result of any sudden change in the prices of commodities due to some cause or another; likewise, in order to put an end to the exploitation of a debtor's inability to fulfill his debt. As for surplus *riba*, it is forbidden in order to prevent people from taking it as a means to committing forbidden acts, that is, to prevent people from taking it as a means of arriving to credit *riba* thereby, for that which is forbidden due to its own intrinsic nature is never made permissible except in dire necessity, just as the eating of dead flesh, blood, and swine is only permitted for preservation of life, while that which is forbidden in order that it not become a means to the forbidden, may be made permissible due to a serious need for such recourse, or if it serves an interest which outweighs the negative effects thereof;[92] and each Muslim is capable of assessing on his own any dire necessity or serious need he may have.

Finally, we may say that the impermissibility of surplus *riba* is not simply because it is a means to credit *riba*, but rather because it itself is true *riba*, based upon the saying of the Prophet (peace and blessings of Allah be upon him) to Bilal, "The essence of *riba*" when he sold two *sa*'s of low-quality dry dates for a *sa'* of high-quality dry dates of Barni; for such *riba* is at times dependent upon the exploitation of people's ignorance of the different categories and types of commodities, and at other times upon exploiting their need of a particular kind or another.

Notes

* Translated from Zuhayli, Wahba, *Al-Fiqh al-Islami wa Adillatuhu*, vol. 4 (Damascus: Dar al-Fikr, 1st edn, 1404/1984) pp. 668–702 by Dr Iman Abdul Rahim, Conference & Business Services Center with Abdulkader Thomas.

1 Al-Khatib Al-Shirbini, *Mughni Al-Muhtaj* (Egypt: Matba'at Al-Babi Al-Halabi, n.d.), 2.61; Al-Ramli, *Nihayat Al-Muhtaj* (Egypt: Al-Matba'at Al-Bhiyyah, n.d.), 3.29.

2 *Radd al-Muqtar*, 4.184.

3 This *Quranic* verse is Allah's reply *to* the Arabs of the pre-Islamic period (*Jahiliya*) who used *to* say, "a non-*ribawi* sale is the same as one which is *ribawi*," that is, the increase that occurs at the end of the of the debt's period is the same as the principal cost price. Thus Allah demonstrated the difference between the two types of transactions, in that the increase in one of them is due *to* postponement of the debt, and in the other due to the sale, in addition to the fact that a sale is the trading of an exchangeable object, because the cost price is in compensation for the object of value; while *riba* is an increase without compensation due to the postponement of the payment, or a surplus in kind. (See the *Quranic* exegesis of Ibn Rushd Al-Qurtubi, *Al-Muqaddimat Al-Mumahhidat* (Matba'at Al-Sa'adah, n.d.).)

4 Related by Muslim on the authority of Abu Huraya, that the Prophet of Allah (peace and blessings of Allah be upon him) said, "Avoid the seven most grievous sins." They asked: "what are they, O'Messenger of Allah?" He (peace and blessings of Allah be upon him) replied, "Associating anything with Allah, magic, killing a soul which Allah has declared inviolate without a just cause, devouring the property *of* an orphan, dealing in *riba*, fleeing on the day of fighting, and culminating the chaste, innocent, believing women." (See Ibn Daqiq al-'Id, *al-Ilman bi ahadlth al-ahkamn* (Damascus: Dar Al-Fikr, n.d.), 518.)

5 Related by Abu Dawud and others on the authority of the Prophet (peace and blessings of Allah be upon him) who said, "Cursed is the one who practices *riba*, his constituent, the one who acts as a notary to it, and his two witnesses," and he said, "they are all alike." Bukhari narrates a similar *hadith* on the authority of Abu Jahlfa, and Tirmidhi and Ibn Majah on the authority of Anas who said, "The Prophet of Allah (peace and blessings of Allah be upon him) cursed ten people who deal with alcohol" to the end of the *hadith*. (See Al-Haythami, *Majma' Al-Zawa'id* (Egypt: Maktabat Al-Qudsi, n.d.); 4.118; Al-Sana'ani, *Subul Al-Salam* (publication data unavailable), 3.36; Al-Shawkani, *Nayl Al-'Awtar* (Egypt: Al-Matba'a Al-'Uthmaniyya Al-Misriyya, n.d.), 5.154.)

6 Related by Ibn Majah in a shortened version, and by Hakim in its complete form, deeming it rigorously authenticated. There are many other *hadith*s of the same meaning, some of which include the phrase, "*Riba* consists of seventy categories," and in others, "*Riba* consists of seventy two categories." (See Al-Haythami, op. cit., 4.117; Al-Sana'ani, op. cit., 3.37.)

7 Al-Khatib Al-Shirbini, op. cit., 2.21, 4.1; Al-Shirazi, Abu Ishaq, *Al-Muhadhdhab* (Egypt: matba'at Al-Babi Al-Halabi, n.d.), 1.270; Al-Sarakshi, *Al-Mabsut* (Matba'at Al Sa'adah, 1st edn, n.d.), 12.109; Ibn Al-Humam, *Fath Al-Qadir, Sharh Al-Hidaya* (Cairo: Mataba'at Mustafa Muhammad, n.d.), 5.274; *Hashiyat al-qalyubi wa 'umayra*, 2.166.

8 See Muhammad, Mustafa, ed., 4.40, *Al-Muwafaqat of Shatibi* (no publication data).

9 Al-Kasani, Bada'i Al-Sana'i (publication data unavailable), 5.183; Ibn Rushd, M., *Bidayat Al-Mujtahid wa Nihayat Al-Muqtasid* (Beirut: Dar Al-Ma'rifa,1997), 2.129; *Hashiyat al-Dasuqi*; 3.47; Al-Khatib *Al-Shirbini*, op. cit., 4.1; Ibn al-Qayyim, *A'lam al Muwaqqi'in*, Vol. 2 (Cairo: Maktabah al-Kulliyyat al-Azhariyyah, 1968), 2.135.

10 Ibn al-Qayyim calls it the hidden *riba*, which is forbidden as a prevention to pretexts to committing forbidden acts *sadd al-dhara'i'*, as is stated in the *hadith* related by Abu Sa'id al-Khudari (may Allah be well pleased with him) that the Prophet (peace and blessings of Allah be upon him) said: "Do not sell one dirham for two, for I fear for you that you fall into *riba.*"

11 Ibn al-Qayyim, op. cit., 2.140.

12 Ibn al-Qayyim calls it "clear *riba*": namely, that which was practiced in the pre-Islamic period, such that the creditor says to the debtor at the conclusion of the deferred period, "Will you pay the debt, or increase?" this being compound profit.

13 That is, and obviously even more so when of like kind.

14 Al-Kasani, op. cit., 5.183; *Radd al-muhtar*, 4.184 and on.

15 A *sa'* is a classical measure akin to a bushel.

16 The physical increase which the seller shall receive after a period of time is against the immediate delivery of a bushel of wheat to the buyer, this is what is meant by the preference of immediacy (immediate payment) to postponement (delayed payment); that is, that the thing given as payment in the present time is of more importance than that which shall be paid in the future. As for the meaning of "assets are more significant than debts," it is that a commodity which is specified by delineation of the commodity itself is of more importance than that which is merely specified by mention of its kind, since individual particulars of that kind may be different than the given description; moreover, the seller may not deliver the agreed upon commodities; for example, the purchase of a particular amount of wheat, sugar, etc. though which particular goods will be given are not specified, against a specified amount of a particular barley; in this scenario, the object of sale is equivalent to a debt rather than asset, and the price represents the assets. Thus, it becomes clear that equality between the two substitutes in relation to similar specification of assets is necessary to avoid a suspected surplus, which is *riba*, because assets are preferable to debts, even if the debt is immediately due. It is for this reason that the *zakat* of an asset may not be taken from a debt. The condition of specification is taken from the *hadith*, which says, "hand in hand," because the hand is the instrument which specifies, by bringing something forth or pointing. Similarly, the condition of equality is taken from his saying (peace and blessings of Allah be upon him), "in equal amounts"; thus, specification of the two *ribawi* counter-values becomes obligatory, due to the necessity of confirming their equality between them, just as the specification of one of the two counter-values is a condition of any sale, in order to avoid selling a debt for a debt, which is credit for credit, this being *riba*.

17 Shatibi, op. cit., 4.42.

18 The generations of Muslims who lived immediately after those who would have known personally the Prophet, peace be upon him.

19 See Al-Sarakshi, op. cit., 12.112; Subki, *Takmilat al-majmu'*, 10.48.

20 Also known as *riba al-fadl*.

21 Al-Ramli, *Nihayat Al-Muhtaj* (Egypt: Al-Matba'at Al-Bhiyyah, n.d.), 3.39; Al-Shirbini op. cit., 2.21; *Hashiyat al-qalyubi wa 'umayra*, 2.167; *Hashiyat al-sharqawi*, 2.30 and on.

22 See *Tafsir Ibn Kathir*, 1.327.

23 Ibn al-Qayyim, op. cit., 2.136.
24 Al-Kasani, op. cit., 5.183; Ibn Al-Humam, op. cit., 5.274; *Mukhtasar al-tahawi.* 75; al-Sarakshi, op. cit., 12.110; *al-Durr al-mukhtar wa Radd al-muhtar*, 4.186.
25 The followed standards for materials measured by volume or by weight are the conventional practice of the Muslims at the beginning of the Islamic era, due to what has been related by Abu Dawud and al-Nasa'i on the authority of Ibn 'Umar (may Allah be well pleased with him) that the Prophet of Allah (peace and blessings of Allah be upon him) said; "Weight is the measure of the people of Makka, and dry-measure is that of the people of Madina" (see *Jami' al-Usul*, 1.371, *al-Talkhis al-habir*, 183). Abu Yusuf is of the opinion that the criterion of *ribawi* kinds is that of the custom of that day and that it changes with the change of custom in every time and locale. (Professor Zarqa, F, al-Madkhal al-fiqhi, 514.)
26 That is, the sale of gold for gold.
27 Professor Zarqa, *al-Madkhal ila nadhariyat al-iltizam*, 139; *al-Durr al-mukhtar*, 4.185.
28 Shatibi, op. cit., and its commentaries, 4.42; Ibn al-Qayyim, *al-Qiyas*, 114; Al-Jaziri, A., *Al-Fiqh 'ala Al-Madhahib Al-'Arba'a* (Cairo: Dar 'Ihya' Al-Turath Al-'Arabi, 1986), 2.247 an on; *al-Madkhal al-fiqhi*, op. cit.
29 Half a *sa'* equals 1350 grams; that is, one kilo and 1.75 ounces, or 6.75 ounces, or 540 dirhams.
30 Humam, op. cit., 5.278; *al-Durr al-mukhtar*, op. cit., 4.188.
31 A handful: is the amount that fills one's hands if cupped.
32 What is meant here is the size of an average grain of barley, any abnormalities being cut from the ends, keeping in mind that one dirham equals 50 and 2/5 grains, that is, 2.975 grams.
33 *Radd al-muhtar*, op. cit., 4.189, 4.191.
34 Related by Abu Dawud and Nasa'i on the authority of Abdallah ibn 'Umar; it is also related by Bazzar, and deemed rigorously authentic by Ibn Hibban and Daraqutni. [Shawkani, op. cit., 5.198].
35 Humam, op. cit., 5.282; *al-Durr al-mukhtar*, op. cit., 4.189; *al-Furuq, al-Qarafi*, 3.264 and on; *al-Qawanin* 254; Al-Khatib Al-Shirbini, op. cit., 2.24, 4.17; *al-Umm*, 3.70.
36 The Hanafis mention this as a *hadith*, which is strange, as mentioned by Zayla'i. The meaning from the *hadith* of Ibn Musayyib from Abu Sa'id al-Khudari and Abu Hurayra concerning the *sa'* of good quality for dates of bad quality from Khaybar, and the Prophet's saying (peace and blessings of Allah be upon him), "Don't do that, but rather sell this, then buy from the other with the profit" (Al-Zayla'i, Al-Hafiz, *Nasb Al-Rayah fi Takhrij ahadith al-hidayah* (publisher data unavailable), 4.36–7).
37 Qayyim, op. cit., 2.143; Al-Sanhuri, Abd Al-Razzaq Ahmad., *Masadir Al-Haqq fil-Fiqh al-Islami*, 6 Parts in 2 Volumes, Part 3. (Egypt: n.d.), 3.206.
38 Kasani, op. cit., 5.183; Humam, op. cit., 5.289; *Mukhtasar al-tahawi*, op. cit., 75. What is intended by "the agreed upon amount" is that the two counter-values be of one group, either the group of commodities which are measured by volume or those measured by weight. As for "the same type": what is meant is that the type of one of the counter-values be of the same type as the other, such as wheat against wheat, or gold against gold, for example.
39 The wisdom of the permissibility of selling one bushel of wheat for two of barley for immediate payment, while it is impermissible if on credit, is that what is intended by the sale in the first scenario is not exploitation but rather fulfilling a need; if it was obligatory to trade in equal amounts, this obligation would be harmful to people. In the second scenario, however, the sale is more like a loan, and it would appear that such would be done as a way of exploiting people in need, for the increase is against the delay. Thus, credit *riba* is forbidden in order to prevent any pretexts to committing the forbidden "Either pay, or increase." If, however, the wheat, for example, is sold for dirhams on credit, that is permissible, as people are in need of such transactions.

40 Ibn al-Qayyim, *Al-Qiyas*, p. 114; Jaziri, op. cit., 2/246; Qayyim, op. cit., 2.137 and on; *al-Durr al-mukhtar*, op. cit., 4.189; Humam, op. cit., 5.286, 5.278.

41 Jaziri, op. cit.

42 Humam, op. cit., 5.297 and on; *al-Durr al-mukhtar*, 4.193 and on.

43 A *qafiz* is a measure. It equals eight drinking cups. One drinking cup equals one (*sa'* and a half, i.e. 2700 grams).

44 Al-Sarakhsi, op. cit., 12.116; Kasani, op. cit., 5.184; Humam, op. cit., 5.277.

45 Sanhuri, op. cit., 3.180.

46 Kasani, op. cit., 5.187; al-Sarakhsi, op. cit., 12.122.

47 *Al-Muntaqa 'ala al-muwatta'*, 4.158; Ibn Rushd, op. cit., 2.131; *Hashiyat al-Dasuqi*, 2.47; Al-Hattab, *Mawahib Al-Jalil*, (publisher data unavailable), 4.346; Jaziri, op. cit., 2.251.

48 Ibn Juzayy, *Al-Qawanin Al-Fiqhiyyah* (Fes: Matba'at Al-Nahdah, n.d.), 253.

49 Related by Muslim and Ahmad on the authority of Mu'ammar ibn Abdallah (see *Nasb al-raya*, 4.37; *al-Talkhis al Habir*, 235; *Nayl al-'awtar*, 5.193).

50 Al-Shirbini, op. cit., 2.22–5; *Hashiyat al-qalyubi wa 'umayra*, 2.167 and on; *Hashiyat al-sharqawi*, 2.32 and on; Shirazi, op. cit., 1.272.

51 Al-Shirbini, ibid., 2.32 and on; *al-Muhadhab*, 1.272.

52 Related by Ahmad and Tabarani in *al-Kabir* and others. Haythami said, "The chain includes Abu Janab, and he is trustworthy, but a *mudallis*" (see *Jami' al-Usul*, 1.469; Al-Haythami, op. cit., 4.113; Al-Zayla'i Al-Hafiz, op. cit., 4.56).

53 Related by Daraqutni on the authority of al-Hasan on the authority of Ubada and Anas ibn Malik (see *Nayl al-'awtar*, 5.193).

54 Al-Khatib Al-Shirbini, op. cit., 4.3–5; al-Qayyim, op. cit., 2.136 and on; *Ghiyat al-Muntaha*, 2.54.

55 Related by Daraqutni in his *Suman* on the authority of Sa'id ibn Mussayib, that the Prophet of Allah (peace and blessings of Allah be upon him) said, "There is no *riba* except in gold and silver, or what is measured by volume, or what is weighed, or what is eaten, or what is drank", and it is a *mursal hadith*. It is also related by Bayhaqi, though the chain stops *(mawqufan)* at Ibn Mussayib (see Zayla'i, op. cit., 4.36).

56 See Al-Shirbini, op. cit., 4.20; *Ghayat al-muntaha*, 2.55.

57 As for the Hanafi opinion, the oil of violets and the oil of roses are two distinct kinds, because they are meant to be used for different purposes, even if they are *of* the same origins. Thus, it is permissible to sell one of them for the other with a disparity in amount between them. Likewise, olives and olive oil, sesames and sesame oil, cooked and none cooked oil, are all permitted to be sold at disparate weights because they are of different types. If the types are one, however, it is not permissible to sell them with a disparity in amount (*al-Durr al-mukhar*, op. cit., 4.194).

58 See Ibn Hazm, Al-Muhalla bi-l' athar (Egypt: Matba' at Al-Iman, n.d.), 8.468.

59 Rushd, op. cit., 2.131.

60 al-Qayyim, op. cit., *Alam al-Muwaqqiin*, 2.137.

61 Sanhuri, op. cit., 3.184.

62 Money: gold or silver, or that which replaces them of coined and paper monies; and the word "goods" here refers to non-monetary commodities and stuff.

63 Juzayy, op. cit., 252, 289; Rushd, op. cit., 2.127,2.142; Qayyim, op. cit., 2.135; *al-Riba wa al-mu'amalat fi al-islam*, Shaykh Rashid Rida, 70 (Cairo: Al Manar, n.d.).

64 Humam, op. cit., 5.276.

65 Ibid.

66 Al-Sarakhsi, op. cit., 12.114; Kasani, op. cit., 5.185; Humam, op. cit., 5.279; *al-Durr al-mukhtar*, op. cit., 4.188.

67 The *qafiz* is a measure that equals approx. 27.817 kilograms; the *jurayb* is a measure that equals four *qafizes*. Furthermore, the *qafiz* is equal in area to one tenth the area of the *jurayb*, which in turn equals 10,000 *ells* (*dhira'*) [Editor: each *ell* is equal to 45 inches (about 1.14 meters) in the old English system].

68 Saffron is different from safflower; the first is a plant of yellow flowers and a root like the root of the onion; the second is a well known plant with orange flowers in an epicalyx that has soft thorns.

69 Kasani, op. cit., 5.189; Humam, op. cit., 5.288 and on; *al-Durr al-mukhtar*, op. cit., 4.194 and on; Jaziri, op. cit., 2.254.

70 Rushd, op. cit., 2.136; *Hashiyat al-Dasuqi*, 3.53; Jaziri, op. cit., 2.253.

71 Shirazi, op. cit., 1.271; Shirbini op. cit., 2.23; Jaziri, op. cit., 2.255.

72 Shirbini, op. cit., 4.24; Humam, op. cit., 2.255.

73 Humam, op. cit., 5.290; *al-Durr al-mukhtar*, op. cit., 4.192; Kasani, op. cit., 5.189.

74 Rushd, op. cit., 2.136; *Hashiyat al-Dasuqi*, 3.54; Shirazi, op. cit., 1.272; Shirbini, op. cit., 2.29, 4.32; Qayyim, op. cit., 2.145.

75 Related by Malik in the *Muwa.tta'*, on the authority of Sa'ld ibn al-Mussayib with a broken chain (*mursalan*). There are other *hadith*s which support the meaning in this one, such as the *hadith* on the authority of Ibn Umar related by Bazzar, and on the authority of al-Hasan on the authority of Samara related by Hakim and Bayhaqi and Ibn Khuzayma. Another narration has another wording, "He forbade the sale of one that is alive for one that is dead." It is said in Shawkani, op. cit., 5.203: "It is not hidden that this *hadith* rises in standing, and is capable of being used as a textual proof, in all of its various narrations" (see *Jami' al-Usul*, op. cit., 1/413; Zayla'i, op. cit., 4.39).

76 Related by Bayhaqi on the authority of a man from the people of Medina. Bayhaqi says, "This *hadith* which has a broken chain (*mursalan*) confirms the *hadith* of Ibn Mussayib which also has a broken chain," that is, the previous *hadith* (see Zayla'i, op. cit., 4.39).

77 *Takhrij al-furu' 'ala al-usul*; 71.

78 That is, the price is an unspecified commodity; thus, *riba* occurs, because an asset is better than a debt, since the debt might not be identical with the description, and the debtor may not deliver what he had pledged.

79 Limestone is the name give to stone of lime, and later it was used to designate other mixes like arsenic and many other materials which are added to lime. It is used as a depilatory material.

80 *Ar.* nuqra, a small, amalgamated piece of silver or gold, collected and formed from the remnants after a jeweler fashions jewelry from the raw ores.

81 *Mithqal*: 1 3/7 dirhams, being 24 karats, equaling 4.8 grams.

82 See Kasani, op. cit., 5.186 and on.

83 Humam, op. cit., 5.276, 5.280; Sarakshi, op. cit., 12.122 and on; *Mukhtasar al-Tajawi*, op. cit., 75; Shirazi, op. cit., 1.271 and on.

84 Related by Bukhari, Muslim, and Nasa'i. It is a rigorously authenticated *hadith*. There are narrations with other wordings; of which are, "*Riba* is in credit," "*riba* is truly in credit," "there is no *riba* if payment is immediate." Bayhaqi said, "It is possible that the narrator abbreviated it, such that the Prophet (peace and blessings of Allah be upon him) was asked about *riba* in two differ categories of commodities, gold for silver, or dry dates for wheat," to which he (peace and blessings of Allah be upon him) replied, "Verily, *riba* is in credit," and thus did the narrator relate to us the *hadith*, without mentioning the question of the questioner (see *Jami' al-Usul*, op. cit., 1.469; Zayla'i, op. cit., 4.37).

85 Kasani, op. cit., 5.187.

86 Rushd, op. cit., 2.132.

87 Related by Ahmad, Abu Dawud, Daraqutni by its general meaning, and Hakim in his *Mustadrak*, who said, "It is rigorously authenticated, according to the conditions of Muslim, but the two (i.e. Bukhari and Muslim) did not relate it." Some scholars have deemed it weak due to the presence of Muhammad ibn Ishaq in the chain, except that Hafiz Ibn Hajar strengthened the chain of the *hadith*. It is also related by Bayhaqi in his *Sunan*, by way of 'Amr ibn Shu'ayb on the authority of his father on the authority of his grandfather (see Zayla'i, op. cit., 4.47; Shawkani, op. cit., 5.304; *Jami' al-Usul*, op. cit., 1.473).

88 Related by Imam Malik in the *Muwatta* (Al-Suyuti, *Tanwir Al-Hawalik, Sharh Muwatta Malik* (Cairo: Matba'at Al-Halabi, n.d.), 2.184; *Jami' al-Usul*, op. cit., 1.474).

89 Ibid., Related by *Muwatta* and Bukhari on the authority of Abdallah ibn Umar.
90 Shirazi, op. cit., 1.271.
91 Shirbini, op. cit., 1.271.
92 See the book Sayyid Rashid Rida, op. cit., 97, 99; and its introduction, Bahjat Bitar, 5; also see *Nadharlyat al-qariiura a-shari'ya* by the author (Professor Wahba Zuhayli) in order to know the difference between necessity and need.

4 An overview of the *Sharia'a* prohibition of *riba*

*Emad H. Khalil**

Introduction

Umar ibn al-Khattab reported, "I wish that the Prophet had not been taken from us until he had given us a satisfactory explanation of *riba* . . . We have forsworn things nine tenths of which were permissible, for fear of *riba*."[1]

The rule concerning *riba* articulated in both the *Quran* and *hadith* may be concisely stated as follows, "God has . . . forbidden *riba*."[2] It is reported by Umar ibn al-Khattab, a companion of the Prophet Muhammad and the second caliph, that the *Quranic* verses condemning and prohibiting *riba*[3] were among the last revelations received by the Prophet Muhammad, who died several days later. "The last verse to be revealed was on *riba* and the Prophet, peace be upon him, passed away without explaining it to us; so give up not only *riba* but *ribah* [i.e. whatever is doubtful]."[4] Thus, the controversy over *riba* is not whether it is legal or not, for the *Quran* clearly prohibits it. Rather, the debate is over the proper definition of *riba* and its application to certain transactions, particularly those involving banks and loans. And at the heart of the debate, as the statements by Umar indicate, is a great deal of doubt.

Although Islamic scholars have yet to reach an absolute agreement on the definition of *riba*, the traditional view is that *riba* is the prohibited payment or receipt of interest on loans of money.[5] The liberal view, generally speaking, seeks to restrictively define *riba* to usurious rates of interest and tolerates it on the basis of necessity, at least until an alternative financial Islamic System has been constructed.[6] While historically *riba* has had a much wider field of application, the crux of the modern debate concerns this point: Does *riba* mean interest or usury? If *riba* simply means usury then, as Mallat points out, as long as interest rates have not hit some exorbitant rate as determined by the *fiqh* then most modern commercial transactions are valid. However, if *riba* is, in essence, defined as interest then the entire present civil and commercial structure is tainted with illegality.[7]

This chapter and the next attempt to analyze this modern debate over *riba* by focusing on Egypt for three reasons: (1) Egypt has had a vibrant debate over *riba* in the twentieth century; (2) Egypt is still regarded in the Arab World as a leader in legal matters. In fact, the 1980 Kuwaiti Civil and Commercial Codes were drafted by a Committee headed by three Egyptian lawyers and the more recent Jordanian Civil Code was drafted by a single Egyptian jurist; (3) There are at least four other

Arab countries, Syria, Libya, Iraq, and Kuwait, whose Civil and Commercial Codes were either written by Abd al-Razzaq Ahmad al-Sanhuri, the architect of the Egyptian Civil Code, or largely based upon his Codes. Moreover, lawyers and judges alike, in the Arab World, rely extensively on Sanhuri's two great treatises: *Al-Wasit* (*The Middle Way*), a multi-volume work on every aspect of civil law, and *Al-Masadir al-Haqq fil Fiqh al-Islami* (*The Sources of Law in Islamic Jurisprudence*), a six-part work, now published in two volumes, which contains a comparative summary of the history of obligations and which also lays out Sanhuri's views on *riba*. While the debate over *riba* is carried on at many levels, these chapters seek to focus on how it has manifested itself in the Civil and Commercial Codes as well as in the jurisprudence of Egypt, Syria, Libya, Iraq, and Kuwait. As a result, these chapters do not concentrate on either the linguistic or historical debate over *riba* as such. Rather, this side of the controversy is described in the context of the jurisprudential debate.

This chapter attempts to provide an overview of the *Sharia'a*'s prohibition of *riba* as it is traditionally understood by the four major schools of Islamic Law. This chapter seeks to provide a historical backdrop against which to understand the modern polemic. Chapter 5 explores this debate as it has developed in Egypt and as it has been "resolved" in the Egyptian Civil Code and its expected implications for the rest of the Arab World, all of whose codes are greatly indebted to Sanhuri. Chapter 5 also concludes with postscripts covering the most recent Azharite *fatawa*. The book concludes with an appendix covering the parallel debate in Pakistan.

Definition of *riba*

Riba is usually translated into English as usury or interest but it has a much broader meaning, as its literal definition of increase, addition, expansion, or growth, suggests.[8] In general it expresses the broad notion of "any unjustified increase of capital for which no compensation is given."[9] And in its *Sharia'a* context it, "refers to the 'premium' that must be paid by the borrower to the lender with the principal amount as a condition for the loan or for an extention in its maturity."[10]

Items subject to the prohibition of *riba* (*Mal Ribawi*)

As we have seen, the *Quran* did not provide a definition of *riba* much less specify rules regarding it. Some argue that this was because at the time *riba* was declared unlawful its meaning was known.[11] That this would seem to contradict the statements attributed to Umar would not trouble some, like Fazlur Rahman, who find these traditions as well as all the *hadith* relating to *riba* to be unauthentic.[12] Nevertheless, it is clear that the complex rules concerning *riba* developed gradually from the *hadith*.[13]

The basic rules regarding *riba*, which became authoritative, derive from several similar *hadith* relating to sale which specify that the prohibition extends to gold, silver, wheat, barley, dates, and salt.[14] While the *Quranic* prohibition of *riba* and the traditions which accompany it are generally unquestioned by all four Islamic schools of law, there is disagreement regarding their interpretation and application. All four schools consider the items mentioned in the traditions only as examples of the kinds of things which are prohibited and, therefore, agree that the prohibition extends by analogy (*qiyas*)[15] to other items.[16] However, there is a difference of opinion as to what other items the prohibition against *riba* extends. Specifically, they disagree on the underlying reason (*'illa*)[17] for the prohibition of the items mentioned in the traditions and therefore disagree as to which items the prohibition can be generalized.

The four schools take two basic approaches to determining the *'illa*. The first approach is characterized by the Shafi'is who hold that gold and silver represent the class of precious metals and the other four items the class of foodstuff. The Malikis essentially hold the same view as the Shafi'is except for them the foodstuff must be necessary for subsistence and capable of being stored or preserved for a reasonable time, that is, not perishable. The second approach is characterized by the Hanafis who hold that gold and silver represent examples of the types of things defined by weight, and the other four items, sold by measure. While the Hanbalis' position is somewhat less clear, the generally accepted view is that they held the same position as the Hanafis.[18]

While barter transactions were undoubtedly prevalent when the rules on *riba* were developed, they no longer play a significant role in today's commerce, making many of these rules appear obsolete. The relevant question today, however, is does money or currency, by analogy, fall under the ambit of *mal ribawi*? The answer, most agree, is probably yes.[19] Based on the characteristic of gold and silver as determinants of value or price at the time of Prophet Muhammad, money today, by analogy, would likely come within the classification of *mal ribawi*. Ibn Qayyim, a well known Hanbali jurist, suggests this conclusion as well:

> Dirhams and dinars are the prices of articles sold and the price is the standard by which the evaluation of property is recognized. It must therefore be fixed and regulated so that it does not go up or down, since were the price to go up or down like commodities, we would not have a price with which to value the articles sold. Indeed, everything is a commodity and the people's need for a price by which to value the articles sold is a general and compelling one. Such valuing is not possible save on the basis of a rate by which to know value. This requires a price on the basis of which things are assessed, which continues upon one state of affairs, and which is not (itself) assessed by reference to anything else. If it becomes a commodity which goes up and down, then the transactions of the people will be impaired...[20]

Categories of *riba*

That the prohibition against *riba* likely extends to money is further bolstered by the fact that the *Quranic* verses on *riba* appear to have been aimed at proscribing a particular type of transaction occurring at that time which involved the charging of interest on loaned money. During this period Makka was a commercial trading center[21], and businessmen there were concerned about leaving their capital (money or goods) unproductive while awaiting the departure or arrival of caravans.[22] Consequently, they entered into loan agreements. However, if the debtor defaulted they would grant him an extension but double the original debt and/or double the original rate of interest, which would again be doubled if the debtor were to subsequently default.[23] This pre-Islamic *riba* or *riba al-jahiliyya* is regarded by many[24] as the one directly referred to in the *Quran*.[25]

But, as we have observed, the *Quran* does not give any specific definition or rules regarding *riba*. Rather, it was the *hadith* that expounded upon it. As a result of these traditions *riba* was classified into two categories: *riba al-fadl* and *riba al-nasi'a*.[26] While the four schools of Islamic law differed in their particular views regarding each of these categories, they generally understood them as follows:[27]

1 *Riba al-Fadl*: This occurs when one type (*jins*)[28] of *mal ribawi* is exchanged for an unlawful excess of the same type of *mal ribawi*. In order to be lawful, the exchange must occur immediately and there must be no disparity in amount. If, however, the two *mal ribawi* items are of different types there is no *riba* and the exchange is permitted with or without excess.[29]
2 *Riba al-Nasi'a*: This occurs when there is a delay in completing the exchange of any two types of *mal ribawi* for one another, whether or not there is an increase or profit. The exchange is permitted with delay, however, if one type is currency and the other is not.[30]

The ambit of *mal ribawi* is not limited to those six commodities mentioned in the *hadith* but is extended by analogy by all four schools of Islamic law to other items. This is based upon their particular understanding of the underlying reason (*'illa*) for the prohibition of each commodity. Therefore, it is easy to see that the schools' views regarding both kinds of *riba* substantially differ as a result of their *contrasting definitions* of *mal ribawi*. Moreover, there are considerable differences between the schools' views because they differ in how they determine whether two *ribawi* items are of the same type (*jins*).[31]

Riba and loans (*Qard*)

The rules regarding *riba*, as we have seen, derive from traditions which are primarily directed at sales transactions.[32] Hence, as a practical matter it makes very little difference whether money is considered *mal ribawi* or not, since with regard to currency the *hadith* only speaks to its sale, that is, money exchanges. In order to avoid *riba al-nasi'a* money exchange operations would need to be conducted on the spot without any delay, but this is already possible and presents no real impediment to modern commercial transactions. Furthermore, money exchange operations do not run afoul of *riba al-fadl* because, as it will be recalled, if the two *mal ribawi* items are of different types (e.g. gold and silver) then in a hand-to-hand transaction there is no threat of *riba*. So if the currencies to be exchanged are of different types (e.g. dollars for francs), then as long as the exchange occurs on the spot the transaction is lawful.[33] Thus, the critical question from the standpoint of modern commercial transactions and at the center of the modern debate over *riba* is how does the *Sharia'a* treat loan transactions in light of the rules on *riba* which seem to only address sales?

The *Sharia'a* recognizes the *qard* loan which,

> involves the loan of fungible commodities: that is, goods which may be esti-
> mated and replaced according to weight, measure or number. In this case the
> borrower undertakes to return the equivalent or likes of that he has received. The
> most likely object of a *qard* loan would be currency or other standard means of
> exchange.[34]

The *Sharia'a* regards *qard* as essentially a gratuitous transaction and consequently not
under a conclusive presumption of *riba*.[35] It may appear strange at first that the
Sharia'a does not deem loans *ribawi* contracts, but as we observed, sales, not loans,
were the basis for the prohibition of *riba*.[36] "[N]evertheless a loan contract does
become a *ribawi* transaction, by analogy with sale, when it secures to the lender an
interest or a premium."[37]

"*Riba* in loan exists not only when one insists upon the repayment of a larger quantity, but if any advantage at all is demanded."[38] But because loans are not essentially
ribawi contracts, but only deemed as such by analogy, it is generally agreed that the
debtor can voluntarily give the creditor a gratuitous bonus.[39] For fear that it might
lead to *riba*, though, creditors were not allowed to accept a gratuitous bonus prior to
repayment of the debt.[40] However, most schools agree that after repayment it is
lawful for the debtor to voluntarily give back more or better than he has borrowed,
provided that the increase (in the quantity or quality) was not a prerequisite for the
loan.[41]

Because interest-bearing loans are not prohibited for themselves but by analogy
to sales and because, it is argued, the nature of loans has changed since the days
of Prophet Muhammad from consumption loans to mostly production loans, some
Islamic scholars contend that at least those contemporary loans not charging exorbitant rates of interest can be legal.[42] While many disagree that the classical texts
support such a view, one commentator believes that an argument justifying interest-
bearing loans might be made based on the need to compensate the lender for inflation.[43] He admits, however, that the validity of such an analysis is hard to determine
because Islamic scholars have yet to adequately address the subject.[44]

Validity of a loan with a *riba* stipulation

Essentially, the question here is whether a *riba* stipulation in a loan agreement nulli-
fies the entire contract or whether it can be severed leaving the transaction valid?
While this issue appears to be under-researched, the views of each school of law can
be summed up as follows.[45] For the Hanafis[46] and Hanbalis,[47] a loan agreement is not
invalidated by a *riba* stipulation; the objectionable term is simply deleted and the
transaction would appear to remain valid as a gratuitous loan. For the Malikis,
whether the entire loan agreement is canceled depends upon whether the *riba*
stipulation is material enough.[48] If it is material then the whole contract is cancelled;
if it is not then only the *riba* stipulation itself is severed. The Shafi'is on the other

hand, as Nabil Saleh points out, appear to be split on this issue:

> For some, a loan agreement impaired with *riba* is void: for, first, the Prophet
> himself has said that "Any *qard* which stipulates an advantage to the lender is
> *riba*" and secondly, when a *qard* is made contingent upon a condition which is
> not fulfilled, it is considered only just to cancel the whole agreement. The oppo-
> site view is also sustained on the ground that the objective of *qard* is charity and
> this objective can only be enhanced by removing the void special condition and
> retaining the agreement.[49]

Methods of evading the prohibition of *riba* (*Hiyal*)

Various methods of evasion (*hiyal*, sing. *hila*) were developed to bring the strict
prohibition of *riba* more into agreement with customary commercial practices.[50]
According to Schacht:

> *hiyal* . . . can be described, in short, as the use of legal means for extra-legal ends,
> ends that could not, whether they themselves were legal or illegal, be achieved
> directly with the means provided by the *Sharia'a*. The "legal devices" enabled
> persons who would otherwise, under the pressure of circumstances, have had to
> act against the provisions of the sacred Law, to arrive at the desired result while
> actually conforming to the letter of the law.[51]

A common example of these *hiyal* is the double sale. If, for example,[52] a lender and
a borrower agree on a loan of $1,000 for one year at an interest rate of 20 percent,
they can circumvent the prohibition on *riba* by setting up the transaction as two
separate sales. In the first sale the lender sells to the borrower some item (it does not
matter what the item is since, as it will be seen, it is only a token) for $1,200 payable
in one year. This transaction is perfectly legal, since based on the earlier description
of *riba al-nasi'a*, the deferred payment of a sale price is valid. A second sale immediately follows in which the borrower sells back to the lender the same item for $1,000
payable at once. Consequently, the object of the two sales is back where it began, with
the lender, while the borrower has obtained $1,000 in cash for which he must pay to
the lender $1,200 in one year. In other words, "[t]wo separate sales transactions,
in themselves formally and perfectly valid, have been combined by the mutual agreement of the parties to effect . . . a loan"[53] of $1,000 by the lender to the borrower at
a fixed interest rate of 20 percent repayable in one year.

As with other areas, the four schools of law have conflicting views regarding *hiyal*.
Some Shafi'is and Hanafis appear to allow their use.[54] First, they argue, man can never
be sure that he understands the actual purpose behind the divine laws.[55] Similarly,
they contend that it is not the court's function to go behind seemingly genuine transactions to discover their actual purpose because God alone knows men's real motives.[56]
Consequently, to some, it is sufficient that one follows the letter of the *Sharia'a*'s
prohibition of *riba* even if this appears to defeat the prohibition's apparent purpose.[57]
In contrast, the Hanbali and Maliki schools completely reject *hiyal*.[58] For them the

motive and intent of the parties involved is what determines the legality or illegality of a transaction.[59] As Coulson points out, the difference between the schools on this issue of motive is essentially one of procedure and evidence.[60] Motive and intent are important for all the schools. The Hanafis and Shafi'is, however, "regard the outward visible sign of the act or statement as the exclusive determinant of intent," while the Hanbalis and Malikis "search for the reality of the inner intent or motive."[61]

The Gulf States, where the Hanbali and Maliki schools are prevalent, have for a long time been economically inferior to those countries in which the Hanafi and Shafi'i schools predominate and in which *hiyal* were developed and employed. Consequently, the use of *hiyal* was not affected much by those countries which rejected them. However, with the modern exploitation of oil in the Gulf the situation has reversed itself and, at least according to one commentator, *hiyal* are now deprived of an important field of application, and the issue of motive and intent is critical in contemporary contract law.[62]

A re-evaluation of *riba*: the seeds for the modern debate

As Umar ibn al-Khattab indicated and as the previous discussion makes clear, from the very beginning there was disagreement over the proper definition of *riba*. And just as early on, there were those who not only differed with the traditional interpretation of *riba* but who also sought to limit the scope of its prohibition. It was their reasoning that modern scholars would later draw upon to justify the charging of interest in commercial transactions.

One of the Prophet Muhammad's cousins, Abdulla ibn Abbas, considered pre-Islamic *riba* (*riba al-jahiliyya*) to be the only unlawful type of *riba*.[63] Ibn Abbas who was well-known for his vast knowledge of tradition relied on the following *hadith* which he himself reported and whose authenticity is generally accepted to substantiate this view: "No *riba* except in the *nasi'a*" (*nasi'a* here refers to pre-Islamic *riba*, i.e. *riba al-jahiliyya*). He maintained that this last *hadith* on *riba* superseded the previous ones. Those who disagree with Ibn Abbas contend that this *hadith* only puts more emphasis on the prohibition of *riba al-nasi'a* but does not supersede the prior *hadith*s.

It is mainly the views of Ibn Qayyim al-Jawziyya, the fourteenth century Hanbali jurist, however, that contemporary liberal scholars draw upon in justifying their restricted interpretation of *riba*.[64] Ibn Qayyim maintained that there were two types of *riba*: manifest and hidden.[65] According to him, manifest *riba* is prohibited because of the great harm it causes, while hidden *riba* is prohibited because it is a means to manifest *riba*. Thus, the prohibition of manifest *riba* is one of ends, while the prohibition of hidden *riba* is one of means. Relying on the same *hadith* as Ibn Abbas, Ibn Qayyim argued that manifest *riba* is *riba al-nasi'a*, and like Ibn Abbas, by *riba al-nasi'a* he appears to have meant pre-Islamic *riba*, that is, *riba al-jahiliyya*.[66] He defined hidden *riba* as *riba al-fadl*. It is prohibited, he argued, in order to prevent access to a greater evil – *riba al-nasi'a*. His reasoning being that if *riba al-fadl* were permitted then eventually people would be tempted to conduct commerce with *riba al-nasi'a*.[67]

It is not clear, however, whether Ibn Qayyim regarded this pre-Islamic practice of doubling the debt (*riba al-jahiliyya*) as itself being *riba al-nasi'a*, or as just a subset *of riba al-nasi'a*, which he viewed as encompassing any delayed profit generally. Or perhaps as the following passage suggests, he may have only regarded *riba al-jahiliyya* as being under a direct prohibition, with *riba al-fadl* prohibited merely as a means to *riba al-nasi'a*, which itself was prohibited only because it was a means to *riba al-jahiliyya*:[68]

> So he forbade *riba al-fadl* because of his fear for their sake of *riba al-nasi'a* ... To permit them *nasi'a* between them is an avenue to "you pay or you increase" [*riba al-jahiliyya*]. So it is perfect protection of their interests that he restricts them to selling hand-to-hand as they wish, so they attain to the benefit of exchange, while they are preserved from the evil of "You pay or you increase."[69]

The significance of these distinctions is that, according to Ibn Qayyim, those things which are prohibited in order to prevent access to evil become permissible when they result in a greater benefit. As an example, he noted that despite the totality of the rule prohibiting women from being seen by men, they are allowed to be seen by a fiancé, witness, doctor, or counterpart in a business transaction. He then concluded that a prohibition to prevent access to evil is less stringent than a prohibition of the evil itself and, therefore, hidden *riba* is permitted when there is merely a need while manifest *riba* is permitted only if there is a compelling necessity. For example, because of the need to compensate the manufacturer for his labor, manufactured ornaments made from gold and silver may be sold for more than their weight despite implicating *riba al-fadl*. And because there is a compelling need, Ibn Qayyim argued, an item may be sold with delay in return for dirhams or for another weighed substance despite implicating *riba al-nasi'a*; similarly, a sale with advance payment for an object not yet in existence is also permitted. And as it was pointed out previously, Ibn Qayyim regarded: "[N]*asi'a* ... [as] a proximate avenue to the evil of *riba*."[70] So if by this, he meant that *riba al-nasi'a* was not under a direct prohibition, one could argue, as Sanhuri and others do, that for *riba al-nasi'a* to be permissible it need only meet the lesser requirement for *riba al-fadl* of a "mere need" rather than the higher threshold for *riba al-jahiliyya* of a "compelling necessity." As it will be seen, this reasoning permits Sanhuri and others to allow the charging of interest on loans.

Following this discussion regarding *riba*, Ibn Qayyim interestingly goes on to add that: "The interest of the people cannot be achieved except thereby or by legal artifices [*hiyal*], and legal artifices are void in the *Sharia'a*."[71] This seems to indicate that he may have relaxed the absolute prohibition on *riba* in an effort to stem the rampant use of *hiyal* occurring at that time. The following passage appears to confirm this as his objective:

> If those practicing legal artifices permit the sale of 10 for 15 [a credit transaction by which an object is sold currently for 10 and resold at term for 15] using a ring worth a copper coin, and they say the five is in return for the ring, then how can they forbid the sale of the ornaments by their weight, with the increase equaling the manufacture? And how does the *Sharia'a*, perfect, virtuous, which surpasses reason in its wisdom, justice, mercy, and sublimity, bring permission for the former and prohibition of the latter? Is this anything but the opposite of

what is reasonable, true to nature, and beneficial? ... They bring *riba al-nasi'a* to *riba al-fadl*, and they allow to the use of legal artifices every opportunity, sometimes by *'ina* [double sale]... God, and those who write the transaction, the two parties, and all present, know that it is a contract by which *riba* is intended ... How strange! How can this means to *riba al-fadl* be prohibited and those means, utterly closer to *riba al-nasi'a*, be permitted? What is the harm in the sale of ornaments for their genus with countervalue for the manufacture in price, in comparison to the evil of legal artifices in *riba*, which are the basis for every evil and the root of every calamity?[72]

While Ibn Qayyim clearly sought to restrict the scope of *riba*'s prohibition, he never actually stated that charging interest on loans was legal. This conclusion, as has been pointed out, was reached only later by modern scholars drawing upon his work. And as the following passage suggests, it can be argued that Ibn Qayyim never intended for his reasoning to extend to currency:

> If *riba al-fadl* were made permissible in dirhams and dinars ... then they become subject to trade, or this attracts *riba al-nasi'a* in them, inevitably. Money is not sought as individual objects, but what is sought is use of it as a means to commodities. If it itself becomes a commodity sought as an individual object, then the affairs of people become corrupted. This is the rational concept peculiar to money not extending to the rest of weighed objects.[73]

In fact, Ibn Qayyim, relying on the reasoning mentioned previously, rejected the argument that coins (at the time made of gold and silver) could be sold for an excess in compensation for the minting process, despite the similarities to his example involving manufactured ornaments.

Thus even at this early stage one can discern the main arguments that later appear in the contemporary debate over *riba*. Those in favor of allowing interest will contend that the necessities of modern transactions and finance require it. Moreover, they will argue as Ibn Qayyim did, "There is nothing prohibited except that which God prohibits [and] ... To declare something permitted prohibited is like declaring something prohibited permitted."[74] Those seeking an absolute prohibition of *riba*, however, will argue that any form of *riba* corrupts all transactions.

Notes

* Originally submitted as The Modern Debate over *Riba* in Egypt and its "Resolution" in the Codes of Sanhuri, the original components have been reconstituted as separate chapters in this book. The paper was prepared by Mr Khalil whilst a student at the Harvard Law School May 1990.

1 W.M. Ballantyne, "The Second Coulson Memorial Lecture: Back to the *Sharia'a*," *Arab Law Quarterly* 3, 1988, pp. 318, 325.

2 "The Qur'an," *Sura al-Baqara* (2:275); see C. Mallat, "The Debate on Riba and Interest in Twentieth Century Jurisprudence," in C. Mallat (ed.), *Islamic Law and Finance* (London: Graham & Trotman, 1988), p. 69.

3 "The Qur'an," ibid. (2:275–281) "Those who consume *riba* shall not rise except like the one who has been struck by the Devil's touch. This is because they say that trade is like *riba*, whereas God has permitted trade and has forbidden *riba*. Whosoever receives an admonition from his Lord and desists, he shall keep (the profits of) that which is past, and his affair is committed to God; but whosoever reverts (to usury) shall be the inhabitants of the fire and abide therein for ever. (275) God destroys *riba* but makes charity prosper. God does not love the ungrateful sinner. (276) [But] those who believe and do good deeds and perform the prayer and pay the alms, their reward is with their Lord, and there shall be no fear for them nor shall they grieve. (277) O you who believe! Fear God and remit what remains of riba if you are believers. (278) If you do not then be prepared for war from God and His Messenger. Wrong not and you shall not be wronged. (279) If the debtor is in difficulty, let him have respite until he is able to pay, although it is better for you to forego out of charity if you are wise. (280) And fear the day when you shall be returned to the Lord and every soul shall be paid in full what it has earned and they shall not be wronged. (281)"

Translations from the *Quran* are a composite of M. Asad, (tr.), *The Message of the Qur'an* (Gibraltar: Dar Al Andalus, 1980), the author's and the editor's, the latter two are unpublished.

4 "This report is recorded in the Musnad of Ahmad ibn Hanbal, the Sunan of ibn Majah, Musannaf of ibn Shaybah, Dala'il al-Nubuwwah of al-Bayhaqi and similar other compilations of the *hadith* scholars of the later period." F. Rahman, *Riba and Interest*, Islamic Studies, (Karachi) 3(1) March 1964; see also M. Asad, op. cit., pp. 622–3 n.35; A.I. Qureshi, *Islam and the Theory of Interest* (Lahore: Ashraf, 1974), p. 70; M.U. Chapra, *Towards a Just Monetary System* (Leicester: The Islamic Foundation, 1985), pp. 60–1, 238. See F. Rahman, op. cit., pp. 8–12 (rejecting the validity of this report and the contention that the verses prohibiting *riba* were the last revealed to the Prophet Muhammad); see also J. Schacht, "Riba," *First Encyclopedia of Islam* (Leiden: Brill, 1987), p. 1148 (attributing the prohibition on *riba* found in *Sura al-Baqara*, op. cit., note 3, to the early Medinese period). Regardless of whether the passages in *Sura al-Baqara* were the last of all the *Quranic* verses revealed to the Prophet Muhammad as Umar ibn al-Khattab relates or only the last verses prohibiting *riba* as Rahman contends, there are unquestionably three other references to the prohibition of *riba* that appear in the *Quran*. The first of these, most agree, occurred in Makka, "Whatever you give in *riba* to gain interest from men's wealth shall not bear interest with God, but what you give as charity in seeking the face of God, these shall gain double." *Sura al-Rum* (30:39). The second of these, most believe, occurred in Medina around 3 AH prior to the revelation of *Surat al-Baqara*, supra note 3, "O you who believe do not consume riba with continual doubling and fear God that perhaps you may prosper." *Sura al-Imran* (3:130) and finally, the third revelation, most concur, occurred early in the Medinese period prior to 5 AH, however there is disagreement whether it came before or after the revelation of *Sura al-Imran*, supra and whether it came before or after *Sura al Baqara*: "And for their [The Jews] taking *riba* which was prohibited to them and for wrongfully consuming the wealth of the people, We have prepared for the disbelievers among them a painful doom." *Sura al-Nisa* (4:161). See M.U. Chapra, op. cit., p. 56 (placing this revelation prior to both those of *Sura al-Imran*, i.e. prior to 3 AH and *Sura al-Baqara*). But, F. Rahman, op. cit., pp. 11–12 argues that this revelation must have occurred prior to *Sura al-Baqara* and also that this revelation had to have occurred before the Jewish tribes left Medina in 5 AH, therefore, both it and *Sura al-Baqra* had to have occurred prior to 5 AH; J. Schacht, *Riba*, op. cit., p. 1148.

5 See N. Saleh, *Unlawful Gain and Legitimate Profit in Islamic Law* (Cambridge: Cambridge University Press, 1986), pp. 35–48.

6 F. Rahman, op. cit., pp. 1–43.

7 C. Mallat, op. cit., p. 69.

8 Please see Chapter 1.

9 J. Schacht, *Riba*, op. cit., note 4, p. 1148; see also J. Schacht, *An Introduction to Islamic Law* (Oxford, 1964), p. 145. "*Riba* is defined as 'a monetary advantage without a counter-value which has been stipulated in favour of one of the two contracting parties in an exchange of two monetary values"; see also N. Coulson, *Commercial Law in the Gulf States*

(London: Graham & Trotman, 1984), p. 11: "*Riba*...seems to express the broad notion of illicit gain or unjustified profit and enrichment."

10 M.U. Chapra, op. cit., pp. 56–7, M. Asad, op. cit., pp. 622–3 n. 35 ("In the terminology of the *Quran*, it [*riba*] signifies any unlawful addition, by way of interest, to a sum of money or goods lent by one person or body of persons to another"). N. Saleh, op. cit., p. 13, gives a more technical definition:

> *Riba*, in its *Sharia* context, can be defined, as generally agreed, as an unlawful gain derived from the quantitative inequality of the counter values in any transaction purporting to effect the exchange of two or more species (*anwa'*, sing. *naw'*), which belong to the same genus (*jins*) and are governed by the same efficient cause ('*illa*, pl. '*illal*). Deferred completion of the exchange of such species, or even of species which belong to different genera but are governed by the same '*illa*, is also *riba*, whether or not the deferment is accompanied by an increase in any one of the exchanged countervalues.

11 Z. Ahmad, "The Our'anic Theory of Riba," *Islamic Law Quarterly* 20 (1978), pp. 3, 4.

12 F. Rahman, op. cit., p. 30.

13 J. Schacht, *Riba*, op. cit., p. 1148; W.M. Ballantyne, *The Commercial Law in the Arab Middle East: the Gulf States* (London: Lloyds of London Press, 1986), p. 22.

14 A representative example of these *hadith* is as follows: "gold for gold, silver for silver, wheat for wheat, barley for barley, dates for dates, salt for salt, the same thing for the same thing, like for like, measure for measure; but if these things are different, sell them as you please if it is (only) done measure for measure." J. Schacht, *Riba*, op. cit., p. 1148. Another representative example provides: "Gold for gold, silver for silver, wheat for wheat, barley for barley, dates for dates, salt for salt, each kind for each kind, in hand; he who increases or asks for increase commits *Riba*, alike whether he gives or takes." C. Mallat, op. cit., p. 69.

15 "Analogy or *qiyas*, is a process of deduction by which a rule of law is applied to cases which, although not expressly, are by implication governed by a legal text, on the basis of a common efficient cause ('*illa*)." N. Saleh, op. cit., p. 14.

16 Note, however, that the Zahris, who are not one of the four major schools of Islamic law, but an important minority school, confine the prohibition of *riba* to the six commodities specifically mentioned in the *hadith*. The Zahris believed that the law could only be derived from the literal text of the *Quran* or *Sunna*. Therefore, they rejected analogy (*qiyas*) as a way of determining the law.

17 N. Saleh, op. cit., p. 14. This ['*illa*] has several meanings, among which one is particularly relevant to the present study, namely to designate the underlying principle or objective of a *Sharia'a* injunction ('*illat al-hukum*). In the context of (*qiyas*), which...play a decisive part in widening the *riba* prohibition...a common '*illa* should connect together the two elements of the analogy, namely the object of the analogy and its subject, in order to produce the analogical reasoning.

18 See Chapter 3 for Sh. Wehba Al Zuhaili's comprehensive discussion of the concept of '*illa* relating to the definition of *riba* in the main schools of Islamic jurisprudence.

19 See W.M. Ballantyne, *Commercial Law in the Arab Middle East*, op. cit., p. 123, "It would probably be advisable to assume that it [*riba*] includes paper currency"; Chapra, op. cit., p. 58, "It has generally been concluded that all commodities used as money enter the sweep of *riba*..."; N. Saleh, op. cit., p. 48, "*riba* in practice amounts simply to the forbidding of payment and receipt of interest on loans of money."

20 W.M. Ballantyne, *Commercial Law in the Arab Middle East*, op. cit., p. 123.

21 That the *Quranic* prohibition against *riba* derived from Muhammad's experience in Makka is not accepted by all. This is reflected in the following passage from J. Schacht, *Riba*, op. cit., p. 1148:

> The fact that the principle passages against interest belong to the Medina period and that the Jews are reproached with breaking the prohibition, suggests that the Muslim prohibition of riba owes less to the conditions in Makka than to the Prophet's closer acquaintance with Jewish doctrine and practice in Medina.

22 N. Saleh, op. cit., p. 10. citing H. Lammens, *La Mecque a la Veille de l'Hegire* (1924), p. 27.

23 There is disagreement over whether the original loan stipulated an interest rate or not. Some argue that the first loan was granted free of interest and that the increase for the extension came from the doubling of the capital due. Also Z. Ahmad, op. cit., p. 5; F. Rahman, op. cit., pp. 5–6 (citing and referring to Sayyid Abu'l Ala Mawdudi, *Sud* (1961), 258, n.2). Furthermore, it is not clear that if there was an initial interest charge, whether it was the interest rate that was later doubled or just the capital due or both. See J. Schacht, *Riba*, op. cit., p. 1148; A.E. Mayer, "The Regulation of Interest Charges and Risk Contracts: Some Problems of Recent Libyan Legislation," *International and Comparative Law Quarterly*, 28 (October 1979), pp. 541, 543–4. (contending that the interest rate only doubled); F. Rahman, op. cit., p. 6 (contending that the capital only doubled). The answer to this question is important in helping determine whether the *riba* prohibited in the *Quran* is the equivalent of the interest charged in modern commercial transactions.

24 A. Sanhuri, *Masadir Al-Haqq fil-Fiqh al-Islami*, Vol. III, p. 217; Z. Ahmad, op. cit., pp. 4–5; N. Saleh, op. cit., p. 13.

25 The *Quran* appears to be referring to this *riba* in at least two passages: *Sura al-Imran* (3:130) and *Sura al-Rum* (30:39).

26 Nonetheless, some commentators divide *riba* into a third category, namely *riba al-jahiliyya*, most notably Ibn al-Qayyim, *I'lam al Muwaqqi'in*, Vol. II, p. 156. Others who did so included al-Sanhuri, as well as Muhammad Abdu and Rashid Rida. N. Saleh, op. cit., p. 13 n.21.

27 For purposes of this study, it is not necessary to examine each school's view in its nuances and technical language. For a detailed analysis of each schools views, however, see Chapter 3.

28 N. Saleh, op. cit., p. 14, provides an excellent definition of "type" (*jins*), or as he refers to it, genus, in this context:

> The prohibition of *riba* applies ... by analogy (*qiyas*), to a species (*anwa'*, sing. *naw'*) which are jointly governed by the same efficient cause ('*illa*) or belong jointly to any of the genera (*ajnas*, sing. *jins*) to which the six articles named in the Traditions are subordinated. Genus (*jins*), in the present context, may be defined as a class of articles containing several subordinate classes or species; and species (*naw'*) may be defined as a group of articles, having certain common attributes or qualities, subordinated to genus. The various Islamic schools of law and often scholars of the same school, disagree on the practical interpretation ...

29 N. Saleh, op. cit., pp. 13–26; W.M. Ballantyne, *Commercial Law in the Arab Middle East*, op. cit., p. 124; M.U. Chapra, op. cit., pp. 58–61; F. Rahman, op. cit., pp. 12–30; A.I. Qureshi, op. cit., pp. 68–71; A. Sanhuri, op. cit., Vol. III, pp. 187–9.

30 N. Saleh, op. cit., pp. 13–26; W.M. Ballantyne, *Commercial Law in the Arab Middle East*, op. cit., p. 124; M.U. Chapra, op. cit., pp. 57–8; F. Rahman, op. cit., pp. 12–30; A.I. Qureshi, op. cit., pp. 68–71; A. Sanhuri, op. cit., Vol. III, pp. 189–94.

31 N. Saleh, op. cit., pp. 16–18. He discusses the determination of type (*jins*), or as he refers to it genus, for each of the major schools of Islamic law.

32 Recall, however, that the *Quranic* prohibition of *riba*, while not specific, seems to have been aimed at what were essentially loan transactions.

33 At least one commentator, however, believes that all modern paper currencies belong to the same type (*jins*) for the purposes of *riba*. W.M. Ballantyne, *Commercial Law in the Arab Middle East*, op. cit., p. 124. If this is so, then an exchange of two different currencies (e.g. dollars for francs) might implicate *riba al-fadl*, since when the two *mal ribawi* items are of the same type no increase is permitted in a hand-to-hand exchange. Thus, the exchange of $100 for F600 might be viewed as tainted by *riba al-fadl* and therefore unlawful. Nevertheless, an argument can be made that if the exchange rate of francs to dollars was 6:1 then there was no unlawful increase because there was no disparity of amount in the exchange: you simply received the equivalent in francs of $100. Whether such an argument

would be accepted is unclear. But, see N. Saleh, op. cit., p. 48 (implying that modern paper currencies are of different types and that their exchange does not run afoul of *riba al-fadl*).

34 N. Saleh, op. cit., pp. 35–6.

35 Ibid., p. 35.

36 See A. Sanhuri, op. cit., Vol. 3, p. 237 ("This question appears strange, since loan is the primary *riba* contract in modern laws. But the fact is that the loan in the Islamic *fiqh* is not one of the bases for analogy in *riba* contracts... sale is the basis for analogy....").

37 N. Saleh, op. cit., p. 35 (citing Sanhuri, op cit., note 30, Vol. 3, p. 237).

38 J. Schacht, *Riba*, op. cit., p. 1150. It is reported that Muhammad said, "Every loan that attracts a benefit is *riba*." al-Asqalani, al-Hafiz Ahmad ibn-Hajar, *Bulugh al Muram min Adillat al Ahkam*, (Multilithed material, I 25).

39 N. Saleh, op. cit., p. 35; J. Schacht, *Riba*, op. cit., p. 1149.

40 W.M. Ballantyne, *Commercial Law in the Arab Middle East*, op. cit., p. 125.

41 N. Saleh, op. cit., p. 35; and W.M. Ballantyne, *Commercial Law in the Arab Middle East*, op. cit., p. 125. "After repayment, such a voluntary gift is permitted." For a more detailed account of each school's views on *qard* see N. Saleh, op. cit., pp. 37–47.

42 See Chapter 5.

43 According to W.M. Ballantyne, *Commercial Law in the Arab Middle East*, op. cit., pp. 125–6:

> When an article loaned is neither weighed nor measured, there is a choice between requiring the return of an equivalent at the date of repayment or requiring a return of the article's value as at the date of the loan. Ibn Qudama held that, with objects not measured or weighed, there could be no equivalents, so the debtor had to restore to the creditor the value of the article as it was when the obligation originally arose, that is, at the time of the loan contract. An argument could be constructed on this basis that a creditor should at least be able to recover a sum equivalent to the amount by which the original principal lent has depreciated in real terms during the period of the loan... Ibn Taimiya, an independent Hanbali whose views have often been approved by legal modernists [also]... believed that the lender should recover the original value...
>
> It would be possible to argue with some force that Ibn Taimiya's view is the one which ought to be adopted, because the lender is not engaging in *riba* -he is not making a real profit out of the transaction. If he could not recover for losses sustained as a result of inflation, he would be much less inclined to grant a gratuitous loan.

44 Ibid., p. 126.

45 Contrary to the analysis provided in the text that follows, Ballantyne claims that Coulson says that the Hanbali, Maliki, and Shafi'i schools would declare a loan with a stipulation of interest to be entirely void. Ballantyne's cite to Coulson, however, is not accurate and so it is difficult to determine the validity of this statement. See W.M. Ballantyne, *Commercial Law in the Arab Middle East*, op. cit., note 15, at 127 and n.42.

46 N. Saleh, op. cit., pp. 44–5. (citing S. Mahmasani, The General Theory of the Law of Obligations and Contracts under Islamic Jurisprudence (1972) 461–2; S. Baz, Sharh al-Majalla art. 23 (1923)).

47 Ibid., p. 45.

48 Ibid., pp. 45–6.

49 Ibid.

50 See J. Schacht, *Introduction*, op. cit., pp. 78–9; J. Schacht, *Riba*, op. cit., p. 1150; W.M. Ballantyne, *Commercial Law in the Arab Middle East*, op. cit., p. 126.

51 J. Schacht, *Introduction*, ibid., pp. 78–9.

52 This example is based upon two similar hypotheticals: one in N. Coulson, op. cit., p. 45, and the other in N. Coulson, *Conflicts and Tensions in Islamic Jurisprudence* (Chicago, IL: University of Chicago Press, 1969), pp. 87–8.

53 N. Coulson, op. cit., p. 45.

54 Ibid., N. Saleh, op. cit., p. 36; J. Schacht, *Riba*, op. cit., p. 1150; J. Schacht, Introduction, op. cit., pp. 81–2; W.M. Ballantyne, *Commercial Law in the Arab Middle East*, op. cit., p. 126;

M.S.A. Khan, 'The Mohammedan Laws Against Usury and How They Are Evaded', *Journal of Comparative Legislation and International Law*, 3d. ser., 11 (1929), pp. 233–44.

55   J. Schacht, *Riba*, op. cit., p. 1150; see also Anderson, "Islamic Law Today The Background to Islamic Fundamentalism", *Arab Law Quarterly* 2 (1987), pp. 339, 344–5.

56   N. Coulson, op. cit., p. 46; M.S.A. Khan, op. cit., p. 234.

57   Anderson, op. cit., p. 345.

58   N. Coulson, op. cit., pp. 45–6; J. Schacht, *Riba*, op. cit., p. 1150; J. Schacht, *Introduction*, op. cit., pp. 81–2; W.M. Ballantyne, *Commercial Law in the Arab Middle East*, op. cit., p. 126; M.S.A. Khan, op. cit., pp. 233–44.

59   N. Coulson, op. cit., p. 46; W.M. Ballantyne, *Commercial Law in the Arab Middle East*, op.cit., p. 126; M.S.A. Khan, op. cit., p. 234.

60   N. Coulson, op. cit., p. 46.

61   Ibid.

62   Ibid., see also N. Saleh, op. cit., p. 48.

63   This section on Ibn Abbas is drawn primarily from N. Saleh, op. cit., pp. 26–7.

64   For example, Muhammad Abdu, Rashid Rida, Abd al-Razzaq Sanhuri; see Chapter 5.

65   Ibn Qayyim, op. cit., pp. 153–64.

66   "As for the evident [manifest *riba*], it is *riba al-nasi'a*. It is what they did in the *Jahiliyya*. For example, one delays his debt and increases it in value..." Ibn Qayyim, op. cit., p. 47.

67   "[If they sold a dirham for two dirhams... they would move by degrees from current profit in them to delayed profit, which is precisely *riba al-nasi'a*." Ibn Qayyim, op. cit., p. 49.

68   For Sanhuri and other scholars with a less restrictive view towards *riba* this is the proper interpretation. See Chapter 5.

69   Ibn Qayyim, op. cit., pp. 49–51.

70   Ibid., p. 52.

71   Ibid., p. 55.

72   Ibid., pp. 55–6.

73   Ibid., pp. 50–1.

74   Ibid., p. 58.

5 The modern debate over *riba* in Egypt

Emad H. Khalil* and Abdulkader Thomas

Muhammad Abdu and Rashid Rida

In Egypt, in 1883, Jamal al-Din al-Afghani and his student Muhammad Abdu formed the Salafiyya Party with the purpose of bringing about an Islamic renaissance. In 1897, Abdu helped his star pupil Rashid Rida to establish a monthly magazine called *Al-Manar* (The Lighthouse), which was to serve as the doctrinal organ of the party.[1] In 1899 Abdu was appointed the Grand Mufti of Egypt, a position he held until his death in 1905. Abdu and Rida issued numerous opinions on various points of Islamic Law (*fatawa*, sing. *fatwa*). These opinions often were extremely controversial but none more so than those regarding *riba*. Rida continued to elucidate upon his and Abdu's views until his death in 1938. However, determining precisely what Abdu's views were regarding *riba* is difficult because Rida has been suspected of attributing his own opinions to Abdu.[2] Moreover, perhaps realizing the volatility of the subject, many of Rida's accounts of his own views as well as Abdu's are vague.

The *Sanduq al-Tawfir* Affair, which has reached us primarily through Rida, demonstrates this difficulty well. Early this century, the Egyptian Government created a Postal Savings Account (*Sanduq al-Tawfir*), similar to those in Europe, which yielded to the depositors a fixed rate of interest. According to Rida, over 3000 depositors, on the grounds of piety, refused to accept the interest which had accrued in their accounts.[3] As a result, certain government officials including the Postal Director, informally asked the Mufti, Muhammad Abdu, if there was any way, in accordance with the *Sharia'a*, that would allow Muslims to accept the interest earned in these accounts.[4] Abdu responded that such interest was not lawful since the Postal Administration was exploiting money which it did not borrow out of need; however, if the money were invested according to the rules of *mudaraba*, then the profits generated would be legal.[5]

Apparently, a rivalry existed between the Khedive, Abbas II, and Abdu because they were vying for the intellectual leadership of Egypt.[6] The Khedive, who, as the head of the Postal Administration, had established the savings accounts and set the interest rates on them, was upset by Abdu's disapproval.[7] So, he appointed a group of scholars from Al-Azhar University to devise a justification for the interest earned on these accounts.[8] But, according to Rida, their opinion was essentially the same as Abdu's.[9] Nevertheless, their opinion was acceptable to the Khedive who, set on embarrassing Abdu, ironically proceeded to accuse him of wanting to force *riba* on pious Muslims.

Perhaps, partly because of the Khedive's actions, Abdu is often quoted as having found bank interest as well as interest generated by insurance policies to be lawful under the *Sharia'a*.[10] And when Rida was asked whether Abdu had ever issued a written *fatwa* in this regard, he did not categorically deny it but gave the previous account of the *Sanduq al-Tawfir* Affair and curiously premised it by saying: "If there was an official *fatwa* issued by the Imam in the *Sanduq al-Tawfir* Affair, it would be with his *fatwa*s which are deposited in the Ministry of Justice, from which it can be sought. I did not [however] see a *fatwa* by the Imam in that regard..."[11] Additionally, although Abdu spoke of *mudaraba* he does not appear to have elaborated upon it.[12] And while there is some evidence that there was nominal compliance with Abdu's opinion, the *Sanduq al-Tawfir* activities seem to have continued essentially unchanged.[13] Moreover, at least according to one commentator, although Abdu did not make his opinion public, he was the first Islamic scholar to have justified the exclusion of the loan for interest from the ambit of *riba*'s prohibition.[14]

But as Mallat points out, it is Abdu (as narrated by Rida) who, in language very reminiscent of ibn Qayyim's,[15] put forth the main argument that would continually be used against interest in the modern debate:

> Money, says Abduh, in his comments on the verses on *riba* in the second *Sura* of the *Quran*, is merely an indicator of the value (*Qima*) of commodities. If this is altered to making money the object (*Maqsud*) of the production of wealth, "then this will lead to the stripping of wealth from the hands of most people and to concentrating it in the hands of those who limit their works to the exploitation (*istighlal*) of money by money. Thus, money expands (*yarbu*) with them ('*Indahum*), and is hoarded in the safes (*sanadiq*, plural of *sanduq*) and in financial houses (*buyut maliyya*) known as banks (*bunuk*), and the labourers ('*amilun*) are stripped from the value of their labor, because most of the profit would then derive from the money itself (he [i.e. Abduh; the narrator is Rida] means that most of the profit goes to the capitalist (*rabb al-mal*), not to the worker), and thus die the poor."[16]

The most likely source for the confusion regarding Abdu's views is Rashid Rida. Rida often incorporated statements made by Abdu in his *fatwa*s and replied to questions posed by subscribers of Al-Manar, giving the impression that his responses conformed to Abdu's opinions. At times it is even difficult to determine whether it is Abdu who is being quoted or Rida who is speaking. Consequently, while we can be certain that Rida's views were to some extent shaped by his teacher, Muhammad Abdu, it would be a mistake to unquestioningly accept all of his accounts of Abdu's thinking, much less attribute all of his views to Abdu.

With this in mind, Rida's and perhaps some of Abdu's views as well, regarding *riba* can be gleaned from Rida's *fatwa*s and writings in Al-Manar. Essentially, Rida viewed *riba al-jahiliyya* as being under a conclusive presumption of *riba* with *riba al-fadl* and *riba al-nasi'a* being under a rebuttable presumption of *riba*.[17] Building upon ibn Qayyim's reasoning, Rida argued that only *riba al-jahiliyya* is manifest *riba* and therefore prohibited in and of itself.[18] *Riba al-fadl* and *riba al-nasi'a*, on the other hand, are hidden *riba* and prohibited only when they lead to manifest *riba* – *riba al-jahiliyya*.[19] And according to Rida, *riba al-jahiliyya* only occurs when interest accrues on the interest originally stipulated in a contract.[20] As a result, Rida regarded the original interest rate set on a loan as lawful, despite being in consideration for the delayed term of payment. If, however, at maturity, another interest charge is made in consideration for deferring the payment further, that interest charge constitutes unlawful *riba al-nasi'a* which if repeated constitutes *riba al-jahiliyya*.[21] According to Sanhuri, Rida's logic makes it clear that he thought the prohibition of manifest *riba* could be lifted only in the case of pressing necessity, whereas *riba al-nasi'a* and *riba alfadl* are regarded merely with aversion and not as under a direct prohibition.[22]

Once again we can see the main outlines of the contemporary debate over *riba* taking shape.[23] On the one hand we have Rida arguing that the *Quranic* prohibition of *riba* is, in modern parlance, only on compound interest. And we have Abdu giving the impression in the *Sanduq al-Tawfir* Affair that had the Postal Administration borrowed the money out of necessity that the interest earned on the accounts would have been lawful. On the other hand we have the argument, as also put forth by Abdu, that for interest charges to be lawful they have to be earned according to the rules of *mudaraba* or else they will lead to exploitation.

Ibrahim Zaki Badawi

In 1939, Ibrahim Zaki Badawi was working with the new Egyptian Civil Code's Preparatory Commission in its Islamic Law Section. According to Badawi, early that year, Sanhuri, who was the head of the Commission, approached him with the idea of somehow reconciling the projected articles on interest in the Code with the *Sharia'a*'s injunctions against *riba*.[24] With the issue of codification, the debate over *riba* reemerged, but this time there would be a "resolution." Badawi claims that, at first, he intended to write a report for the Commission which simply summarized the ideas of certain Islamic scholars (presumably ibn Abbas, ibn Qayyim etc.) that might allow them to bring the projected articles in accordance with the *Sharia'a*. In fact, he claims to have originally entitled his work, "Opinions on Prohibited *Riba* in the *Sharia'a*" ("*Ara fil Riba al-Muharram Shar'an*").[25] In the process of researching and writing, however, Badawi says he discovered that these scholars' ideas reflected a general theory of *riba* of which he became convinced. So he set about rewriting his original paper and retitled it, "The Theory of Prohibited *Riba* in the *Sharia'a*" ("*Nazariyyat al-Riba al-Muharram. fi al-Sharia'a al-Islamiyya*").[26] Sanhuri was so impressed with Badawi's study that he had it published in the Fuad University (later Cairo University) law journal – *The Journal of Law and Economics* (*Majallat al Qanun wal-Iqtisad*), then and still the most prominent Arabic law journal.[27]

Badawi's article was a long intricate analysis of *riba* but, it was his conclusions justifying interest in modern transactions that so pleased Sanhuri.[28] Like ibn Qayyim, Badawi reminded his reader that, "nothing is prohibited except that which God prohibits."[29] It is improper, he said, to prohibit transactions which are only regarded with aversion particularly if these are financial transactions which the people need.[30] He approved of ibn Abbas' understanding of the *hadith* which says there is, "No *riba* except in the *nasi'a.*"[31] Consequently, Badawi only viewed *riba al-jahiliyya* as being under a direct prohibition. And like Rida, he defined *riba al-jahiliyya* as the increase in the principal at the time of maturity in order to postpone the due date.[32] He then cited approvingly to ibn Qayyim's reasoning that *riba al-fadl* is prohibited only because it is a means to *riba al-nasi'a*; and that a prohibition of means is less stringent than a prohibition of ends and therefore can be lifted in cases of need.[33]

Loans which attract a benefit, he argued, should not be analogized to *riba al-jahiliyya* because the forbidden increase of *riba al-jahiliyya* is forced upon the borrower at the time of maturity in order for him to postpone the due date; while in the loan for interest the increase occurs at the time of contracting and so does not involve compulsion.[34] Even if one were to accept the analogy, he said, its strength has weakened over time. Loans have evolved from being primarily unproductive consumption loans to today being profit-generating production loans for the borrower. Hence, it is only fair to allow the lender to share in these profits.[35]

Sanhuri immediately adopted Badawi's conclusions in the proposed articles for the new Egyptian Civil Code. Badawi, on the other hand, apparently became more discontent with his views as time passed. And as discussed in the next section, in an incredible reversal 25 years later, he published a 300-page book completely reversing his original conclusions.

Abd Al-Razzaq Ahmad Al-Sanhuri

From a modern standpoint, Sanhuri is perhaps the most important person in this debate over *riba*. Sanhuri was, as Enid Hill acknowledges, "Egypt's most distinguished scholar of modern jurisprudence."[36] He was not only the architect of the Egyptian Civil Code of 1948 but subsequently of the Civil Codes of Syria, Iraq, and Libya and the Commercial Code of Kuwait, whose provisions regarding *riba* are very similar to those of Egypt. And as the discussion on Badawi showed, Sanhuri was deeply concerned with making sure that the Codes, as much as possible, were in accordance with the *Sharia'a*. Sanhuri himself declared, regarding the Egyptian Civil Code, "I assure you that we did not leave a single provision of the *Sharia'a* which we could have included in this legislation without so doing."[37] Despite the general consensus that Sanhuri's Codes for the most part were not Islamic,[38] the sections on interest were, in his view, certainly in accordance with the *Sharia'a*.[39] Consequently, his views regarding *riba* and the debate surrounding it, as well as the fate of the interest provisions in the Egyptian Civil Code, in this era of Islamic codification, are critical. For in this respect at least, as Egypt goes so does much of the Arab World.

Before examining the interest provisions of the Egyptian Civil Code, it is instructive to look at Sanhuri's views on *riba* in his *Masadir al-Haqq fil Fiqh al-Islami (Sources of Law in Islamic Jurisprudence)* of which they are a reflection.[40] This six-part work now published in two volumes was developed from lectures he gave at the Arab Studies Institute in Cairo between 1954 and 1957.[41] In it Sanhuri provides a short but detailed analysis of *riba* which clearly owes a great deal to Badawi. Unlike Rida who regarded *riba al-nasi'a* and *riba al-fadl* merely with aversion,[42] Sanhuri viewed *riba* as being prohibited in all of its forms for three main reasons: (1) to prevent people from hoarding their foodstuff; (2) to prevent speculation in currency so that it does not become a commodity and therefore upset prices; and (3) to protect people from fraud and exploitation.[43]

However, the distinction between *riba al-jahiliyya, riba al-fadl* and *riba al-nasi'a* was still critical for Sanhuri. *"Riba al-jahiliyya* is prohibited in its essence, the prohibition being one of ends [or objectives]."[44] *Riba al-nasi'a* and *riba al-fadl* are not prohibited in their essence but merely because they are means to *riba al-jahiliyya*. Thus, theirs is not a prohibition of ends but of blocking the avenues to evil (*saddan li-al-dhara'i*)[45] – "a prohibition designed to close the loopholes which might lead to pre-Islamic *riba* [*riba al-jahiliyya*]."[46] The significant result of this distinction for Sanhuri was that while *riba al-jahiliyya* is permitted only for pressing necessity, *riba al-fadl* and *riba al-nasi'a* are permitted for a mere need.[47]

A loan with interest, he argued, is not under a direct prohibition of *riba* since sales are the basis for the prohibition and loans have traditionally been regarded as essentially gratuitous transactions.[48] However, "a loan contract does become a *ribawi* transaction, by analogy with sale, when it secures to the lender an interest or a premium."[49] "But this is not because the stipulated excess is *riba*, rather it is because it resembles *riba*."[50] Consequently, he put interest on loans in the same category as *riba al-fadl* and *riba al-nasi'a*, prohibited not for itself but because it is a means to *riba al-jahiliyya*.[51] "Thus the prohibition is lifted if a need arises."[52] And according to Sanhuri, loan contracts are no longer essentially gratuitous transactions but have evolved into a means for providing the necessary capital for production.[53]

Sanhuri equated *riba al-jahiliyya* with modern compound interest:

> This is similar to what we now today call interest upon interest, or compound gain. It is when the lender claims interest independently upon interest which has accumulated, so he says to the debtor, either you pay the principal and the interest accumulated upon it, or you increase, such that the frozen interest is included in the capital, and the whole becomes new capital, increased by the interest which is produced from the period by which the term of the loan is lengthened.[54]

As was mentioned, for such a transaction to be lawful, he argued, there needed to be a pressing necessity similar to one that would permit the eating of carrion or blood.[55] While it may be possible to imagine such a situation for the borrower, Sanhuri argued, it was hard to conceive of any reason other than covetousness and greed that would impel a creditor to this type of exploitation.[56]

Recall, however, that for Sanhuri, a mere need lifted the prohibition on *riba al-fadl, riba al-nasi'a*, and simple interest on loans. According to him:

> Need [*haja*] here means, as ibn Qayyim defined it, a greater benefit in one specific type of *riba*, which would be lost if the prohibition remained according to the general principle. In such a case that type is permitted as an exception to the rule of prohibition, and to the degree of the existing need.[57]

Based on this concept of need Sanhuri went on to justify interest in modern commercial transactions:

> In the capitalist economic system, like the system existing at the present time in most countries, which is distinguished by capital being owned by individuals, institutions and banks, and not by the state, general and universal need calls for the worker to obtain capital so that he might exploit it by his work. *Mudaraba, qirad* [another name for *mudaraba*], and other transactions become insufficient to obtain the necessary capital. Share and commandite [*tawsiya*] companies permit in most cases that the owner of the capital invest his property in purchase of shares of these companies, with the result that he participate in the profit and loss. Nonetheless, loans are the primary means in the existing capitalist economic system to obtain capital. Even in the companies just mentioned there exists besides shares, which are the shares of the partners who participate in the profit and loss, bonds, which are loans advanced to these companies. The borrower here, as has been previously said, is the stronger party, and the lender is the weak party whose protection is required. So long as the need exists to obtain capital by means of loan or otherwise, and so long as capital is not owned by the state, but rather is the property of the individual who accumulates it by his work and his effort, then it is his right that he not oppress concerning it and that he not be oppressed; as long as the need exists for all of this, then interest on capital within the mentioned limits is permitted as an exception to the basic rule of prohibition.[58]

By "mentioned limits" Sanhuri meant that the interest needed to be simple not compound. And even with simple interest, he argued, in order to insure that the prohibition was being lifted only to the extent of the need, it was necessary for the Legislature to develop laws regarding its maximum rate, method of accrual, and the total sum which could be demanded.[59] If the need is removed, however, the prohibition should be restored. For example, he argued, if the economic system were to change from capitalist to socialist, where capital was in the hands of the state not individuals then the need may not arise and *riba* would return to its basic principle of prohibition.[60] Many would argue later that with the newly found prosperity of the oil-rich states and with the advent of Islamic banking one could no longer contend that there was a need for interest in modern transactions and so the prohibition on *riba* should be restored.[61]

The treatment of interest in the Civil Code

Sanhuri's views on interest are reflected in the provisions of the Egyptian Civil Code. While there are no fewer than 35 articles in the Civil Code which deal with interest, the basic elements of Sanhuri's views can be discerned by just examining a few of them.

Articles 226 and 227 reflect Sanhuri's view that interest rates should be within limits determined by the Legislature to insure that the prohibition of *riba* is being lifted only to the extent of the need. Article 226 provides that if the debtor defaults, as damages for the delay, he will be charged an interest rate of 4 percent in civil transactions and 5 percent in commercial transactions. Article 227, however, provides that the parties can agree on an interest rate up to 7 percent as damages for a delay in payment or in any other situation (e.g. interest on a loan). The parties, though, cannot agree on any higher rate of interest.

> Article 226: When the object of an obligation is the payment of a sum of money of which the amount is known at the time when the claim is made, the debtor shall be bound, in case of delay in payment, to pay to the creditor, as damages for the delay, interest at the rate of four percent in civil matters and five percent in commercial matters. Such interest shall run from the date of the claim in Court, unless the contract or commercial usage fixes another date. This article shall apply, unless otherwise provided in law.

> Article 227: The parties may agree upon another rate of interest either in the event of delay in effecting payment or in any other case in which interest has been stipulated, provided that it does not exceed seven percent. If the parties agree to a rate exceeding seven percent, the rate will be reduced to seven percent and any surplus that has been paid shall be refunded.
>
> Any commission or other consideration of whatsoever nature stipulated by the creditor which, together with the agreed interest, exceeds the maximum limits of interest set out above will be considered as disguised interest and will be subject to reduction, if it is established that this commission or this consideration is in respect of a service actually rendered by the creditor or of a lawful consideration.

Similarly, Article 229 is a determination by the Legislature that in instances of bad faith by the creditor a Judge may reduce the legal or contractual interest rate or even eliminate it altogether.

> Article 229: If a creditor, whilst claiming his rights, has in bad faith prolonged the duration of the litigation, the Judge may reduce the legal or contractual interest or may refuse to allow interest for the whole period during which the litigation has been unjustifiably prolonged.

Article 232 reflects Sanhuri's view that what is absolutely prohibited is compound interest. And by providing that total interest can never exceed the principal, Sanhuri codified the *Quran*'s injunction not to consume *riba* with continual doubling. But because of the need for long-term production loans, Sanhuri argued, this prohibition should not extend to them.[62]

> Article 232: Subject to any commercial rules or practice to the contrary, interest does not run on outstanding interest and in no case shall the total interest that the creditor may collect exceed the amount of the capital.

Reflecting the *Sharia'a*'s view that loans are basically gratuitous transaction, Article 542 provides that if the parties do not agree on an interest rate the loan is considered interest free. Nevertheless, if the debtor defaults, the creditor is entitled to delay interest as provided in Article 996.[63]

> Article 542: The borrower is under liability to pay the agreed interest as it falls due; in the absence of an agreement as regards interest, the loan is deemed to be without consideration.

Article 544 reflects another policy decision by the Legislature, lifting the prohibition of *riba* only to the extent of the perceived need. It provides the debtor with a guaranteed right of prepayment any time after six months from the date of the loan. And the debtor has six months from the date he gives notice of his intention to prepay the loan, to effectuate that intention. However, he incurs the interest that accrued on the debt before he announces his intention to prepay and the interest that accrues on the debt during the period following his announcement until he actually executes his intention.

> Article 544: If interest is agreed, the debtor may, after six months from the date of the loan, give notice of his intention to terminate the contract and to restitute the thing taken on the loan, provided that the restitution takes place within a term not exceeding six months of the date of the notice. In such a case the debtor shall be liable to pay the interest due for the six months following the notice. He will not, in any case, be bound to pay interest or to perform a prestation of any kind by reason of the fact that payment is made before due date. The right of the borrower to effect restitution cannot be forfeited or limited by agreement.

The key element to all these provisions according to Sanhuri is that they are a legislative determination of how far the prohibition of *riba* should be lifted to accommodate the present need for interest in society. The Legislature, therefore, must always have the ability to modify these provisions to reflect the changing level of the need for interest in society. And if a need no longer existed for interest-bearing transactions, then these provisions should be eliminated and *riba* should return to its basic principle of prohibition.[64]

Badawi's about face

In 1964 Badawi published a book with the same title as his 1939 article.[65] In it he reexamined the concept of *riba* in even more depth than his original study. And in an incredible about-face, after acknowledging that his 1939 conclusions were wrong, he reached exactly the opposite conclusions. He then went on to criticize Sanhuri's treatment of interest in the Egyptian Civil Code, which ironically were largely based on Badawi's 1939 report to the Preparatory Commission.

Badawi's new conclusions embraced the traditional view of *riba*'s absolute prohibition. He now defined the *Quranic* prohibition of *riba al-jahiliyya* as any increase in the debt for a delay in payment.[66] This included any increase in the debt that occurred at the time the loan agreement was signed or subsequently at the time of maturity. Thus, Badawi now regarded the prohibition of *riba al-jahiliyya* as including a loan with interest.[67] Moreover, he now argued, that the *Quranic* prohibition of *riba* and the *hadith's* prohibition of *riba*, that is, *riba al-fadl* and *riba al-nasi'a*, are essentially the same. Both are prohibited in order to prevent the exploitation which occurs when one obtains a benefit without due consideration.[68] He also now regarded the six commodities mentioned in the *hadith* as only practical examples, relevant at the time of the Prophet and not intended to define or limit the contours of the prohibition or its underlying reason.[69] Additionally, Badawi now understood ibn Abbas as only permitting *riba al-fadl*; and similarly he now understood ibn Qayyim as only permitting *riba al-fadl* in cases of need. Neither man, now in Badawi's maturer view, ever permitted *riba al-nasi'a* and consequently ever permitted a disparity of amount in a delayed exchange.[70] Rashid Rida's views on *riba*, therefore, he argued, were wrong because they were based on a mistaken understanding of both *riba al-jahiliyya* and the views of ibn Abbas and ibn Qayyim.[71]

Moreover, Badawi contended, Sanhuri's understanding of *riba* as well as his treatment of it in the Egyptian Civil Code was incorrect.[72] Article 232, he argued, reflected the unduly narrow view that only compound interest is absolutely prohibited. And by exempting long-term productive investments because of the need for them from Article 232's requirement that total interest not exceed the principal, Sanhuri made the mistaken assumption that loans with interest are prohibited merely because they are a means to *riba al-jahiliyya* and can be permitted if a need arises.[73] Badawi concluded that the rules regarding loans with interest in the Egyptian Civil Code contravene the *Sharia'a's* prohibition of interest.[74]

Muhammad Abu Zahra

Abu Zahra in his *Tahrim al-Riba* (*Riba's Prohibition*) also provides some of the traditional responses to the reasoning Sanhuri used to justify permitting interest in the Egyptian Civil Code.[75] First, Abu Zahra attacks the argument that interest may be permitted because of the need for it. He denies that the present need for interest is of the same magnitude as the need to lift the prohibition of pork or wine in critical situations.

> It is not of the same kind, and even if it were, it would work only on an individual, and not on a social level. Even in the case [of necessity favoring *Riba* on a personal basis], which is an exception, this cannot be accepted. On the institutional level, necessity would apply to the borrower, never to the lender.[76]

Abu Zahra recognizes that there is a distinction between a pressing necessity and a mere need but he also distinguishes between borrowing and lending. Abu Zahra argues that all those involved with *riba* are condemned. But there is a legal difference, he says, between borrowing and lending.

Borrowing with *riba* is prohibited in order to block the avenues to evil, whereas lending for *riba* is absolutely prohibited. He concludes that borrowing may be allowed in the case of a compelling necessity. In the case of a mere need, however, both lending and borrowing are prohibited, but the lender is in double infringement and his responsibility for the violation is of the first degree, whereas the borrower is merely an accessory.

Abu Zahra also criticizes those who loosely interpret Umar's statements on *riba*. He understood Umar as saying that it was difficult to precisely determine when *riba* was implicated, so one should be extremely careful when engaging in matters relating to *riba*. It was better to avoid any doubtful practice which might even minimally lead to it. Thus according to Abu Zahra, Umar was not saying that *riba* should be allowed just because we were left in the dark as to its exact meaning. In any event, he says, Umar knew exactly what *riba al-jahiliyya* meant and this is precisely the type of *riba* involved in the present loan for interest. Abu Zahra also criticizes the distinction made by those who argue that interest should be allowed on production loans but not on consumption loans. He agrees that being able to raise capital is necessary to build and maintain an economy. But there are other ways to raise capital, he argues, without having to resort to fixed interest rates. For example, he says, one could raise sufficient capital through *mudaraba*.

The legislative debate

The legislative as well as judicial debate over *riba* begins with the Egyptian Constitution of 1971. Prior to 1971 there was no provision in the Egyptian Constitution on the sources of law or their hierarchy. Article 1 of the Egyptian Civil Code, however, instructed a judge in any civil matter to apply the provisions of any applicable law, and in their absence, custom and in the absence of custom, the principles of the *Sharia'a*. Thus, the *Sharia'a* was relegated to a subsidiary role in the hierarchy.[77] In fact, there are virtually no cases other than personal status cases before 1970 in which judges refer to the *Sharia'a*.[78] But the *Sharia'a* was significantly strengthened and more frequently referred to by judges and lawyers alike when, after intense debate, Article 2 was inserted in the Constitution of 1971.[79] Article 2 provided that, "The principles of the *Sharia'a* are a principal source of law." Initially, the Committee on Constitutional and Legislative Affairs in Parliament, chaired by Gamal al-Oteifi, fielded most of the proposals seeking to implement Article 2.

Early in 1976, Shaykh Salah Abu Ismail, a Member of Parliament, introduced a bill calling for an amendment to the Civil Code making interest illegal.[80] Investment loans, however, made according to the rules of *mudaraba* would be permitted. Hoping to block Shaykh Ismail's bill, the Government asked al-Oteifi to introduce a counterproposal into Parliament.[81] At first, it appeared to be more restrictive than even the original bill because it not only prohibited interest, but also made it a criminal offense to agree to its stipulation. Upon closer analysis, however, it was clearly less severe, because it only applied to private dealings. Commercial transactions involving corporations, banks, the Government, and other institutions were exempt. Through this maneuver, the Government successfully blocked Shaykh Ismail's bill. And despite being approved by his committee, Oteifi's bill was never discussed in full Parliament and was not passed.[82]

With pressure mounting on the Government by Islamic parties to enforce the *Sharia'a*, on November 20, 1975, the Ministry of Justice set up a committee chaired by the president of the Court of Cassation (*Mahkamat al-Naqd*) and charged it with preparing legislation in accordance with the *Sharia'a*. Between 1976 and 1978 the Committee produced a number of proposals.[83] In this environment a proposal was made to amend Article 2 of the Constitution to say that the principles of the *Sharia'a* are "the" principal source of law, and not just merely "a" principal source of law. This amendment was adopted by referendum on May 22, 1980. Most observers felt that this amendment was simply an instruction to the Legislature to conform future legislation to the *Sharia'a*. Some, however, argued that Article 2, as amended, made all existing legislation not in accordance with the *Sharia'a*, including provisions in the Civil Code, unconstitutional. This conflict would eventually come to a head in the judiciary with regard to the Civil Codes' treatment of *riba*.

On December 17, 1978 the Ministry of Justice disbanded the committee it created in 1976 and replaced it with a special Parliamentary committee, chaired by the Speaker Sufi Abu Talib.[84] This Committee was entrusted with codifying the *Sharia'a* by preparing new codes in accordance with it. The Committee was instructed to consult the University of Al-Azhar, the various faculties of law and the judiciary.[85] By 1982 the Committee had drafted six codes including a Civil Code, which was presented to Parliament on July 1 of that year.[86] The Draft Civil Code provided that any stipulation of interest was null and void. Interest was defined broadly to include any commission for which no services had been rendered or any delayed benefit. Only investment through *mudaraba* was allowed.

The Government, however, sidestepped the entire issue by immediately burying the Draft Codes in committee. But after loud protest by the opposition, Parliament resolved to debate the matter on May 4, 1985 as part of the discussion of the Committee for Religious and Social Affairs and Religious Endowments' annual report. Although the Committee's report contained a section dealing with conforming existing laws to the *Sharia'a*, it did not discuss the Draft Codes. The Committee recommended that existing laws be "gradually and scientifically" cleared from all provisions conflicting with the *Sharia'a*.[87] During the debate, the opposition demanded that the Draft Codes be discussed. The Speaker, however, dodged the issue, arguing that the Draft Codes had not been properly put on the agenda and could not be considered in that session.[88] So, the Draft Codes were once again buried in committee and the Government succeeded in avoiding the issue of codifying the *Sharia'a*.

The judicial debate

The *Maglis al-Dawla* (the Council of State), the highest administrative court in Egypt, had, as early as 1948, regarded the Constitution to be superior to ordinary law, so that if a conflict occurred the Constitution would prevail.[89] Administrative courts and, to some extent ordinary courts, developed the concept of a "lack of constitutionality" (*adam dusturiyya*) and assumed the *ad hoc* right of judicial review.[90] In 1969 this power of judicial review was consolidated and given to the *Mahkamat al-Ulya* (Supreme Court). With the passage of Article 2 in 1971, the Court was presented with numerous challenges to the constitutionality of laws not in accordance with the *Sharia'a*.[91]

In April 1976 the *Mahkamat al-Ulya* was presented with a constitutional challenge made under Article 2 to certain personal status legislation[92] enacted in 1920 and 1929 which made it possible to imprison a husband who refused to pay maintenance to his wife in spite of being able to do so.[93] The Court ruled that under Article 2 the *Sharia'a* was one of the criterion for testing the constitutionality of legislation, even if this legislation had been enacted before the promulgation of the Constitution. This ruling is impressive because it was made even before Article 2 had been amended so the Constitution still contained the weaker wording making the principles of the *Sharia'a* only "a" principal source of legislation rather than "the" source of legislation. The Court went on to uphold the provisions of this legislation, however, ruling that it was in accordance with the *Sharia'a*.

The *Mahkamat al-Ulya* was replaced in 1979 by a more independent and non-political tribunal: *al-Mahakamat al-Dusturiyya al-Ulya* (The Supreme Constitutional Court (herein "SCC")).[94] With the 1980 amendment to Article 2 a large number of cases came before the SCC in which the constitutionality of legislation was called into question. However, it was a 1982 Court of Cassation (*Mahakamat al-Naqd*) decision which would provide a glimpse of how the SCC would later deal with the issue of interest.[95] A lower court convicted two police officers for assaulting a suspect during an interrogation. Since the victim's testimony was the only evidence in the case, the officers appealed the decision arguing that it conflicted with Article 2 of the Constitution because the *Sharia'a* does not admit as evidence the testimony of a victim in a criminal case. The court dismissed their appeal on the grounds that Article 2, as amended, was no more than an instruction to the Legislature and the *Sharia'a* could not be applied by the judiciary until the Legislature has heeded this instruction and formulated the principles of the *Sharia'a* in precise legislation:

> ... Whereas the provision of Article 2 of the Constitution to the effect that the principles of the *Sharia'a* are the principal source of legislation has no legal force in and of itself, but is only an instruction to the legislator to take the *Sharia'a* as a principle source of the law he enacts;
>
> ... Whereas, consequently, the *Sharia'a* can only be applied after the Legislature has obeyed this instruction and has formulated its exalted principles in well-defined and precise enactments according to which the judiciary must pass judgment as from the date fixed by the Legislative Authority for their coming into force;
>
> ... Whereas the opposite view would lead to a blending of, on the one hand, the oblig-ation of the judiciary to enforce the existing legal enactments and, on the other hand, the enactment of the legal principles that are incompatible with a precise definition of its jurisdiction, not to mention the fact that the application of the *Sharia'a* requires that it should be determined which exactly of the manifold con-flicting views of the founders of the schools of Islamic law, existing with regard to one single case, must be used as a basis for judgements.[96]

Nevertheless, after 1980, there were courts which, invoking Article 2, refused to apply provisions in laws which were contradictory to the *Sharia'a* and advocated its immediate application. According to one observer, the issue in nearly half the cases was the lawfulness of interest.[97] For example, one case involved a defendant who had been fired and was now being sued by his former employers for the principal and legal interest on the amount missing from the money entrusted to him while he was an employee. The District Court of Mit Ghamr refused to grant the interest saying:

> The Court feels embarrassed in front of God – be He praised and exalted – to give judgment for the plaintiffs... or even to consider their claim, since this is in reality claiming *riba* which, in all its forms, is made unlawful in the *Sharia'a*. This is pointed out by God's words: "O' believers, devour not *riba*, doubled and redoubled."[98]

On May 4, 1985, the same day that Parliament was side-stepping the debate on the Draft Codes, the SCC ruled on the legality of interest in light of Article 2, as amended.[99] Fouad Gouda brought an action before an administrative tribunal against the Rector of Al-Azhar University for Egyptian Pounds (LE) 592 and 112 milliems along with interest for the balance owed on surgical instruments purchased by the Medical Faculty of Al-Azhar. The court ruled in favor of Mr Gouda and in accordance with Article 226 of the Civil Code allowed him to collect interest on the debt at the rate of 4 percent, starting from the date of the legal action. The Rector of Al-Azhar appealed the decision to the Supreme Administrative Tribunal. During the appeal the Rector raised the question of Article 226's constitutionality, and on April 3, 1978, the Tribunal suspended the proceedings before it in order to enable the Rector to raise this issue before the SCC, which he did.

The Rector argued that Article 226 of the Civil Code was null and void because it conflicted with the principles of the *Sharia'a* which by virtue of the amendment to Article 2 of the Constitution became "the" principal source of legislation. Specifically, the Rector argued that Article 226 was contrary to the *Sharia'a*'s absolute prohibition of *riba*. The Court rejected this claim without ever having to address it on the merits. It ruled that only legislation enacted after Article 2 was amended needed to be in accordance with the *Sharia'a*. In other words, the amendment to Article 2 did not apply retroactively. Consequently, Article 226 of the Civil Code promulgated in 1948 could not be attacked on the grounds that it was contrary to Article 2, as amended, of the Constitution.

In support of its decision the Court pointed to the 1980 report of the committee responsible for drafting the amendment's language.[100] It also noted that the 1981 report of the General Committee in Parliament which addressed the effects of Article 2, as amended, on legislation, supported the Court's decision as well.[101] The Court reasoned, if the Legislature had meant to specifically incorporate the principles of the *Sharia'a* into the Constitution, or if they had meant these principles to be enforced by the Court without awaiting any legislative enactments formulating these principles, then they could have done so clearly and unambiguously. The Court also pointed out the enormous contradictions, confusion, and instability that would result in the judicial process were it responsible for formulating and implementing on an *ad hoc* basis these *Sharia'a* principles. Moreover, the Court argued that a contrary decision by it would invalidate a great deal of legislation that forms the basis for the, "civil and criminal law and governs the social and economic life of the community."[102]

Thus, as Saba Habachy says in his commentary on the case, the Court ruled that Article 2, as amended, did not automatically make the *Sharia'a* the law of the land, it merely made it the main source of future legislative enactments. And the responsibility for implementing Article 2, as amended, now rested with the Legislature not with the Judiciary.[103] Nevertheless, this did not mean that the Legislature was freed from all responsibility concerning past legislative enactments not in accordance with the *Sharia'a*. On the contrary, the Court said, Article 2 as amended, "imposes on the Legislator, from a political point of view, the duty of purifying the texts of such past legislation and clearing them from any trespass against these principles."[104]

So, as Habachy points out, although,

> The Supreme Court of Egypt did not add or subtract anything from the centuries-old arguments on both sides of the substantive law question of interest... [it] saved, not merely Article 226, but the entire new Egyptian Code of Professor Sanhuri... [which] has served as a model for the Civil Codes of Syria, Libya, Kuwait and Iraq.[105]

Even still, it was not clear how far the SCC decision extended. On its facts it only applied to delay interest in civil matters. It did not address other types of interest dealt with in the Civil Code such as interest in commercial transactions or on loans nor did it refer to bank interest which is not regulated by the Civil Code at all. And as the quote from the 1986 District Court of Mit Ghamr decision shows, even after the SCC decision, a group of judges was still prepared, out of piety, to make rulings which they knew would be likely reversed on appeal but would force the appellate courts to deal with the issue of interest in all its facets. Nevertheless, a 1987 SCC decision made it clear that their 1985 decision, by simple analogy, applied to other provisions dealing with interest in the Civil Code.[106] More controversial was whether the decision covered bank interest, which is regulated by Law 20 of 1975 which predates the 1980 amendment to Article 2 but postdates the original 1971 enactment.[107]

The Sanduq al-Tawfir affair revisited

To some extent, this question became moot when in the fall of 1989, the Government-appointed Mufti of Egypt, Dr Muhammad Sayed Tantawi, ruled that interest on Government Investment Certificates (*Shahadat al-Istithmar*) and similar financial instruments such as Postal Saving Accounts (*Sanadiq al-Tawfir*) was in accordance with the *Sharia'a*.[108] He issued his *fatwa*, apparently at the request of the Government which had been losing out on millions of dollars worth of Egyptians' savings to Islamic Banks and similar institutions. His ruling re-ignited a bitter debate that goes back to the turn of the century with Muhammad Abdu and Rashid Rida.[109]

Tantawi says that he examined the writings of Islamic scholars, and that, despite their prolificacy, there was no agreement by them on this issue. Reflecting this situation, he says, was the split of opinions among the 14 members of a Jurisprudential Studies Committee of an Islamic Studies Institute which convened to discuss this issue in 1976.[110] Tantawi states that four members[111] of the Committee concluded that interest earned on these Certificates was not in accordance with the *Sharia'a*, while nine members held that they were. After examining the personal opinions of some of the various members on the Committee, Tantawi summarizes what he thinks was the essential disagreement.

The main argument put forward against the interest generated by these Certificates, he says, was that they were the result of an imperfect *mudaraba* since their rates and periods of accrual were preset, thus fixing a loss for the bank. Those who consider the interest generated by these Certificates to be in accordance with the *Sharia'a*, he says, respond that presetting the interest rate protects the depositor and prevents any disagreement from occurring between him and the bank; and there is nothing in the *Quran* or in the traditions which prohibits this presetting, so long as it occurs with the consent of both parties. Tantawi then quotes Shaykh Abd al-Wahab Khallaf:

> Thus *mudaraba* takes place according to the agreement of the parties. We are presently in an era in which the uprightness of people has diminished, and if the investor is not guaranteed a fixed return then his partner will take advantage of him.

In addition, Tantawi says, those who regard this interest as lawful point out that the interest is not literally "preset," as evidenced by the fact that the interest rate on these Certificates when they were originally created was 4 percent but have risen today to over 16 percent. Moreover, they argue, the bank does not determine the interest rate until after making precise calculations, for which it alone is responsible and which no one forces upon it. So they conclude, Tantawi says, that there is nothing wrong with this arrangement, so long as it is agreed that if the bank suffers a loss for which it is not negligent, the depositors will take their share of the loss.

Therefore, Tantawi says, because people connect the the word "interest" ("*Fai'dat*") with *riba* he has proposed to the responsible officials at the National Bank (*al-Bank al-Ahly*) to take the steps necessary to rename the profits (*Arbah*) generated by these Certificates from "interest" ("*Fai'dat*") to "investment return" ("*al-A'idat al-Istithmariyya*") or "investment profit" ("*al-Ribh al-Istithmary*").[112] He acknowledges, however, that the lawfulness of a transaction is determined by its actual content not by its name. Tantawi also proposed that the National Bank create a new Investment Certificate with a variable interest rate that would not provide for any preset return. Thus, giving those who doubt the legality of a fixed rate Certificate, an investment option which all agree is in accordance with the *Sharia'a*.

But in the final analysis Tantawi agrees with the majority position of the Committee and concludes that interest earned on Government Investment Certificates (*Shahadat al-Istithmar*) and similar financial instruments such as Postal Saving Accounts (*Sanadiq al-Tawfir*) is in accordance with the *Sharia'a*. This is because, he says, the interest earned is the result of a lawful *mudaraba* transaction, because it is a new transaction beneficial to both individuals and the nation, and it does not involve any exploitation by either party of the other. Tantawi adds, it is admirable for people to invest their money in these Certificates with the intention of aiding the nation in its public projects and to accept as a form of encouragement the profits the nation gives in return by way of interest.

In a December 1989 interview with the Egyptian magazine *October*, Tantawi makes it clear that his reasoning extends much farther than just Government Investment Certificates.[113] Tantawi posits a situation where he has bought a taxi and hired a driver. He tells the driver to research what the expected daily earnings will be. The driver after doing so reaches a figure of LE 10 which Tantawi, based on his own research, agrees is a reasonable estimate. Tantawi then asks what is better, to share whatever earnings the driver brings in or to have the driver pay him LE 5 a day and for the driver to keep whatever he makes above that figure? The first alternative, Tantawi says, will inevitably lead to conflict the first day the driver claims to have made only LE 8 because despite the fact that the driver may be telling the truth, it is natural to doubt him, since he may be tempted to hide some of his income in order to not have to share it. The second alternative, however, Tantawi says, guarantees him a fixed return and assures that the driver will exert his best efforts. Tantawi concludes, therefore, that presetting the rate of return is not prohibited by the *Sharia'a* so long as both parties agree.

So with Tantawi's *fatwa* the twentieth century debate over *riba* seems to have come full circle, right back to where it began with the *Sanduq al-Tawfir* Affair. Tantawi, however, has turned the traditional argument against *riba* on its head. Even Sanhuri agreed with the traditional position that *riba* is prohibited primarily because it results in the exploitation of the borrower by the lender. But Tantawi observes that in the case of Investment Certificates it is the bank which is the borrower and the public the lender. And he makes the very compelling point that it is difficult to argue that a bank is being exploited when it voluntarily offers a fixed interest rate in order to attract capital. On the contrary, Tantawi is saying, if the depositor is not assured a fixed return then it is he who is being exploited. In *Al-Ahram*, Tantawi said that he would be examining other aspects of banking transactions and issuing *fatwa*s on them.[114] These rulings had trickled out of Tantawi during the 1990s without squelching the debate over *riba* in Egypt.

Conclusion

At the turn of the century, the *Sanduq al-Tawfir* Affair forced legislators to address the question of *riba*. How they in fact resolved the issue remains unclear. What is certain is that they were most uncomfortable with it, and that, in practice, interest on Postal Savings Accounts was permitted. And as the Khedive's actions indicate, even at this early stage, there was an acute awareness that the slightest differences over *riba* could be used as a political weapon. Conscious of this threat, Sanhuri was determined, with the help of Badawi, to justify the interest provisions of the new Egyptian Civil Code under the *Sharia'a*. Thus, it would appear that Norman Anderson is mistaken when he says that,

> the significant point, ... is not so much that Sanhuri incorporated in the new Iraqi (Civil) Code much more of the *Sharia'a* than he did in Egypt, but rather that he abandoned it as often and as radically as he did in favour of quite

different principles – and particularly so in matters such as contracts of a "speculative" or allegedly "usurious" character about which Muslim opinion is most sensitive.[115]

On the contrary, the significant point is that in the more *Islamic* Civil Code of Iraq, Sanhuri included the Egyptian interest provisions because he felt they were in accordance with the *Sharia'a*.

Those opposed to Sanhuri's views, however, such as Muhammad Abu Zahra, quickly made their opposition known. The biggest blow, of course, came when Badawi recanted his original views on *riba*, upon which Sanhuri based the interest provisions in the Egyptian Civil Code and which later served as the basis for the interest provisions of the Syrian, Libyan, Iraqi, and Kuwaiti Codes. But the real opposition to the Codes' resolution of the debate over *riba* came in the political arena. With the Islamic political revival in the 1970s there were calls for a return to Islamic Law and to a codification of the *Sharia'a*. The two areas in which this desire was most obviously manifested was in personal status laws and the Civil Codes' provisions on *riba*. But as the memorandum accompanying the 1972 amendments outlawing *riba al-nasi'a* between natural persons in the Libyan Civil and Commercial Codes indicates, the desire for more Islamic provisions regarding *riba* may have had less to do with piety than an intention to make "an easily intelligible gesture of defiance in the face of the West's denigration of Islamic culture and achievement, and a reaffirmation of faith in the indigenous culture, its respectability and viability."[116]

While Libya was the first country adopting Sanhuri's Codes to prohibit *riba* in any meaningful manner, it was Egypt which paved the way, much as it had done earlier, in permitting interest. With the adoption of Article 2 to the Egyptian Constitution in 1970 making the *Sharia'a* "a" source of law and its subsequent amendment in 1980 making the *Sharia'a* "the" source of law, it looked as if Egypt was truly headed towards codifying the *Sharia'a*. In fact, several Draft Codes were prepared in accordance with *Sharia'a* and not surprisingly, given the fundamentalist contribution, the Draft Civil Code outlawed interest. The Judiciary also seemed to suggest, in the 1970s, that even laws written prior to the enactment of Article 2 (which at that time had yet to be even amended and so only contained the weaker language, making the *Sharia'a* simply "a" source of law) if they were not in accordance with the *Sharia'a* were unconstitutional. This, of course, begged the question whether the interest provisions of the Civil Code were contrary to the *Sharia'a* or not. But given the Draft Codes in existence at the time, outlawing interest, the answer that would have been given is clear. In this environment in 1980 Kuwait enacted a new Civil Code which outlawed interest. But not yet prepared to go out on a limb all by itself, and suffer the economic consequences, in its new Commercial Code of 1980 Kuwait preserved interest in commercial transactions.

But, already by 1979, as Rudolph Peters describes it:

The [Egyptian] Government had changed its policy with regard to the enforcement of the *Sharia'a* and was no longer willing to promote the enactment of these proposals. Three factors had contributed to this political volte-face. In the first place the Government's stand towards the Islamic opposition had hardened. After 1979 the Government began to abandon its attempts to render a large part of the Islamic opposition harmless and obtain its support by following policies designed to give greater prominence to Islamic ideals. Particularly after President Sadat's assassination on 6 October 1981, it had sought confrontation.[117] Therefore, there was no longer a need for conciliatory gestures, such as the policy of codifying the *Sharia'a*. Another factor was fear of sectarian clashes... Finally there was some apprehension in Government circles as to possible repercussions in the sphere of foreign, especially economic, relations.[118]

So, it was not surprising when in 1985 the Supreme Judicial Court of Egypt ruled that Article 2, as amended, of the Constitution had no retroactive effect, thereby sidestepping the issue of whether the interest provisions of the Civil Code were in accordance with the *Sharia'a* but in effect saving them and the provisions based on them in the Syrian, Libyan, Iraqi, and Kuwaiti Codes. And it was no more surprising when in 1989, the Mufti of Egypt ruled that interest on Government Investment Certificates and the like, such as Postal Savings Accounts, was in accordance with the *Sharia'a*. Thus the tide of the debate, at least in Egypt, appears to have swung all the way back to where it began at the turn of the century with the *Sanduq al-Tawfir* Affair.

The Mufti of Egypt has promised that he will soon issue *fatwas* on other aspects of *riba*. Whether he will ratify the Civil Code's approach, thereby permitting interest in both civil and commercial matters or whether he might adopt the Kuwaiti compromise and permit it only in commercial matters or perhaps even adopt the Libyan compromise and permit it only for institutional transactions, is not clear. But if this is the level at which the debate is now carried on, then Sanhuri's views have once again prevailed. You will recall, that Sanhuri believed that the Legislature should permit *riba* only to the extent of the perceived need; and if that need diminishes the rules on interest, should as a result, be restricted; and if that need were to not exist at all, then *riba* should return to its basic principle of prohibition. Thus while the legislators of each country may disagree on the perceived need for *riba*, it appears that all those countries whose Codes are indebted to Sanhuri still feel that some need exists for interest in the economy and they agree with Sanhuri, whether implicitly, like Kuwait and Libya, or explicitly, like Egypt, that such a need brings their laws on *riba* into accordance with the *Sharia'a*.

First postscript

The jurisprudential debate over *riba* in the Arab World has primarily taken place in Egypt. The outcome of the debate, however, affects much of the Arab World which looks upon Egypt, with its rich legal history, as a leader in the area of law. This is especially true for those countries whose Civil and/or Commercial Codes were not only based upon Egypt's but which were written by Sanhuri himself: Syria, Iraq, Libya, and Kuwait. In fact, when interpreting their own laws, judges in these and other Arab countries will often cite Sanhuri's treatises and commentaries. In the postcolonial era, a number of these states modified their codes in an effort to reverse what they perceived to be the erosion of the *Sharia'a* introduced by Western governors. Even still, the efforts to combat such influences have not been uniform. For instance, some states have made a distinction between interest on personal loans and commercial loans. More recently, Arab states, notably in the Arabian Gulf region, have been systematically introducing Islamic banking codes parallel to their existing codes, but none as yet has overturned Sanhuri's legacy, keeping the debate over *riba* alive even in those countries which are considered to be conservative.

Second postscript[119]

In the Fall of 2002, the Islamic Research Institute of Al-Azhar University issued a new *fatwa* relating to bank operations, the text of which follows. In this *fatwa* and the question which generated it, the language is fudged so as to make it unclear what is the operation and what is the contract. For instance, the bank simply states prima facie that its activities are permissible and states that the profits are fixed with specific payment dates. Based on this wording, one could come to believe that the permissible activity was something with a stable revenue like a long-term equipment lease and that the profits were a fixed portion of the rent, paid at specific periods. Or, is the permissible activity the co-mingled lending of the bank and the profits the arbitrarily fixed interest paid to depositors. The first could be a *mudaraba* with profit sharing, and the second is only an interest-bearing deposit.

With respect to the *fatwa* text, it does not distinguish between the concept of depositing which in most banking codes is legally recognized as lending and that of investing. Thus, the use of obfuscating language is subtle and allows a false conclusion to be reached.

An insinuation is made in the text that the deposits are simply a form of *wakala* or agency. But, this is neither consistent with the rules of agency practiced historically nor those advised in Malaysia more recently. In these basic rules of *wakala*, the agent has no obligation to pay a return and is actually only safeguarding the depositor's money. Were the agent to invest the funds and earn a return, the agent could at its discretion pay a return to the depositor. Conversely, were the agent to lose money, the agent would be responsible for the full deposit's safe return to the depositor. If this is the relationship that the querying bank means, it does not so specify.

As if to justify the fixing of an interest rate on a deposit, the author of the *fatwa* appears to deliberately confuse upward and downward movement of rates with profit and loss sharing. But, a lower interest rate is an opportunity loss, not a loss of capital. Thus a deposit which is subject to changing interest rates is not compliant with the rules of *mudaraba* which appears to be insinuated by the *mufti*.

Still working with multiple justifications, the *mufti* shifts his focus to indicate that the deposit is a form of investment agency. But, is it? Are the terms of investment clearly disclosed, are the prospective profits and losses clearly indicated? It seems not. And, this too is a false analogy meant to convince the reader that there must be many rules to cover a single contract, other than the one that factually governs it.

Finally, the *mufti* takes cover in *maslaha*, the concept of public good. Neither the facts of the deposit are analyzed and then analogized with its proper home in *Sharia'a*, nor are the *Shari'i* rules defined to correctly apply to the circumstances of the deposit. And, as a result the Mufti of Egypt in 2003 is writing arguments, perhaps at the behest of others, that are little different from those he personally considered in 1989 or his predecessors wrote at the bidding of the Government as far back as 1903.

Finally, as we shall discuss in the concluding chapter of this book, the *mufti* argues that the nature of the deposit in the inquiry is not a matter of creed or faith. Yet, if it is factually *ribawi*, it is fundamentally a question of creed and worship, thereby a matter too great for such shoddy reasoning.

Text of the query and *fatwa*[120]

Re: Investing Funds in Banks that pre-specify profits

Prof. Dr Hassan Abbas Zaki, Chairman of the Board of Directors of the International Arab Banking Corporation sent a letter dated 22/10/2002 to the Honorable Great Imam Dr Muhammad Sayyid Tantawi, Shaykh-ul-Azhar stating the following:

> Honorable Dr. Muhammad Sayyid Tantawi – Shaykh-ul-Al-Jami'-Al-Azhar, As-Salamu alaykum wa raHmatu Allahi wa Barakatuh:
>
> The customers of the International Arab Banking Corporation forward their funds and savings to the bank, which uses said funds and invests them in permissible dealings, earning a profit which is distributed to the customers at pre-specified amounts and agreed-upon time periods. We request that you kindly inform us of the Legal status of this transaction, Chairman of the Board of Directors,
>
> Dr. Hassan Abbas Zaki.

Attached to this letter was a sample document for the dealings between an investor and the bank. (The second page has a small sample document informing a customer that his account of LE 100,000 is renewed for the calendar year 2002, with added "return rate of 10%" in the amount of LE 10,000, thus bringing the account balance to LE 110,000.)

The Honorable Great Imam forwarded the letter and its attachment to the Islamic Research Institute for consideration during its first following meeting. The Institute convened its meeting on Thursday 25 Shaban 1423 (October 31, 2002) during which time the issue was presented. Following the deliberations and studies of the members, the Institute decided: Approval of the ruling that investing funds with banks that pre-determine profits (*tuhaddid al-ribh muqaddaman*) is Islamic-Legally permissible, and there is no harm therein.

Since this topic is of particular importance for citizens who wish to know the Islamic-Legal status of their investments with banks that pre-specify profits, and since there have been numerous questions about this issue, the General Council of the

Islamic Research Institute has decided to prepare an Official *fatwa* backed by the Legal Proofs, as well as a summary of the Institute Members' reasoning, to give citizens a full picture of the issue and instill confidence [in the decision].

The general council presented the full text of the *fatwa* to the Islamic Research Institute meeting on Thursday 23 Ramadan 1423, equivalent to November 28, 2002. After reading the *fatwa* and taking account of the members' comments on its language, they approved the *fatwa*.

This is the text of the *fatwa*:

> Those who deal with the International Arab Banking Corporation, or other banks, thus giving their funds and savings to the bank as an agent (*wakil*) in Legally permissible investments in exchange for a pre-specified profit that is given to them at agreed-upon periods.
>
> This dealing, in this form (*Surah*) is Legally permissible, and there is no Legal suspicion (*shubha*) associated with it. This follows from the fact that there is no Canonical Text (*naSS*) in the Book of Allah or the Prophetic Sunnah that forbids this type of transaction, wherein the profit or return is pre-specified, as long as both sides mutually consent to this type of transaction.
>
> Allah (Most High) said: "O people of faith, do not devour each other's property unjustly, but let there be among you trade by mutual consent" (Al-Nisaa 4:29).
>
> In other words, O you who have the proper faith in Allah, it is not permissible for you, and not proper for any of you, to devour the property of another in invalid and forbidden ways that Allah (Most High) has forbidden – such as theft, usurpation, *riba*, and other acts that Allah (Most High) has forbidden. However, it is permissible for you to exchange benefits among yourselves through transactions initiated by mutual consent in a manner that does not make permissible what has been forbidden, or make forbidden what has been permitted.
>
> This applies whether the mutual consent is established verbally, in writing, by physical signaling, or in any other way that implies mutual acceptance and agreement of the two parts.
>
> In this regard, there is no doubt that mutual agreement over pre-specification of the profit is acceptable legally and logically, so that each party may know his rights.
>
> It is well known that when banks pre-specify for their customers their profits and returns, those profits/returns are fixed after a detailed study of the international and domestic market conditions, and the economic circumstances in society, in addition to the special conditions and nature of each transaction, and the average profitability of each such transaction.
>
> Furthermore, it is well known that those fixed rates of return may be adjusted upward or downward. For instance, Investment Certificates at their inception paid 4 percent returns, whose rate of return later increased to over 15 percent, and then more recently declined to approximately 10 percent.
>
> The party that specifies this rate of return that is subject to upward and downward revision has the responsibility of determining that rate, according to the instructions of the specific authorizing national agency.

Advantages of this pre-specification of the rate of return – especially during this time in which deviation from Truth and truthfulness is rampant – accrue to the funds-owner, as well as the managers of banks that invest those funds:

- The funds-owner benefits by knowing his rights without any degree of ignorance or uncertainty (*jahala*), and thus can plan his life accordingly.
- The managers of banks also benefit from this specification [of rates of return] since it gives them the incentive to maximize their profits to exceed the amount they guaranteed for the funds-owner. Thus, the excess profits after paying the funds-owners their rights accrue to the bank managers as compensation for their effort and diligence.

It may be said in this regard: But banks may lose, so how can banks pre-specify profits to those who invest with them?

In answer [we say]: If a bank loses on any one transaction, it makes a profit on many others, and thus covers its losses with its profits. This fact notwithstanding, in case of an overall loss, the matter can be referred to the legal system.

In summary, pre-specification of profits for those who invest their funds through an investment agency (*al-wakala al-'istithmariyya*) with banks or other institutions is Legally permissible, and above Legal suspicion (*la shubhat fiha*). This transaction belongs to the domain of benefits that were neither explicitly permitted nor explicitly forbidden (*min qabil al-masalih al-mursalah*), and does not belong to the domains of creeds or formal acts of worship, wherein change and alteration is not allowed.

Based on what has been stated [we rule that] investing funds with banks that pre-specify profits or returns is Legally permissible and there is no harm therein, and Allah [only] knows best.

(Shaykh-ul-Azhar Dr Muhammad Sayyid Tantawi,
27 Ramadan 1423 AH, 2 December 2002 AD)

Notes

* Originally submitted as The Modern Debate over *Riba* in Egypt and its "Resolution" in the Codes of Sanhuri, the original components have been reconstituted as separate chapters in this book. The paper was prepared by Mr Khalil whilst a student at the Harvard Law School May 1990.

1 N. Saleh, *Unlawful Gain and Legitimate Profit in Islamic Law* (London: Graham & Trotman, 1992), p. 28.

2 Ahmad, Ziauddin Khan, M. Fahim and Iqbal, Munawar (eds) *Money and Banking in Islam* (Jeddah: International Center for Research in Islamic Economics, King Abdul Aziz University, 1983), p.__; S.H. Homoud, *Islamic Banking* (London: Arabian Information, 1985), p.__; I.H. Badawi, "Nazariyyat al-Riba al-Muharram" (Cairo: *Al-Majles al-A'la li-Ri'yat al-Funun*, 1964), p. 223; C. Mallat, (ed.) "The Debate on Riba and Interest in Twentieth Century Jurisprudence," *Islamic Law and Finance* (London: Graham & Trotman, 1988), pp. 69–88.

3 *Al-Manar* February 22, 1917, p. 528 and December 5, 1903, p. 717.

4 Ibid.

5 While Abdu did not elaborate on what he meant by *mudaraba*, according to Saleh op. cit., p. 103:

> Nearly all schools of law have understood *mudaraba* in the following sense: "A contract between at least two parties whereby one party, called the investor (*rabb al-mal*) entrusts money to the other party called the agent-manager (*mudarib*) who is to trade with it in an agreed manner and then return to the investor the principal and a pre-agreed share of the profits and keep for himself what remains of such profits." The division of profits between the two parties must necessarily be on a pro-portional basis and cannot be lump sum or a guaranteed return. In a valid *mudaraba* the investor is not liable for losses beyond the amount of the capital he has paid. Conversely the agent-manager, who does not normally partake in the investment in terms of money, does not bear any share of the losses, losing only his time and effort.
>
> And *Al-Manar,* op. cit.

6 C. Mallat, *Islamic Law and Finance* London: Graham & Trotman, 1988, p. 71.

7 *Al-Manar,* op. cit.

8 Ibid.

9 Ibid.

10 Peters, "Divine Law or Man-Made Law? Egypt and the Application of the Sharia'a," *3 Arab Law Quarterly*, 1988, p. 231–4; Edge, "Comparative Commercial Law of Egypt and the Arabian Gulf," *34 Clev. St. L. Rev.*, 1985–86, pp. 129–37.

11 *Al-Manar,* op. cit., p. 528.

12 Ibid., *Al-Manar,* op. cit., p. 717.

13 I.H. Badawi, op. cit., p. 223. He claims to have found in the Postal Administration's files a notation made in the margin of a Sanduq al-Tawfir document which read:

> Voluntary declaration specifically for Muslim depositors who wish to invest their money according to specific conditions: 'I, the undersigned, ——————————, have entrusted the Director General for the Postal Administration with powers of attorney to use the sums deposited by me in such a manner which is in accordance with the *Sharia'a* and free of any type of *riba*, and to commingle my money with other depositors' money; I acknowledge accepting to share with the rest of the depositors the profits in proportion to my deposit.

Badawi goes on to add that transactions conducted according to this declaration are in accordance with the *Sharia'a* so long as the depositor shares in the losses as well as profits. However, he also says that this declaration is not applied in practice.

14 Ibid., p. 223.

15 I.H. Badawi, op. cit., p.223.

16 C. Mallat, *Islamic Law and Finance*, Law op. cit., p. 73 quoting *Al-Manar* May 24, 1906, p. 348.

17 N. Saleh, op. cit., p. 28.

18 *Fatawa al-Imam Muhammad Rashid Rida*, vol. II, 1970, p. 608.

19 Ibid.

20 Ibid.

21 Ibid., pp. 608–9.

22 A. Sanhuri, Al-Sanhuri, Abd Al-Razzaq Ahmad. *Masadir Al-Haqq fil-Fiqh al-Islami*, 6 Parts, Part 3. III, p. 220.

23 C. Mallat, *Islamic Law and Finance*, op cit., p. 74.

24 I.H. Badawi, op cit., p. 223.

25 Ibid.

26 Ibid.

27 Ibid.

28 I.H. Badawi, op. cit., p. 223, and Badawi, I.Z., "Nazariyyat al-Riba al-Muharram," *Majallat al-Qanun wal-Iqtisad*, April and May 1939, Cairo, Part I, pp. 387–446, and Part II, pp. 533–66.

29 Ibid.

30 Ibid.

31 Ibid.

32 Ibid.

33 Ibid.

34 Ibid.

35 Ibid.

36 Hill, Enid, "'Al-Sanhuri and Islamic Law: The Place and Significance of Islamic Law in the Life and Work of 'Abd al-Razzaq Ahmad al-Sanhuri, Egyptian Jurist and Scholar 1895–1971 Part II," *Arab Law Quarterly*, No. 3, 1988, pp. 182–5.

37 Anderson, J.N.D., "The Sharia'a and Civil Law (The Debt Owed by the New Civil Codes of Egypt and Syria to the Sharia'a)," *1 Islamic Quarterly* 29, 1954 (quoting al-Qanun al-Madani: Majmu'at al-A'mal al-Tahdiriyya), p. 85.

38 Anderson, ibid., pp. 29–46; Hill, op. cit., pp. 182–5.

39 A. Sanhuri, op. cit., p. 244.

40 A. Sanhuri, op. cit., pp. 234–44 (Chapter 2, note 30, hereinafter cites are made to the translation in the Multilithed Material I. pp. 36–46).

41 Hill, op. cit., note 125, p. 202.

42 N. Saleh, op. cit., p. 28.

43 A. Sanhuri, op. cit., pp. 38–9, 44.

44 Ibid., p. 39.

45 Ibid.

46 N. Saleh, op. cit., p. 29.

47 A. Sanhuri, op. cit., p. 40.

48 Ibid., p. 43.

49 N. Saleh, op. cit., p. 35.

50 A. Sanhuri, op. cit., p. 43.

51 Ibid., pp. 43–4.

52 Ibid., p. 44.

53 Ibid., p. 241.

54 Ibid., p. 44.

55 Ibid., p. 45.

56 Ibid.

57 Ibid.

58 Ibid., p. 47.

59 Ibid.

60 Ibid.

61 W.M. Ballantyne, *Commercial law in the Arab Middle East*, op. cit., p. 127.

62 A. Sanhuri, op. cit., pp. 245–6.

63 Ibid., p. 245.

64 Ibid., p. 249.

65 I.H. Badawi, op. cit.

66 Ibid., pp. 269–70.

67 Ibid., p. 270.

68 Ibid.

69 Ibid.

70 Ibid.

71 Ibid.

72 I.H. Badawi, 1964, op. cit., pp. 251–8.

73 Ibid., p. 254.

74 Ibid., p. 270.

75 C. Mallat, *Islamic Law and Finance*, op. cit., pp. 76–9. Neither the author nor the editor were able to obtain copies of Abu Zahra's book, and, therefore, rely on Mallat's account.
76 Ibid. (citing to Abu Zahra, *Tahrim al-Riba*, p. 53).
77 Edge, "Shari'a and Commerce in Contemporary Egypt," *Islamic Law and Finance* (C. Mallat ed. 1988), p. 44.
78 Ibid.
79 Ibid.
80 Peters, op. cit., p. 234 (citing Proposal in 58 *al-Muhama*, vol. 34, 1978, p. 154).
81 Ibid. p. 235; Altman, "Islamic Legislation in Egypt in the 1970's," *African and Asian Studies*, 13, (1979), p. 212.
82 Peters, op. cit., p. 235; Altman, op. cit., p. 213.
83 Peters, op. cit., p. 236. Most of these proposals dealt with penal law.
84 Peters, op. cit., p. 236; Edge, op. cit., p. 39; Hill, op. cit., p. 210.
85 Peters, op. cit., p. 236.
86 *Madbatat Maglis al-Sha'b*, Session 70, 1982, pp. 32–41.
87 Peters, op. cit., pp. 239–40 (citing to *Madbatat Maglis al-Sha'b*, Session 74, 1985, pp. 14–35).
88 Ibid.
89 Edge, op. cit., p. 44.
90 Ibid.
91 Ibid.
92 *Sharia'a* Courts' Ordinance (*La'ihat al-Mahakirn al-Shar'iyya*).
93 Edge, op. cit., p. 44 (citing *Majmu'at Ahkarn wa Qararat al-Mahkarvit al-'Ulya*, pp. 432–41); Peters, op. cit., p. 241 (citing to *Al-Ahram*, April 4, 1976).
94 Edge, op. cit., p. 45.
95 Peters, op. cit., pp. 241–2.
96 Ibid., p. 242, n.33 (citing to *Al-Ahram*, July 4, 1982).
97 Ibid.
98 Ibid. (citing to *Al-Jumhuriyya*, May 5, 1986).
99 Habachy (tr.), Supreme Constitutional Court (Egypt), *Sharia'a* and *Riba*: Decision in Case No. 20 of Judicial Year No.1, *Arab Law Quarterly* 1, 1985, pp. 101–7 (Also *in al-Mahkarnat al-Dusturiyya al-'Ulya*, 1984–86, pp. 209–24; *Al-Garida al-Rasmiyya* Vol. 20, May 16, 1985 pp. 992–1000).
100 Ibid., p. 104 (Citing to the Amending Committee's report of July 19, 1979). The purpose of the amendment, the Committee said, was that:

> It enjoins the Legislature to have recourse to the rules of the *Sharia'a* in its quest for the rule of law which it is seeking, to the exclusion of any other system of law; and in case it does not find in the *Sharia'a* a clear ruling, then it should apply the approved methods of deducting legal rules from the authorized sources of endeavor in Islamic jurisprudence. These may help the Legislator in reaching a ruling which does not contradict the principles and the general framework of the *Sharia'a*.

101 Ibid., p. 105 (citing the General Committee Report approved September 15, 1981). The General Committee' report said:

> The Constitution of 1971 was the first constitution in our modern history which explicitly provides that the *Sharia'a* is a principal source of law. Then later on, the Constitution was amended in 1980 so that the *Sharia'a* became the principal source of legislation. This amendment means that it is no longer possible in the future to enact any legislation which contradicts the rulings of Islamic law. It also means that it is imperative to review the laws which were in effect before the application of the Constitution of 1971 and to amend these laws in such a manner as to make them conform to the principles of Islamic law.

The report went on to say, however, that:

> The departure from the present legal institutions of Egypt, which go back more than one hundred years, and their replacement in their entirety require patient efforts and careful consideration. Hence, legislation for changing economic and social conditions which were not familiar and were not even known before, together with the innovations in our contemporary world and the requirements of our membership in the international community, as well as the evolution of our relationships and dealings with other nations – all these call for careful consideration and deserve special endeavors. Consequently, the change of the whole legal organization should not be contemplated without giving the lawmakers a chance and a reasonable period of time to collect all legal materials and amalgamate them into a complete system within the framework of the *Quran*, the *Sunna*, and all the opinions of the learned Muslim jurists and Imams.

102 Ibid., p. 106.
103 Habachy, "Commentary on the Decision of the Supreme court of Egypt given on 4 May, 1985 Concerning the Legitimacy of Interest and the Constitutionality of Article 226 of the New Egyptian Civil Code of 1948," *Arab Law Quarterly* 1, 1986, pp. 239–40.
104 Ibid., p. 106. It is interesting that the SCC in its decision did not refer to the 1976 *Mahkamat al-Ulya* decision, which it implicitly overruled in this case. Perhaps, as Ian Edge says, this is "because the S.C.C. is considered a new court and not a mere continuation or rearrangement of the *Mahkamat Ulya*. In any event, the S.C.C. is not bound by precedent and only occasionally refers to its own or any other judgments of other courts." Edge, op. cit., p. 45–6.
105 Habachy, op. cit., p. 240.
106 In this case the SCC affirmed its 1985 decision and held that its reasoning extended to Article 458 of the Civil Code which provides, "Subject to an agreement or custom to the contrary, the vendor is not entitled to legal interest on the price, unless he has placed the purchaser in default by a formal summons, or unless the thing sold is productive of fruits or other profits and he has delivered the thing sold to the purchaser." *Al-Garida al-Rasmiyya*, vol. 25, June 20, 1987, pp. 2071–5.
107 Ian Edge refers to a case that he says was before the SCC in 1987 that would have forced it to address the issue of whether bank interest was in accordance with the *Sharia'a* and therefore constitutional. I. Edge, op. cit., pp. 46–7. I have been unable to locate this case and it does not appear that a decision was ever given. However, it is possible that the 1989 decision of Egypt's Mufti affirming that bank interest was in accordance with the *Sharia'a* was in part prompted by this case. The Mufti's decision, though, would not cover the facts of the case Edge refers to, which he says concerned a bank loan at a variable interest rate secured by a mortgage.
108 *Al-Ahram*, September 8, 1989, p. 13.
109 The debate became so heated that the Mufti himself was the subject of bitter personal attacks, which *Al-Ahram* felt obliged to condemn in two separate editorials. *Al-Ahram* September 22, 1989, p. 13; October 1, 1989, p. 7.
110 According to Tantawi, the members of the Committee, chaired by Muhammad Faraj al-Sanhuri, broke down as follows: 5 members represented the Hanafi School: Abd Allah alMashad, Muhammad al-Husayni Shahata, Abd al-Hakirn Radwan, Muhammad Salarn Madkur and Zakariyya al-Barri; 4 members represented the Maliki School: Yasin Soaylim, Abd al-Jalil Issa, Khalil al-Jarahi and Sulayman Ramadan; 3 members represented the Shafi'i School-Muhammad Jerat Allah, Tantawi Mustafa, Jad al-Rab Ramadan; and 1 member represented the Hanbali School: Abd al-Azim Barakat. *Al-Ahram*, op. cit., p. 13.
111 Muhammad Jerat Allah, Tantawi Mustafa, Jad al-Rab Ramadan and Sulayman Ramadan. Ibid.
112 Tantawi was severely criticized for this suggestion by many who accused him of trying, through a word game, to permit what is prohibited.

113 *October*, December 24, 1989, p. 7.
114 *Al-Ahram*, op. cit.
115 N. Anderson, *Law Reform in the Muslim World* (London: Athalone Press, 1976), p. 84.
116 Mayer, "The Regulation of Interest Charges and Risk Contracts: Some Problems of Recent Libyan Legislation," International and Comparative Law Quarterly 28 (October 1979), pp. 541–59.
117 Mayer, op. cit., p. 552.
118 Peters, op. cit., p. 239.
119 This Postscript is authored by Abdulkader Thomas.
120 Translated by Dr Mahmoud El-Gamal on December 11, 2002 and posted on the Internet at www.ibfnet.com

6 Why has Islam prohibited interest?

Rationale behind the prohibition of interest

*M. Umer Chapra**

Introduction

Since the entire international financial system is based on interest, the question that is often raised is why Pakistan should adopt a different mechanism for financial intermediation. The answer, of course, is the Islamic injunction against interest and Pakistan's constitutional commitment to Islam. This, however, leads to the related question of why Islam has prohibited interest. Is there any solid rationale behind the prohibition? The rationale would be difficult to understand unless we take into account the *maqasid al-sharia'a* or the goals of Islam. The strategy has to be commensurate with these goals. If it is not, the goals may not be realized. If we desire to go to Lahore from Karachi, we have to go north. If we travel eastward or westward, we will not reach Lahore, no matter how good the road is and how proficient the driver is. Hence, the first thing that we need to see is the goals of Islam.

Establishment of justice: the central goal of Islam

The *Quran* and the *Sunna* have both placed tremendous stress on justice, making it one of the central objectives of the *Sharia'a*. According to the *Quran*, establishment of justice is one of the primary purposes for which God has sent His prophets (*al-Quran*, 57:25). The *Quran* places justice nearest to righteousness or *taqwa* (*al-Quran*, 5:8) in terms of its importance in the Islamic faith. Righteousness is naturally the most important because it serves as a springboard for all rightful action, including justice. The Prophet, peace and blessings of God be on him, equated the absence of justice with "absolute darkness" and warned: "Beware of injustice for injustice will lead to absolute darkness on the Day of Judgement."[1] This is but natural, because injustice undermines brotherhood and solidarity, accentuates conflict, tensions, and crime, aggravates human problems, and thus leads ultimately to nothing but misery in this world as well as in the Hereafter. Brotherhood, which is another primary objective of the *Sharia'a*, would be a meaningless jargon if it were not reinforced by justice in the allocation and distribution of God-given resources.

All leading jurists throughout Muslim history have therefore, without any exception, held justice to be an indispensable ingredient of *maqasid al-sharia'a*. For example, Abu Yusuf (d. 182/798) laid considerable stress on justice in his letter to the

Caliph Harun al-Rashid (d. 193/809) by saying that: "Rendering justice to those wronged and eradicating injustice, raises tax revenue, accelerates development of the country, and brings blessings in addition to reward in the Hereafter."[2] Al-Mawardi (d. 450/1058) stressed that comprehensive justice "inculcates mutual love and affection, obedience to the law, development of the country, expansion of wealth, growth of progeny, and security of the sovereign," and that "there is nothing that destroys the world and the conscience of the people faster than injustice."[3]

Ibn Taymiyyah (d. 728/1328) considered justice to be an essential outcome of *tawhid* or belief in one God.[4] To him justice was a very wide concept –

> everything good is a component of justice and everything bad is a component of injustice and oppression. Hence, justice towards everything and everyone is an imperative for everyone and injustice is prohibited to everything and everyone. Injustice is absolutely not permissible irrespective of whether it is to a Muslim or a non-Muslim or even to an unjust person.[5]

He zealously upheld the adages prevailing in his times that: "God upholds the just state even if it is unbelieving, but does not uphold the unjust state even if it is Islamic," and that "the world can survive with justice and unbelief, but not with injustice and Islam."[6]

Ibn Khaldun (d. 808/1406) stated unequivocally that it is not possible for a country to develop without justice,[7] something that has now been belatedly recognized by the pundits of development economics after a long flirtation with injustice.[8] He goes to the extent of emphasizing that "oppression brings an end to development and the end of development becomes reflected in the breakdown and destruction of the state,"[9] and that "a decline in prosperity is the necessary and inevitable result of injustice and transgression."[10] He elaborated further that

> oppression does not consist merely in taking away wealth and property from its owner without cause or compensation. Oppression has rather a wider connotation. Anyone who seizes the property of others, forces them to work for him against their will, makes unjust claims on them, or imposes on them burdens not sanctioned by the *Sharia'a*, is an oppressor.[11]

The implications of justice

Given the importance of justice in Islam, there arises the question of what its implications are? Justice is a comprehensive term in Islam and covers all aspects of human interaction, irrespective of whether it relates to the family, the society, the economy, or the polity, and irrespective of whether the object is a human being, animal, insect, or the environment. This has wide implications, one of the most important of these is that the resources provided by God to mankind are a *trust* and must be utilized in such a manner that the well-being of *all* is ensured, irrespective of whether they are rich or poor, high or low, male or female, and Muslim or non-Muslim. In the field of economics, one could assert that justice demands the use of resources in such an equitable manner that the universally cherished humanitarian goals of general need-fulfillment, optimum growth, full employment, equitable distribution of income and wealth, and economic stability are realized.

These humanitarian goals are recognized by all societies. They are the outcome of moral values provided by most religions. However, it is the strategy for realizing these that makes a difference. It is the contention of this paper that these humanitarian goals cannot be realized without a humanitarian strategy. The strategy requires, among other things, the injection of a moral dimension into economics in place of the materialist and self-indulgent orientation of capitalism. Abolition of interest is a part of this moral dimension. This is perhaps one of the reasons why Islam is not alone in condemning interest.[12] All other major religions, including Judaism, Christianity, and Hinduism have also condemned it. The Bible makes no distinction between usury and interest and brands those who take interest as wicked.[13]

There are, nevertheless, some Muslims who try to argue that bank interest is not prohibited by Islam. Their rationale is that the rate of interest during the days of the Prophet, peace and blessings of God be on him, was usurious and led to the exploitation of the poor. Islam was against such exploitation and, therefore, it prohibited usury and not interest. Even though the extension of help to the poor and the raising of their socioeconomic condition enjoys a high profile in *maqasid al-Sharia'a*, confining the rationale behind the prohibition of interest to just this limited objective is not only factually wrong but also unduly restrictive in terms of the concept of justice in Islam.

During the Prophet's time, peace and blessings of God be on him, the Muslim society had become so well-organized in terms of mutual care that the needs of the poor were automatically taken care of by the rich. To the extent that this did not happen, there was the *bayt al-mal* to fill the gap. The poor were not, therefore, constrained to borrow to fulfill their basic needs. Since there was no conspicuous consumption or extravagance in marriages and other festivities, there was no need to resort to borrowing for this purpose either. Therefore, borrowing was primarily undertaken by tribes and rich traders who operated as large partnership companies to conduct large-scale long-distance trade. This was necessitated by the prevailing circumstances. The difficult terrain, the harsh climate, and the slow means of communication made the task of trade caravans difficult and time-consuming. It was not possible for them to undertake several business trips to the east and the west in a given year. Funds remained blocked for a long time. Hence, it was necessary for the caravans to muster all available financial resources to purchase all the locally available exportable products, sell them abroad, and bring back the entire import needs of their society during a specific period. Before Islam, such resources were more often than not mobilized on the basis of interest. Islam abolished the interest-based nature of the financier–entrepreneur relationship and reorganized it on a profit-and-loss-sharing basis. This enabled the financier to have a just share and the entrepreneur did not get crushed under adverse conditions, one of which was the caravan being waylaid on the journey.

However, even justice to the trader and entrepreneur does not go far enough to show the rationale behind the prohibition of interest and the harsh verdict against it by all major religions. If it is desired to utilize all God-given resources in such a way that the universally cherished humanitarian goals mentioned previously are fully realized, then it is necessary to reorganize the economic system accordingly. Financial intermediation on the basis of equity and profit-and-loss sharing is an essential part of such reorganization. It would make the financier share in the risks as well as the rewards of business and thereby introduce a greater discipline in the use of financial resources. Since financial intermediation plays a more important role in modern economies than it did during the Prophet's days, it is all the more important to organize it on the basis of equity and profit-and-loss sharing. Let us see why.

Need-fulfillment

Financial intermediation on the basis of interest tends to promote living beyond means by both the private and public sectors. Financial resources become available to borrowers on the criteria of their ability to provide acceptable collateral to guarantee the repayment of principal, and sufficient cash flow to service the debt. End use of financial resources does not constitute the main criterion. Hence, financial resources go to the rich, who fulfill both criteria, and also to governments who, it is assumed, will not go bankrupt. The rich, however, do not borrow only for investment but also for conspicuous consumption and speculation, while governments borrow not only for development and public well-being, but also for chauvinistic defence build-up and white-elephant projects. The relatively easy availability of borrowed funds contributes to a rapid expansion in claims on resources (partly for unproductive and wasteful spending) and, besides accentuating macroeconomic and external imbalances, squeezes resources available for need-fulfillment and development. This explains why even the richest countries in the world like the United States have been unable to fulfill the essential needs of all their people in spite of abundant resources at their disposal.

Pakistan is a very clear example of how excessive borrowing squeezes resources for need-fulfillment. Governments in Pakistan have borrowed right and left until debt-servicing (interest plus amortization) reached 46 percent of total central government spending in the 1998/99 budget. Since another 24 percent of the total is allocated to defence and 12 percent to administration, only 18 percent remains for development spending, including education, health, and infrastructure construction. This is far less than what Pakistan needs to fulfill its dream of becoming an Asian tiger. If the Government of Pakistan had taken the Islamic injunction against interest seriously, it would have tried to reduce its deficits with a view to minimizing its borrowing. It would have streamlined the tax collection system and also reduced its unproductive and wasteful spending. A number of the white-elephant projects which were undertaken by the Government and which have proved to be sour would have been avoided. The Far Eastern countries adopted fiscal discipline, while Pakistan, which should have done so all the more because of its commitment to Islam, did not.

Pakistan is, of course, not alone in this predicament. A number of other countries are in a worse condition as is clear from Table 6.1, which shows interest payments (excluding amortization) as a percentage of total central government expenditure. The higher the interest payment as a percentage of total government expenditure, the

Table 6.1 Interest payments as percent of total
central government expenditure in
some selected countries, 1997

Country	%
Brazil (1994)	40.04
Germany	7.08
Greece (1996)	36.06
India	22.94
Israel	12.73
Italy	18.74
Malaysia	11.67
Mexico (1996)	43.14
Pakistan	30.43
Singapore	2.66
Thailand	1.68
United Kingdom	8.83
United States	15.03

Source: International Monetary Fund (IMF),
Government Finance Statistics, 1998, pp. 8–9 for all countries except Pakistan, for which the 1994 figure (24.52
percent) is given in this publication. Hence, the 1997
figure has been calculated from data given in
Government of Pakistan, *Economic Survey, 1997–98*,
pp. 59–60.

lesser will be the availability for development purposes and the more serious will be
the socioeconomic problems faced by these countries.

Optimum growth and full employment

The basic ingredients for sustained growth are saving, investment, hard and conscientious work, technological progress, and creative management, along with helpful
social behavior and government policies. As far as saving is concerned, its positive
effect on growth is now well-established.[14] It helps capital formation, which in
turn helps raise output and employment. A well-established fact is that high-saving
countries have generally grown faster than low-saving countries.[15]

The central importance of saving brings into focus the question of what effect
Islamic values in general and the abolition of interest in particular have on it. It is
now well-recognized that since Islam prohibits extravagance, status symbols, and
living beyond means, there should be a positive effect of Islamic values on saving.
Moreover, studies conducted in conventional economics have indicated a strong link
between the households' access to credit and the saving rate. High-saving countries
like Japan and Germany have tax systems that tend to discourage consumer borrowing.[16] On the basis of these findings, it may be hoped that the adoption of the profit-
and-loss sharing system would help raise saving by curbing the availability of credit

to both the public and private sectors for unproductive purposes, which serve as a major drain on savings.

This leads to the related question of whether the positive effect of Islamic values on saving would be offset by the absence of interest. The generally recognized fact is that people normally save for future contingencies and not necessarily for the purpose of earning interest. It would, nevertheless, be helpful if they were able to invest their savings and earn an attractive return. Islam does not, however, deny a return on savings. While it has prohibited interest, it has allowed profit.

The encouraging fact is that over the last hundred years the equity premium has been substantially high in the United States – average real rates of return on stocks has been 7 percent, about 6 percent higher than that on Treasury bills.[17] It has also been high in Germany and Japan, where the average compounded real rate of return on stocks from 1926 through 1995 were 5.9 and 4.0 percent, respectively. In contrast, the hyperinflation of the 1920s wiped out bondholders altogether in Germany, and the post-Second World War hyperinflation did the same in Japan.[18] The catch, however, is that equity investments involve greater risk, which everyone may not be willing to bear. Some people may prefer to have less risky modes. But these are available within the Islamic framework as well. Hence, what is important is the availability of, and easy access to, investment opportunities of varying risks and maturities to satisfy the different preferences of savers.

If higher interest rates had helped promote saving, the persistently high real rates of interest since the early 1980s[19] would have led to a rise in worldwide saving. On the contrary, gross domestic saving as percent of GDP has registered a worldwide decline over the last quarter century from 26.6 percent in 1971 to 22.6 percent in 1996. The decline in industrial countries has been from 23.6 to 20.2 percent and that in developing countries, which need higher savings to attain accelerated development without a significant increase in inflationary pressures and debt-servicing burden, has been even steeper from 34.2 to 26.1 percent over the same period.[20] There are a number of major reasons for this. One of these is the rise in consumption by both the public and private sectors due to the easy availability of credit in a collateral-linked, interest-based financial system.

While the high real rates of interest have failed to promote saving, they have been one of the major factors responsible for low rates of rise in investment and economic growth. These low rates have joined hands with structural rigidities and some other factors to raise unemployment, which stood at 7.2 percent in the Organization for Economic Cooperation and Development (OECD) countries in 1997, close to two-and-a-half times its level of 2.9 percent in 1971–73. Unemployment in the European Union (11.2 percent in 1997) is even higher.[21] If "discouraged workers" (those who have dropped out of the labor force because of poor job prospects) and workers in involuntary part-time employment are also included, the overall rate of unemployment may be much higher.[22] Even more worrying is youth unemployment of around 25 percent, excluding the "discouraged" youth.[23] This hurts their pride, dampens their faith in the future, increases their hostility towards society, and damages their personal capacities and potential contribution.

Since budgetary discipline has now rightly become a part of conventional wisdom and is also indispensable for the success of the euro, the prospect of reducing unemployment by means of fiscal deficits is not a feasible alternative for the European Union, or even other countries if they do not wish to lose their competitiveness. A decline in government and private sector wasteful spending may perhaps be the most promising way of promoting savings and productive investment. This may not, however, be possible when the value system encourages both the public and private sectors to live beyond their means, and the interest-based financial intermediation makes this possible by making credit available relatively easily without sufficient regard to its end use.[24]

Even if it is accepted that ostentatious and wasteful consumption may decline and raise saving in Pakistan after the implementation of Islamic teachings, there is no guarantee that the saving realized may be invested within the country itself. Investment may rise only if investment opportunities of varying degrees of risk and maturity are available along with security of life and property, guarantees against arbitrary nationalization and confiscation, reasonable tax rates, and relative stability in the internal and external value of the country's currency. The existing realities in Pakistan do not raise one's confidence with respect to all these prerequisites.

However, if the necessary socioeconomic reforms are instituted and a proper investment environment becomes available, Islamic values would tend to have a positive effect on investment.[25] *Zakat* collection should also help because it penalizes idle savings, discourages hoarding, and thereby stimulates investment. Savers would be under constraint to earn enough to at least offset the erosive effect of inflation and *zakat* on the nominal as well as real value of their savings.[26]

Profit-and-loss sharing according to a fair ratio between the financier and the entrepreneur should also help promote a more efficient allocation of resources.[27] The entrepreneur is after all the primary force behind all investment decisions, and the removal of one of the basic sources of injustice is bound to have a favorable effect on his decision-making. By turning "savers into entrepreneurs," using the words of Ingo Karsten, the risks of business may be more equitably distributed, thereby improving the investment climate. Moreover, by making the savers and the banks involved in the success of the entrepreneur's business, greater expertise may become available to the entrepreneurs, leading to an improvement in the availability of information, skills, efficiency, and profitability. More productive entrepreneurship may lead to increased investment.[28] The aggregate level of investment may, therefore, tend to be higher in a profit-sharing system. Since savings and investment are among the crucial determinants of economic growth, the rise in savings and investment in Pakistan resulting from the implementation of Islamic values and institutions may tend to lead to higher growth.

Coming now to hard and conscientious work that is needed for development, there is no doubt that Islam is absolutely positive in these terms.[29] One of the primary obligations of a Muslim is to fulfill his responsibilities conscientiously and diligently with the maximum possible degree of care and skill. The Prophet exhorted: "God has made excellence obligatory upon you"[30] and "God loves that when anyone of you does a job he does it perfectly."[31] This esteem for work along with the urge to improve one's living conditions and those of others, may be highly conducive to growth provided there is an appropriate political and socioeconomic environment.

There is no reason to assume that there may be less incentive for technological progress and creative management in an Islamic economy. In fact the closure of all doors of resort to unfair and dishonest practices to increase one's income may create a greater need for technological innovation and increased efficiency, provided that the technical qualification for this is available along with proper facilities and incentives. All things being equal, this may be the only way for a businessman or an industrialist to reduce costs and raise his honestly earned (*halal*) income. As far as helpful social behavior patterns and government policies are concerned, there seems to be no reason to expect that Islamization of the society, economy, and polity of Pakistan would not help lead Pakistan towards the availability of these.

Equitable distribution

A number of Islamic values and institutions are directed towards making brotherhood, social equality, and equitable distribution a reality in Muslim societies.[32] Of particular significance are *zakat* and the inheritance system. If both of these are effectively implemented in Pakistan, the effect on distribution of income and wealth in the country should be highly positive.

The replacement of interest-based financial intermediation by the profit-and-loss-sharing system should also be of great advantage. The established practice of banks in the conventional banking system is to lend mainly to those individuals and firms who have the necessary collateral to offer large internal savings to service the debt. Credit, therefore, tends to go to those who, according to Lester Thurow, are "lucky rather than smart or meritocratic."[33] The banking system thus "tends to reinforce the unequal distribution of capital."[34] Even Morgan Guarantee Trust Company, the sixth largest bank in the United States, has admitted that the banking system has failed to "finance either maturing smaller companies or venture capitalists," and "though awash with funds, is not encouraged to deliver competitively priced funding to any but the largest, most cash-rich companies."[35] Hence, while deposits come from a broader cross section of the population, their benefit goes mainly to the rich. This tends to accentuate the inequalities of income and wealth. Certain measures have undoubtedly been adopted in a number of countries to redress the situation. Such measures would also need to be adopted in Pakistan. They may, however, tend to be relatively more successful in an equity-based system where the banks would be motivated to give at least as much attention to the profitability of the project as to the collateral and thereby enable small businesses also to compete.[36]

The tragedy, however, is that the Pakistan banking system has aggravated inequalities. Almost 56 percent of resources provided by 28.4 million depositors in 1994 went to only 4,703 privileged borrowers.[37] If we take into account the deplorable fact of the corrupt political system in Pakistan, a number of these borrowers would probably default in spite of having the ability to pay and be able to get away unscathed. This would raise the prevailing inequalities even further.

Economic stability

Economic activity has fluctuated throughout history for a number of reasons, some of which, like natural phenomena, are difficult to remove. However, economic instability seems to have become exacerbated over the last two decades or so as a result of turbulence in the financial markets due to excessive volatility in interest rates, exchange rates, and commodity and stock prices. There is perhaps hardly any part of the world, which has not gone through a serious crisis at some time or other.[38] Such crises tend to accentuate uncertainties, disrupt the smooth functioning of the financial system, create financial fragility, and hurt economic performance.

There are a number of internal and external factors that cause volatility in the financial markets. Not all of these concern us here. They are all, however, closely interlinked and together tend to aggravate the impact. One of these is the excessive build-up of public and private debt as a result of relatively easy access to credit, particularly short-term credit, in an interest-based system of financial intermediation, where the lender tends to rely more on the crutches of collateral than on the strength of the project. The tax system has also indirectly promoted the use of debt rather than equity by subjecting dividend payments to taxation while allowing interest payments to be treated as a tax deductible expense. In addition, the revolution in information and communications technology has led to rapid transfers of funds from country to country on the slightest rumor. This leads to a high degree of volatility in interest rates which has in turn injected a great deal of uncertainty into the investment market and driven borrowers and lenders alike from the long-end of the debt market to the short-end. The result is a steep rise in highly leveraged short-term debt. This has had the effect of accentuating economic instability. The IMF concluded in its 1998 *World Economic Outlook* that countries with high levels of short-term debt are "likely to be particularly vulnerable to internal and external shocks and thus susceptible to financial crises."[39]

One may wish to pause here to ask why a rise in debt, and particularly short-term debt, should accentuate instability. There seems to be a close link between easy availability of credit, macroeconomic imbalances, and financial instability. The easy availability of credit makes it possible for both the public and private sectors to live beyond their means. If the debt is not used productively, the ability to service the debt does not rise in proportion to the debt and leads to financial fragility and debt crises. The greater the reliance on short-term debt, the more severe the crises may be. This is because short-term debt is easily reversible, but repayment may be difficult if the amount is locked in long-term investments where the gestation period is long. While there may be nothing basically wrong in a reasonable amount of short-term debt, an excess of it tends to get diverted to speculation in the foreign exchange, stock, and commodity markets.

The 1997 the East Asia crisis has clearly demonstrated this. The Asian tigers had healthy fiscal policies, which were the envy of a number of developing countries. Since it is well-recognized in macroeconomic literature that the financing of government deficit by bonds or fixed-interest bearing assets promotes instability,[40] the fiscal discipline of these countries should have helped save them from such instability.

However, it did not. The rapid growth in bank credit to the private sector fuelled by inflows from abroad created speculative heat in the equity and property markets and generated a mood of "irrational exuberance," which pushed up asset prices.

The large foreign exchange inflows from abroad enabled the central banks to peg exchange rates. This helped provide the assurance that foreign banks needed to lend and attracted further inflows of funds from abroad in foreign currencies to finance the boom in the assets markets. Since about 60 percent of these inflows were short term, there was a serious maturity mismatch. This joined hands with political corruption and ineffective banking regulations to encourage heavy lending to favored companies, which became over-leveraged. The fast growth of these companies was thus made possible by the availability of easy money from conventional banks who do not generally scrutinize the project minutely because of the absence of risk-sharing.

It was the old mistake of lending on collateral without adequately evaluating the underlying risks. Had there been risk-sharing, the banks would have been under a constraint to scrutinize the projects more carefully and would not have yielded even to political pressures if they considered the projects to be too risky.

There was a reverse flow of funds as soon as there was a shock. Shocks may result from a number of factors, including natural calamities, and unanticipated shifts in terms of trade, interest rates or export prices, and lead to a decline in confidence in the country's ability to honor its liabilities. The rapid outflow, which is not possible in the case of equity financing or even medium- or long-term debt, led to a sharp fall in exchange rates and asset prices along with a steep rise in the local currency value of the debt. Borrowers were unable to repay their debts on schedule.

There was a domestic banking crisis, which had its repercussions on foreign banks because of the inability of domestic banks to meet their external obligations. Governments have only two options in such circumstances. The first is to bail out the domestic banks at great cost to the taxpayer, and the second is to allow the banking system to fail and the economy to suffer a near breakdown. The governments naturally choose the politically preferable first alternative. Since the domestic banks' external liabilities were in foreign exchange, a bailout was not possible without external assistance, which the IMF came in handily to provide.

There was thus a further rise in debt, which would have been difficult to service if these countries had been unable to raise their exports quickly. James Tobin has hence rightly observed that "when private banks and businesses can borrow in whatever amounts, maturities and currencies they choose, they create future claims on their country's reserves."[41] As a result governments and central banks may be forced to adopt monetary and fiscal policies that sacrifice the realization of their goals. The best way to regulate borrowing may not be the imposition of strict controls but rather the introduction of a built-in self-discipline. What could be more effective than the introduction of risk-sharing, which would automatically make foreign as well as domestic banks more careful in lending?

Even industrial, and not just developing, countries can face such crises if there is a heavy reliance on short-term credit or inflow of funds. The 1990s boom in the US stock market has been to a great extent fed by short-term flows of funds just as it had been in East Asia. If these inflows dry up, or get reversed, for some unpredictable reason, there may be a serious crisis. In the late 1960s when there was a decline in confidence in the dollar, there was an outflow of funds from the United States, leading to a substantial depreciation in the external value of the dollar accompanied by a decline in US gold and foreign exchange reserves and a rise in international commodity prices.

The 1990s collapse of US hedge funds like Long-Term Capital Management (LTCM), "Quantum," and "Tiger" was also due to highly leveraged short-term lending. A hedge fund is able to shroud its operations in secrecy because, as explained by the Federal Reserve Chairman, Alan Greenspan, it is "structured to avoid regulation by limiting its clientele to a small number of highly sophisticated, very wealthy individuals."[42] He did not, however, explain how the banks found it possible in a supposedly very well-regulated banking system to provide excessively leveraged lending to such "highly sophisticated, very wealthy individuals" for risky speculation. These hedge funds, which are "nothing more than rapacious speculators, borrowing heavily to beef up their bets," are generally blamed for manipulating markets from Hong Kong to London and New York.[43] These hedge funds do not operate in isolation. If they did, they would not be able to make large gains. They normally operate in unison. This is possible because their chief executives often go to the same clubs, dine together, and know each other very intimately.[44] On the strength of their own wealth and the enormous amounts they are able to borrow, they are able to destabilize the financial market of any country around the world whenever they find it to their advantage. By the time the LTCM was rescued by the Federal Reserve, its leverage had reached 50:1.[45] The Federal Reserve had to arrange its rescue because many of the top commercial banks, which are supervised by the Federal Reserve and considered to be healthy and sound, had lent huge amounts to these funds. If the Federal Reserve had not rescued LTCM, there might have been a crisis in the US financial system with spillover effects around the world.[46]

The heavy reliance on short-term borrowing has also injected a substantial degree of instability into the international foreign exchange markets. According to a survey conducted by the Bank for International Settlements, the daily turnover in traditional foreign exchange markets, adjusted for double-counting, had escalated to $1,490 billion in April 1998, compared with $590 billion in April 1989, $820 billion in April 1992, and $1,190 billion in April 1995.[47] The daily foreign exchange turnover in April 1998 was more than 49 times the daily volume of world merchandize trade (exports plus imports).[48] Even if an allowance is made for services, unilateral transfers and non-speculative capital flows, the turnover was far more than warranted. Only 39.6 percent of the 1998 turnover was related to spot transactions, which have risen at the compounded annual rate of about 6.0 percent per annum over the 9 years since April 1989, very close to the growth of 6.8 percent per annum in world trade. The balance of the turnover (60.4 percent) was related largely to outright forwards and foreign exchange swaps, which have registered a compounded growth of 15.8 percent per annum over this period. If the assertion normally made by bankers that they give due consideration to the end use of funds had been correct, such a high degree of leveraged credit extension for speculative transactions might not have taken place.

The dramatic growth in speculative transactions over the past two decades, of which derivatives are only the latest manifestation, has resulted in an enormous expansion in the payments system. Such a large value of transactions implies that if problems were to arise, they could quickly spread throughout the financial system, exerting a domino effect on financial institutions. Accordingly, Mr Crockett, the General Manager of the Bank for International Settlements, has been led to acknowledge that "our economies have thus become increasingly vulnerable to a possible breakdown in the payments system."[49] The large volume also has other adverse effects. It has been one of the major factors contributing to the continued high real rates of interest, which have tended to discourage productive investment.

Foreign exchange markets, being driven by short-term speculation rather than long-term fundamentals, have become highly volatile. This impedes the efficient operation of these markets, injects excessive instability into them, and creates pressures in favor of exchange controls, particularly on capital transfers. The effort by central banks to overcome this instability through small changes in interest rates or the intervention of a few hundred million dollars a day has generally proved to be ineffective. The Tobin tax on foreign exchange transactions has therefore been suggested to reduce the instability. However, critics of the tax have argued that the imposition of such a tax would be impractical. Unless all countries adopt it and implement it faithfully, trading would shift to tax-free havens. Moreover, even if all countries complied, experienced speculators may be able to devise ways of evading or avoiding the tax because not all countries have an effective tax administration.[50]

If it is not desirable to rely heavily on short-term borrowing to finance large current account deficits normally incurred in the initial phase of economic development, then the more desirable thing would be to rely on long-term borrowing and equity financing. Of these two, equity financing is preferable because it would introduce greater health into the economy through a more careful scrutiny of projects.

It would also have a number of other advantages. The IMF has also thrown its weight in favor of equity financing by arguing that:

> Foreign direct investment, in contrast to debt-creating inflows, is often regarded as providing a safer and more stable way to finance development because it refers to ownership and control of plant, equipment, and infrastructure and therefore funds the growth-creating capacity of an economy, whereas short-term foreign borrowing is more likely to be used to finance consumption. Furthermore, in the event of a crisis, while investors can divest themselves of domestic securities and banks can refuse to roll over loans, owners of physical capital cannot find buyers so easily.[51]

Moreover, as Hicks has argued, interest has to be paid in good or bad times alike, but dividends can be reduced in bad times and, in extreme situations, even passed. So the burden of finance by shares is less. There is no doubt that in good times an increased dividend would be expected, but it is precisely in such times that the burden of higher dividend can be borne. "The firm would be insuring itself to some extent," to use Hicks' precise words, "against a strain which in difficult conditions can be serious, at the cost of an increased payment in conditions when it would be easy to meet it. It is in this sense that the riskiness of its position would be diminished."[52] This factor should tend to have the effect of substantially reducing business failures, and in turn dampening, rather than accentuating, economic instability.

A number of Muslim as well as non-Muslim economists have hence argued that the shift to an equity-oriented financial system may help substantially reduce instability in the financial markets. It has been argued that while the nominal value of deposits tends to be assured in the conventional system, there is no assurance that all loans and advances will be recovered. This leads to a discrepancy between assets and liabilities, and ultimately to a banking crisis if there is a loss of confidence in the banking system. In the profit-and-loss-sharing system, the loss on the assets side gets promptly absorbed by the liabilities side. This should help minimize the risk of bank failures and enhance the stability of the banking system. It has also been argued that since the erratic behavior of interest rates along with the generally accepted instability of credit tend to usher in an atmosphere of uncertainty and instability in the investment climate, greater reliance on equity may tend to inject greater stability into the economy.

A further argument is that interest rate volatility defeats all efforts to create stability in exchange rates. Because of the volatility in interest rates, funds move from country to country to take advantage of the interest rate differential. This worsens the climate of uncertainty in which economic decisions are taken, discourages capital formation, and leads to misallocation of resources.[53] An equity-based economy may tend to remove the daily destabilizing influence of fluctuating interest rates. In such an environment the strength or weakness of a currency would tend to reflect the underlying strength of the economy. Exchange rates may tend to be relatively more stable because all the fundamentals that influence exchange rates, such as structural imbalances and differences in growth rates, are of a medium or long-term nature and do not normally change erratically.[54]

Notes

* Dr Umer Chapra is Research Adviser to the Islamic Research and Training Institute (IRTI) of the Islamic Development Bank (IDB), Jeddah. This paper was prepared by him in his private capacity at the request of the *Shariat* Appellate Bench of the Supreme Court of Pakistan. It is a modified version of a section of chapter 7 of the author's recently published book on the *Future of Economics: An Islamic Perspective* (The Islamic Foundation, Leicester, 2000, pp. 5–20 and has previously appeared in the *Review of Islamic Economics*, No. 9, May 2000) and is reprinted with his permission. He is grateful to Mr Mobin Ahmad and Sheikh Mohamad Rashid for the secretarial assistance provided by them in the preparation of this paper.

1 *Sahih Muslim* (1955), vol. 4, p. 1996:56, *Kitab al-Birr wa al-Silah wa al-Adab, Bab Tahrim al-Zulm*, from Jabir ibn Abdullah. The Prophet, peace and blessings of God be on him, has used the word *zulumat* in this *hadith*. *Zulumat* is the plural of *zulmah* or darkness, and signifies several layers of darkness, leading ultimately to "pitch" or "absolute" darkness, as is also evident in the Quranic verse, 24:40.

2 Abu Yusuf, Yaqub ibn Ibrahim (d. 182/798), *Kitab al-Kharaj* (Cairo: al-Matbaah al-Salafiyyah, 2nd edn, 1352 AH), p. 111; see also pp. 3–17.

3 Mawardi, Abu al-Hasan Ali, al- (d. 450/1058), *Adab al-Dunya wa al-Din*, Mustafa al-Saqqa (ed.) (Cairo: Mustafa al-Babi al-Halabi, 1955), p. 125.

4 Ibn Taymiyyah, *Majmu Fatawa Shaykh al-Islam Ahmad ibn Taymiyyah*, Abd al-Rahman al-Asimi (ed.) (Riyadh: Matabi al-Riyadh, 1st edn, 1381–83/1961–63), vol. 18, p. 165.

5 Ibid. p. 166. See also his *Minhaj al-Sunna al-Nabawiyyah*, M. Rashad Salim (ed.), (Riyadh: Imam Muhammad Islamic University, 1986), vol. 5, p. 127.

6 Ibn Taymiyyah, *Al-Hisbah fi al-Islam*, Abd al-Aziz Rabah (ed.) (Damascus: Maktabah Dar al-Bayan, 1967), p. 94. Also Mukhtar Holland under the title *Public Duties in Islam: The Institution of the Hisba* (Leicester, UK: The Islamic Foundation, 1982), p. 95.

7 Ibn Khaldun, Abd al-Rahman, *Muqaddimah* (Cairo: Al-Maktabah al-Tijariyah al-Kubra, n.d.), p. 287.

8 See Chapra, M. Umer, *Islam and the Economic Challenge* (Leicester, UK: The Islamic Foundation, 1992), pp. 143–56 and 168–9.

9 Ibn Khaldun, op. cit., p. 288.

10 Ibid., p. 288.

11 Ibid., p. 288.

12 For the Judaic and Christian views on interest see Chapter 2; also see Johns, C.H.W., John Dow, W.H. Bennett, and J. Abelson, on the Babylonian, Christian, Hebrew, and Jewish views respectively on "Usury," *Encyclopedia of Religion and Ethics* (New York: Charles Scribner's Sons, n.d.), vol. 12, pp. 548–58; and Noonan, Jr, John T., *The Scholastic Analysis of Usury* (Cambridge, MA: Harvard University Press, 1957); and for the Hindu view, see Bokare, M.G., *Hindu-Economics: Eternal Economic Order* (New Delhi: Janaki Prakashan, 1993), p. 168.

13 See the Bible – Ezekiel, 18:8, 13, 7; 22:12. See also Exodus, 22:25–27; Leviticus, 25: 36–38; Deuteronomy, 23:19; and Luke, 6:35. Also see Chapter 2 for a more detailed discussion of Judeo Christian imperatives.

14 This is the interpretation of data presented in Mankiw, Gregory, David Romer and David Weil, "A Contribution to the Empirics of Economic Growth," *Quarterly Journal of Economics*, May 1992, pp. 407–37.

15 See chapter V on "Saving in a Growing World Economy," in IMF, *World Economic Outlook*, May 1995, pp. 67–89.

16 Poterba, James M. (ed.), *Public Policies and Household Saving* (Chicago, IL: University of Chicago Press, 1994).

17 See Kocherlakota, Narayana R., "The Equity Puzzle: It's Still a Puzzle," *The Journal of Economic Literature*, March 1996, pp. 42–71; and Siegel, Jeremy J. and Richard H. Thaler, "Anomalies: The Equity Premium Puzzle," *Journal of Economic Perspectives*, Winter 1997, pp. 191–200.

18 Siegel and Thaler, op. cit., p. 194.

19 According to the IMF: "The high level of world real interest rates that has persisted since the early 1980s is prima facie evidence of strong demand for investment relative to the supply of world saving" (IMF, *World Economic Outlook*, May 1995, p. 7).

20 Figures have been derived from the table on "Consumption as percent of GDP," in the IMF, *International Financial Statistics, 1998 Yearbook*, pp. 166–7.

21 OECD, *Economic Outlook*, December 1991, table 2, p. 7, and June 1998, table 21, p. 245.

22 Bank of International Settlements (BIS), 64th *Annual Report*, June 1994, p. 17.

23 Ibid.

24 The worldwide tendency now seems to be in favor of reducing fiscal deficits. The European Community has set a limit of 3 percent of GDP for the budgetary deficit and of 60 percent for public debt. However, there are no such limits for the private sector. The US foreign debt rose by $193.8 billion in 1996 to $831.8 billion (*The Economist*, July 12, 1997, p. 42). The main reason for this was the current account deficit of $148 billion, fuelled primarily by the country's economic boom. The household debt in 1996 totaled 89 percent of annual disposable income compared with 83 percent in 1990 and only 67 percent in 1980.

25 See Chapra, M. Umer, *Towards a Just Monetary System* (Leicester, UK: The Islamic Foundation, 1985), pp. 111–25.

26 The literature on the effects of *zakat* on different economic variables is quite extensive. For a detailed bibliography of items in Arabic as well as English, see Suhaibani, M.I., *Athar al-Zakat ala Tashghil al-Mawarid al-Iqtisadiyyah* (Effect of *Zakat* on the Employment of Economic Resources) (Riyadh: al-Ubaykan, 1990), pp. 313–25.

27 Zarqa, M. Anas, "Capital Allocation, Efficiency and Growth in an Interest-Free Islamic Economy," *Journal of Economics and Administration* (Jeddah, Saudi Arabia), November 1982, pp. 98–106; Chapra, op. cit., 1985, pp. 107–17; Presley, J.R. and J.G. Sessions, "Islamic Economics: the Emergence of a New Paradigm," *The Economic Journal*, May 1994, pp. 584–96.

28 Karsten, Ingo, "Islam and Financial Intermediation," *IMF Staff Papers*, March 1982, p. 131 as well as pp. 129–36.

29 See Chapra, op. cit., 1985, pp. 122–3.

30 *Sahih Muslim*, from Shaddad ibn Aws, *Kitab al-Sayd wa al-Dhaba'ih, Bab al-amr bi Ihsan*, vol. 3, p. 1548:57.

31 Cited from *Sayyidah* A'ishah by al-Bayhaqi in his *Shuab al-Iman*, vol. 4, p. 334:5312.

32 See Iqbal, Munawar (ed.), *Distributive Justice and Need Fulfilment in an Islamic Economy* (Leicester: The Islamic Foundation, 1988), and Chapra, op. cit., 1992, pp. 251–76.

33 Thurow, Lester, *Zero-Sum Society* (New York: Basic Books, 1980), p. 175.

34 Bigsten, Arne, "Poverty, Inequality and Development," in Norman Gemmell, *Surveys in Development Economics* (Oxford: Blackwell, 1987), p. 156.

35 Morgan Guarantee Trust Company of New York, *World Financial Markets*, January 1987, p. 7.

36 See Chapra, op. cit., 1985, pp. 107–11 and pp. 200–2.

37 Based on statistics published in State Bank of Pakistan, *State Bank Bulletin*, July 1955, pp. 32–3 and 46–7.

38 The world has experienced a number of crises after the 1987 stock market crash. Some of the most important of these are: bursting of the Japanese stock and property market bubble in the 1990s, the breakdown of the European exchange rate mechanism in 1992–93, the bond market crash in February 1994, the Mexican crisis in 1995, the East Asian crisis in 1997, and the Russian crisis in August 1998.

39 IMF, *World Economic Outlook*, May 1998, p. 83.

40 Christ, Carl, "On Fiscal and Monetary Policies and the Government Budget Restraint," *American Economic Review*, 1979, pp. 526–38; and Searth, Wan, "Bond Financed Fiscal Policy and the Problem of Instrument Instability," *Journal of Macroeconomics*, 1979, pp. 107–17.

41 World Bank, *Policy and Research Bulletin*, April–June 1998, p. 3.

42 See his testimony before the Committee on Banking and Financial Services of the House of Representatives on October 1, 1998, in the *Federal Reserve Bulletin*, October 1998, p. 1046.

43 "The Risk Business," *The Economist*, October 17, 1998, p. 21.

44 John Plender, "Western Crony Capitalism," *Financial Times*, October 3–4, 1998.

45 "The Risk Business," op. cit., p. 22.

46 This was clearly acknowledged by Mr Greenspan in the following words: "Had the failure of the LTCM triggered the seizing up of markets, substantial damage could have been inflicted on many market participants, including some not directly involved with the firm, and could have potentially impaired the economies of many nations, including our own" (*Federal Reserve Bulletin*, op. cit., p. 1046).

47 See table 1 of the Bank of International Settlements (BIS), Press Release of October 19, 1998, giving preliminary results of the foreign exchange survey for April 1998. Such a survey is conducted by the BIS every three years.

48 World trade (exports plus imports) rose from $499 billion in April 1989 to $908.7 billion in April 1998 (IMF, *International Financial Statistics*, CD-ROM and November 1998). The average value of daily world trade in April 1998 comes to $30.3 billion.

49 Andrew Crockett, address at the 24th International Management Symposium in St. Galen on June 1, 1994, *BIS Review*, June 22, 1994, p. 3.
50 See the arguments in favor of and against the feasibility of the Tobin tax by various writers in Haq, Mahbubul, Inge Kaul, and Isabelle Grunberg (eds), *The Tobin Tax: Coping with Financial Volatility* (Oxford: Oxford University Press, 1996).
51 IMF, op. cit., May 1998, p. 82.
52 Hicks, John, "Limited Liability: The Pros and Cons," in Tony Orhnial (ed.), *Limited Liability and the Corporation* (London: Croom Helm, 1982), p. 14.
53 BIS, *Annual Report*, 1982, p. 3.
54 The preceding argument reflects the attempt of a human being with his limited knowledge and capacity to understand the rationale behind God's teachings in the *Quran*. If this argument does not satisfy anyone, it should be borne in mind that "God alone has the convincing argument" (*Quran*, 6:14) and He alone knows the total rationale. What we, as human beings, need to do is to accept His teachings willingly and to trust that their implementation, even if this involves some difficulties in the beginning, will ultimately lead to the well-being of all in a just manner. Such a submission to God's Will undoubtedly requires a deep faith in Him and His teachings. No amount of logic can be a substitute for this. In the end we may do well to join the Prophet, peace and blessings of God be on him, in his following prayer: "O God! Give me the wisdom [needed to accept Your teachings] and save me from the evil [promptings] of the self."

7 An attempt to understand the economic wisdom (*ḥikma*) in the prohibition of *riba*

Mahmoud A. El-Gamal*

Introduction

When Islamic jurists discuss the invalidity (and prohibition) of various *riba* contracts, they most often discuss only the juristic instigating factor for previous rulings forbidding juristically similar contracts (*'illat al-Hukm*). For non-jurists, the juristic language of instigating factor may wrongly seem causal in nature, that is, it may seem like a philosophical explanation of the prohibition. This misunderstanding, in conjunction with the typical juristic usage of the language on justice (*'adl*), prompted many of the early to mid-twentieth-century writers on Islamic Economics and Finance to jump to unwarranted conclusions that are neither supported by the canonical Islamic texts (the *Quran* and the *Sunna* of the Prophet Muhammad (pbuh)) nor accurately representing the expressed views of early Muslim jurists. As a result, misconceptions about the prohibition of *riba* and how it affects contemporary financial transactions permeated not only the academic Islamic Economics language but also the popular discourse on Islam, money, and financial transactions.

Thus, a number of misconceptions have become accepted as "truths" about Islam and the Islamic model of finance. Three main misconceptions must be addressed in this regard:

1   Many have come to believe that the prohibition of *riba* is primarily a prohibition of exploitative lending by loan-sharks. Some thus reasoned that only exorbitantly high interest rates are forbidden. Others argued more generally that the prohibition of *riba* should only be considered to bear on contracts wherein the potential for exploitation is present. Strangely enough, this opinion is held by some of the most knowledgeable Islamic scholars of our time, despite having been thoroughly debunked centuries ago in classical sources of Islamic jurisprudence. Taqiyyuddin Al-Subki, in his continuation of Al-Imam Al-Nawawi's *Al-Majmu' Sharh Al-Muhadhdhab*,[1] reported an opinion of Ibn Kayyisan that "the reason (*al-maqsud*) for the prohibition of *riba* is kindness towards people" (i.e. by not charging an increase). However, he proceeded (in "*far' fi Madhahib al-'ulama' fi bayan 'illat al-riba fi al-'ajnas al-'arba'ah*") to argue that this cannot possibly be an explanation of the prohibition of *riba*, since excessive interest rates can still be imposed when trading goods of different genera. For instance, it is still possible to trade 1 pound of wheat today for 100 pounds of barley in a year, even if the prices of wheat and

barley are very close (provided that wheat and barley are not used as money in this economy). Moreover, non-fungible goods can be traded with inequality; thus it is possible to trade a Volkswagen today for a brand-new Mercedes-Benz in a year, clearly an exploitative trade.

Interestingly enough, some have used this incomplete understanding of the prohibition of *riba* to argue that interest charged and paid by commercial banks today is not the prohibited *riba*. They have argued (e.g. the controversial *fatwas* of Sheikh Dr Tantawi, the past *Mufti* of Egypt and current Shaikh-ul-Azhar, and similar *fatwas* by Sheikh Wasil (the current *Mufti* of Egypt) that conventional banking interest is a share in the profits of growth-inducing investments[2] and not the forbidden *riba*. Islam forbids charging such interest for delays or repayment. Yet both Islamic and conventional banks often renegotiate debt payment schedules, without any compensation, in cases of an obligor's inability to repay. Not only is this argument built on a partial understanding of the prohibition of *riba* based on exploitation, it is also deficient in ignoring the fact that much of the *riba* which was used in pre-Islamic Arabia was indeed for commercial and business financing.[3] This is in contrast to the European view of "usury" (a common but faulty translation of the term *riba*), which evokes the mental image of exploitative consumption loans.

The issue is sometimes complicated by negligent interpretations of the verses of prohibition of *riba* in the *Quran*. For instance, one of the most popular translations of the meaning of the *Quran* by Yusuf Ali,[4] translates the meaning of verses (2:278–279) thus:

> 278. O ye who believe! Fear Allah, and give up what remains of your demand for usury, if ye are Indeed believers.
> 279. If ye do not, take notice of war from Allah and His Messenger: but if ye turn back, ye shall have your capital sums; Deal not unjustly, and ye shall not be dealt with unjustly.

Thus, the English reader who is not familiar with the end of verse 279 "*la tazlimuna wa la tuzlamun*," reads this translation as a proof that the (sole?) objective served by the prohibition of *riba* is the avoidance of injustice (in the sense of exploitation of the poor debtor by the rich creditor). However, the meaning of the ending of the verse – as explained by Abu Ja'far, Ibn 'Abbas, and others[5] – is much closer to: "if you turn back, then you should collect your principal, without inflicting or receiving injustice." The exegetes[6] then explain "without inflicting or receiving injustice" as "without increase or diminution," where both an increase or a decrease of the amount returned relative to the amount lent would be considered injustice.

If we ponder this standard explanation, we see that "injustice" here is a symmetric relation, which depends only on the lent sum and *not* on the relative wealth of the parties or their respective positions as creditor and debtor. In other words, the "injustice" mentioned here is economical: there is no valid justification for any given increase or diminution; thus such increase or diminution lends itself to injustice. We shall see in this section that Ibn Rushd provided a more detailed analysis of this notion of inequity or injustice as the rationale for the prohibition of *riba*. Moreover, while many jurists have argued that *riba al-fadl* (forbidden in the *hadith*) was prohibited due to the fact that it may lead to *riba al-nasi'a* (prohibited in the *Quran*),[7] Ibn Rushd will provide a much more direct economic argument for why both types of *riba* contain the same type of injustice. We shall discuss the implications of Ibn Rushd's analysis later in the paper, but for now, we need to make a few more points clear.

2   Another major misconception that continues to this day is that the forbidden *riba* is identical with "interest," in all its forms as understood by contemporary finan-cial scholars and practitioners. This ideological assertion creates a great deal of con-fusion among Muslims and non-Muslims alike. In particular, when we observe an "Islamic bank" engaging in a one-year credit sale with a credit price that is higher than the cash price, any school child can calculate the implicit annual interest rate (calculated as the price difference divided by the cash price and then multiplied by 100). In order to maintain the ideological slogan of "Islam forbids interest," while allowing this permitted transaction (under the title of *murabaha ma'a bay' bi-thaman 'ajil*, or cost-plus credit sale), jurists, Islamic bankers, and many writers resort to highly technical juristic arguments. However, the solution is much sim-pler: the translation of *"riba"* as interest was wrong. The earlier writers in Islamic Economics[8] may be excused for confusing the two notions, since the only form of finance they observed in their primitive financial sectors took the form of bank loans, in which interest is indeed a form of forbidden *riba*. However, the past five decades have witnessed a great revolution in financing forms, wherein the bound-aries between commercial banks (whose transactions are based on forbidden *riba* through borrowing and lending with interest) and other financial institutions became blurred. Along with that blurring, the Western notion of "interest" evolved to include all profits made on invested capital. The following is one of the definitions in Webster's of "interest" as a noun:

> the profit in goods or money that is made on invested capital." Thus, it is paradoxical for anyone accustomed to this modern notion of interest to hear the claim that Islamic banking involves no interest, when the school child mentioned previously can easily calculate the implicit interest rate in the credit sale and leasing finance models that dominate Islamic bank practices.[9]

The inaccurate ideological statement that "Islam forbids interest" led to patently false conclusions. Thus, many Islamic economists claimed that Islam does not accept the notion of a "time value of money," despite the fact that all eight major schools of jurisprudence recognize that "time has a factor in the price,"[10] for full references and quotations. There are a very large number of papers in Islamic Economics, which address the question whether or not Islam recognizes a time value of money, many of which come to a negative answer. Those assertions by later Islamic economists stem from two notable early denials of time preference and time value of money.[11]

The paradox to which I pointed earlier is that Islamic banking thrived in recent decades on cost-plus sales (*murabaha*) with deferred receipt of the price, and lease financing (*ijara wa iqtina*). Those contracts involve an increase over the cash price that is fully justified as compensation to the trader or financial commercial intermediary for the opportunity cost of deferring the receipt of his compensation (time value of money). Thus, the fact that the same financial firm would sell one item for one price on a cash-and-carry basis and for a higher price on a deferred basis is not un-Islamic, provided that certain conditions are met. Whether or not we wish to call that increase "interest" is idle sophistry unworthy of serious academic discourse, especially since the term has acquired new meanings as we have seen earlier.

I have thus shown that not all "interest" in the modern sense is considered forbidden *riba*. To complete the argument that associating *riba* with interest is faulty, I now argue that not all forbidden *riba* involves interest. This argument is much easier to make. While proving the previous point – that interest payments in the general sense are not necessarily part of the forbidden *riba* – required references to Islamic Jurisprudence, this point requires nothing more than quoting a well-known *hadith*. This *hadith* is narrated in numerous sources, of which we list one.[12] Muslim narrated on the authority of Abu Said Al-Khudriy; The Messenger of God (pbuh) said, "Gold for gold, silver for silver, wheat for wheat, barley for barley, dates for dates, and salt for salt; like for like, hand to hand, in equal amounts; and any increase is *riba*."

This is the famous *hadith* prohibiting *riba al-fadl*. Clearly, the transactions being prohibited here need not involve a temporal element, and therefore, the prohibition of this *riba* is not necessarily related to debts, deferment, or time.

Another *hadith* which further illustrates this fact – that prohibited *riba* and "interest" are not necessarily related – is the following famous story.[13] Muslim narrated on the authority of Abu Said Al-Khudriy:

> Bilal visited the Messenger of God (pbuh) with some high quality dates, and the Prophet (pbuh) inquired about their source. Bilal explained that he traded two volumes of lower quality dates for one volume of higher quality. The Messenger of God (pbuh) said: "this is precisely the forbidden *riba*! Do not do this. Instead, sell the first type of dates, and use the proceeds to buy the other.

The process of selling one type of dates in the market only to use the proceeds to buy the other type may seem to some to be obsessively ritualistic, or – God forbid – a nominal circumvention of the law. However, we shall see next in light of the analysis of Ibn Rushd that there is great wisdom in this legally binding *hadith*.

3   The third major misconception goes back to the early days of Islamic banking in Egypt (Mit Ghamr, 1963), pioneered by the late Dr Ahmad Al-Najjar. He proposed the definition of *riba* as any pre-specified percentage earned over a specified period of time. In a recent interview, the Egyptian Shaikh-ul-Azhar angrily responded to a group of reporters that pre-specification of the rate of return has nothing to do with *riba*. He was right on that account. Indeed, a very simple analysis of Islamically permissible credit-sales and leases shows immediately that the latter forms have a fixed term and a fixed percentage increase over the cash

price. Hence, if an Islamic bank buys a car for $10,000 and sells it with a credit price of $12,000, he would guarantee a rate or return of 20 percent over the term of deferment. The only risk borne by the bank after selling the car is the "credit risk," that the buyer or client will not be able to pay. But that is the exact same type of risk borne by a commercial bank that could have lent the client $10,000 to buy the car, and charged him 20 percent interest over the period of the loan. The extra risk borne by the Islamic bank between the time it buys the car and the time it sells it to the client is negligible since that time period can be a matter of minutes, despite the fact that writers on Islamic banking over-emphasize this difference. The other difference that is highlighted by some Islamic economists and jurists is the relevant one, but requires more analysis: the case of a credit sale is different from the case of a loan, since it involves a direct link to a real transaction (the purchase of a car). However, everyone is aware of the fact that when a client goes to a commercial bank to get an auto-loan, the bank does not simply give him cash. Indeed, the loan issued by the commercial bank is also tied to the automobile, and the bank often writes the check directly to the car dealership. Moreover, the issue of collateralization of the underlying debt is also handled by commercial banks, which hold a lien on the car or financed property. Therefore, we need a deeper understanding of the difference between the two types of financial transactions to get a better economic understanding of the verse: "But Allah has permitted trade, and He has forbidden *riba*."

Ibn Rushd on the objective served by the prohibition of *riba*

We are now ready to set the stage for the argument of Ibn Rushd.[14] This argument was provided in the context of *tarjih*, a choice of one juristic opinion over another, regarding the set of goods to which the prohibition of *riba al-fadl* applies. The Zahiri opinion, not surprisingly, disallowed any reasoning by analogy (*qiyas*) beyond the goods mentioned in the *hadith* cited in the previous section. The Shafi'is and Malikis, on the other hand, restricted such an inference by analogy to gold and silver (for their use to denominate prices; *thamaniyyah*), and foodstuff, with a further restriction by the Malikis to non-perishable foodstuff. The Hanafis went to the extreme in reasoning by analogy, generalizing the prohibition in the *hadith* to all items measured by volume or weight.

Ibn Rushd – despite being of the Maliki school – found the reasoning of the Hanafis to be most compelling. While some contemporary jurists found the logic of Ibn Rushd to be objectionable due to its dramatic enlarging of the scope of *riba*,[15] understanding the economic content of that logic can help us enhance our understanding of the Law, and its economic, as well as its juristic implications.[16]

As justification for his siding with the Hanafi generalization of the scope of *riba*, Ibn Rushd[17] said:

It is thus apparent from the law that what is intended by the prohibition of *riba* is what it contains of excessive injustice (*ghubn fahish*). In this regard, justice in transactions is achieved by approaching equality. Since the attainment of such equality in items of different kinds is difficult, their values are determined instead in monetary terms (*with the Dirham and the Dinar*). For things which are not measured by weight and volume, justice can be determined by means of proportionality. I mean, the ratio between the value of one item to its kind should be equal to the ratio of the value of the other item to its kind. For example, if a person sells a horse in exchange for clothes, justice is attained by making the ratio of the price of the horse to other horses the same as the ratio of the price of the clothes [for which it is traded, tr.] to other clothes. Thus, if the value of the horse is fifty, the value of the clothes should be fifty. [If each piece of clothing's value is five], then the horse should be exchanged for 10 pieces of clothing.

As for [fungible] goods measured by volume or weight, they are relatively homogenous, and thus have similar benefits [utilities]. Since it is not necessary for a person owning one type of those goods to exchange it for the exact same type, justice in this case is achieved by equating volume or weight since the benefits [utilities] are very similar...

Understanding the prohibition of *riba al-fadl* in economic terms: efficiency and pre-commitment

We can now understand the economic logic of Ibn Rushd by converting his language to contemporary Economic terminology. In the first translated paragraph, he proclaimed that justice is obtained if and only if the ratio at which non-fungible goods are traded for one another (e.g. clothes for a horse) is the reciprocal of the ratio of their prices. Thus, a horse worth 50 on the market is to be traded for 10 dresses each worth 5 on the market. Justice in this context is simply "marking to market." In the context of very heterogeneous items (e.g. clothes for a horse), Ibn Rushd implicitly argues that it is obvious that the parties to such a transaction would make sure that the ratio at which they trade is close to the ratio of market prices. Moreover, since non-fungibles vary widely in prices (the ratio of the price of this horse to other horses, etc.), such a ratio can only be determined approximately in any case.

The second translated paragraph talks mainly about fungibles, but sheds significant light on the equality of ratios of barter trading and market prices and its relationship to economic efficiency. In the second paragraph, the discussion centers around the ratio of barter trading and the ratio of utilities (benefits) derived by the traders. Combining the two equalities which "justice" requires in the two paragraphs, we get: ratio of barter trade = ratio of prices = ratio of (?)-utilities. In what follows, I cannot resist the temptation of replacing the mystery square (?) with the term "marginal." Clearly, this is the notion which Ibn Rushd meant when discussing the benefits derived from various goods. However, he obviously lacked the proper language to express it in terms of marginal benefit or utility, writing as he did centuries before the invention of differential calculus.

Considering benefit/utility in the marginal sense, it would stand to reason that the ratio at which a barter trade takes place would roughly equate the two parties' ratios of marginal utilities of the traded objects (with perfect equality if the goods were perfectly divisible), provided that they have access to many other trading partners. The trade will be conducive to economic efficiency if the trading ratio was equal to the ratio of marginal utilities over the entire economy. The latter is ensured – in turn – by equating the ratio of marginal utilities to the ratio of market prices. This is the condition for Pareto efficiency in the market. We can now appeal to the first and second welfare theorems of economics, and conclude that "justice" dictates that the "just" prices and trading ratios are those which maximize allocative efficiency. This does not mean that equality considerations are ignored, for they can be easily addressed *ex post* through Islamic re-allocative mechanisms such as *Zakat* (thus, the common conjunction of the verses of *zakat* and *sadaqat* with the verses of *Riba* in *Al-Rum, Al-Imran*, and *Al-Baqarah* can be understood in this light, in addition to the direct contrast between the two terms "*riba*" and "*zakat*," both of which lexically mean "increase").

Now, we can also understand the Prophet's (pbuh) order to Bilal not to trade dates of low quality for dates of high quality at a mutually agreeable ratio. The second paragraph from Ibn Rushd translated previously clearly states that "it is not necessary for a person" (in this case Bilal) to engage in this exchange. Thus, if he does engage in trading dates for dates, the *hadith* says, he should trade in the same quantities. Otherwise, if he considers them sufficiently different to warrant a trading ratio other than one, then he should be forced to "mark to market" what this ratio should be. Thus, he should sell the one type of dates, and collect its price, presumably getting the fair market price for his goods. At this point, he is not obliged to buy from any particular seller, and thus if he engages in the activity of using the proceeds to buy the other type of dates, he will also get the fair market price in the second trade. The net result is, again, the equality of the ratio of [marginal] utilities of the traders to the ratio of market prices, Pareto efficiency, and the maximization of a certain notion of social welfare. *Ex-post* reallocations of wealth can then address other notions of social welfare (especially, equality) outside the marketplace.

Before we move to *riba al-nasi'a*, it is useful to highlight the two conclusions we derived from the analysis of Ibn Rushd:

1   The objective served by the prohibition of *riba* – justice – is obtained by fairly compensating each party for the value of its goods as determined by the marketplace. This fair compensation is equivalent to the notion of Pareto efficiency familiar to students of welfare economics. Issues of "fairness" which incorporate equality are not ignored in this context; they are only excluded from the marketplace and handled *ex post* by reallocative mechanisms.

Further proof for this conclusion is the well-known prohibition in the following *hadith*, narrated by Muslim and others[18] on the authority of Jabir: The messenger of Allah (pbuh) said: "Let not a city-dweller sell on behalf of an incoming bedouin. Leave the people so that Allah may make them benefit from one another."

The explanation of this *hadith* is thus[19]: A bedouin coming to the market may not know the current market conditions. The prohibition here applies to a city-dweller who knows the market conditions, and asks the bedouin to allow him to sell on his behalf (thus helping the bedouin to earn a higher profit). While most discussions of this *hadith* refer to the case of a shortage in the market, and the city-dweller helping the incoming bedouin to keep supply low and prices high, the *hadith* in itself is quite symmetric, and "benefiting from one another" is a fixed-sum game in which one person's relative loss is another's gain. The *hadith*, indeed, forbids interventions into market conditions which may reduce efficiency (by fostering monopoly as indicated by commentators, or in any other way).

2   The second point we take out of this section is the pre-commitment mechanism recommended in the *hadith* of Bilal and its link to the analysis of Ibn Rushd. For fungibles, the rule is that if the same item is to be traded, it should be in equal quantities; otherwise, the prohibition of *riba al-fadl* forces the traders physically to "mark to market" the ratio at which they trade. The need for such a pre-commitment mechanism avoids inefficient trades due to lack of complete information about the fair market prices of the two exchanged goods. We shall see in the next section that a similar argument illustrates the efficiency-enhancing role of pre-commitment mechanisms which allow economic agents to avoid *riba al-nasi'a*.

Efficiency gains from the prohibition of *riba* and the pre-commitment mechanisms inherent in Islamic financial contracts

The informational argument which applied to *riba al-fadl* applies by extension to *riba al-nasi'a*. However, the dimension of time adds at least another source of inefficiency in the market: the tendency for humans to be dynamically inconsistent. We shall shortly review some of the experimental evidence on so-called discounting anomalies exhibited by humans (as well as animals) and which result in such dynamic inconsistency. Before we do that, however, it is productive to reference a few of the verses of the *Quran* which assert that "man" – generally speaking – does indeed exhibit such dynamic inconsistency and asymmetric treatment of potential gains and losses:

> If Allah were to hasten for men the ill (they have earned) as they would fain hasten on the good, then would their respite be settled at once. (10:11)
> When trouble toucheth a man, he crieth unto us,...But when we have solved his trouble, he passeth on his way as if he had never cried to us for a trouble that touched him. Thus do the deeds of transgressors seem fair in their eyes. (10:12)

> They ask thee to hasten on the evil in preference to the good:...(13:6)

> (Inevitably) cometh (to pass) the Command of Allah: seek ye not then to hasten it:...(16:1)

> The prayer that man should make for good, he maketh for evil; for man is given to haste. (17:11)

> When distress seizes you at sea, those that ye call upon – besides himself – leave you in the lurch. But when He brings you back safe to land, ye turn away (from Him). Most ungrateful is man. (17:67)

Man is a creature of haste: soon (enough) will I show you My Signs; then ye will not ask Me to hasten them. (21:37)

He said: "Oh my people! why ask ye to hasten on the evil in preference to the good? . . . ." (27:46)

They ask thee to hasten on the Punishment (for them): . . . (29:53)

They ask thee to hasten on the Punishment . . . (29:54)

When trouble touches men, they cry to their Lord, turning back to Him in repentance: but when He gives them a taste of Mercy as from Himself. Behold, some of them pay part-worship to other gods besides their Lord . . . (30:33)

Do they wish (indeed) to hurry our Punishment? (37:176)

They say: "Our Lord! hasten to us our sentence (even) before the Day of Account" (38:16)

When some trouble toucheth man, he crieth unto his Lord, turning to Him in repentance: but when He bestoweth a favour upon him from Himself, (man) doth forget what he cried and prayed for before, . . . (39:8)

Now, when trouble touches man, he cries to Us; but when We bestow a favour upon him as from Ourselves, he says, "This has been given to me because of a certain knowledge (I have)!" . . . (39:49)

"Taste ye your trial! This is what ye used to ask to be hastened!" (51:14)

Truly, man was created very impatient. (70:19)

Fretful when evil touches him; (70:20)

and niggardly when good reaches him. (70:21)

Nay, (ye men!) But ye love the fleeting life (literally: that which is sooner) (75:20)

Woe to those that deal in fraud. (83:1)

Those who, when they Have to receive by measure from men exact full measure, (83:2) but when they have to give by measure or weight to men, give less than due. (83:3)

Those verses assert four aspects of human behavior: (1) they are impatient, that is, they discount the near future too heavily; (2) they treat potential gains and losses asymmetrically; (3) they do not follow through with their plans (to repent or otherwise); and – most surprising of all – (3) they wish to "hasten the evil." While this set of irrational dispositions of mankind may strike economists accustomed to working with models of perfectly rational agents as irrelevant, another body of research in Economics and Psychology independently reached the same conclusions under the banner of so-called discounting anomalies.

Experimental evidence of idiosyncratic human behavior

Perhaps the most comprehensive analysis of discounting anomalies to date is that of Loewenstein and Prelec.[20] They classified anomalous experimental findings on discounting of future benefits and losses into four categories and then offered a unifying model which accounts for all four anomalies. We now state the four anomalies which they consider, and show that they are in accordance with the positive behavioral assumptions we cited in the previous section:

1   *Common difference effects*: Individuals have been observed to determine their "time preference" based not only on the period of time between two choices but also on the distance between the time a choice is made and the time of the two options. For example, Thaler found that a person may prefer one apple today to two apples tomorrow, while preferring two apples in 51 days to one apple in 50.[21]

    This observation is in agreement with the behavioral implication of the Quranic verses cited previously. In the religious domain, humans are criticized for their preference to enjoy material goods immediately and postponing costly righteous deeds into the future. When young, they see the advantages of righteous deeds in their old age, but are unwilling to undertake them now, even though the rewards of righteous deeds when they are young are higher. Thus, events deferred one year in the immediate future is discounted much more heavily than ones deferred one year in the distant future. This is the common difference effect.

2   *Absolute magnitude effects*: Large benefits suffer less discounting than smaller ones. Thus, Thaler found individuals may on average be indifferent between $15 immediately and $60 in a year; and be on average indifferent between $3,000 immediately and $4,000 in a year. This result was replicated with different designs.[22]

    The verses (75:20, 21) assert: "Nay, (ye men!) but ye love the fleeting life (that which is sooner) and leave alone the hereafter." Similarly, the verse (76:27) asserts: "as to these, they love the fleeting life [the one that is sooner] and put away behind them a day (that will be) hard." The behavior depicted in these verses is consistent with high discounting for lower benefits (of this fleeting life), but low discounting for higher benefits associated with higher pursuits. Other things being equal, such behavioral distortions would make the individuals invest an excessive amount of effort to obtain material benefits as soon as possible, but delay working for the higher payoffs and pursuits to later times.

3   *Asymmetry between gains and losses*: Individuals were observed to discount losses less severely than they discounted gains. An extreme case was found in Thaler (1981), where several subjects exhibited negative discounting of losses, preferring an immediate loss to a later loss of equal value.

    This "anomaly" is in perfect agreement with Quranic assertions about irrational human behavior quoted earlier in this chapter. The verse (10:11) explicitly disparages humans for different treatment of gains and losses. The extreme form of this anomaly, where individuals prefer immediate loss to later loss of equal value corresponds to the verses which refer to "hastening the evil" and "hastening the punishment" (13:6, 27:46, 29:53, 29:54, 37:176, 38:16, 51:14). Such behavior gives rise to dynamically inconsistent behavior, which is precisely the implication that the cited verses carry. Implicit, thus, is an understanding that dynamic consistency is normatively desirable, as contrasted with the positively verifiable dynamically inconsistent behavior.

4   *Asymmetry of delays and speedups*: Subjects were found in Loewenstein (1988) to discount delays more heavily than they discount speedups. Thus, the compensation they demanded to accept a delay of consumption was two to four times the amount they were willing to sacrifice in order to speed up consumption over the same period.

This asymmetry appears to be similar to many preference reversals[23] where the individual demands more compensation for an object if he owns it than he is willing to pay for it if he does not. This is the behavior depicted in verse (83:3) as well as others. When an individual is in possession of an object, even the infinite "Treasures of the Mercy of God," he would "hold back for fear of spending them" (17:100). Thus, an individual will always demand more for what he holds than he truly thinks it is worth. On the other hand, when he does not possess an object, and when asked how much of what he has he is willing to exchange for the object, he will always be willing to pay less of what he has to get it. The two attitudes are opposite sides of the same coin characterized by the fear of not being sufficiently compensated for one's possessions. When applied to delays and speedups, one may interpret a delay as giving up the time value of the goods whose delivery is being delayed and speedups as obtaining that time value. Asymmetric pricing of that "time value" depending on whether one "has it" or not is yet another manifestation of preference reversals.

Dynamic inconsistency: the inability to follow one's plan

It is well-known that individuals who have this idiosyncratic behavior act in dynamically inconsistent ways. The best way to explain dynamic inconsistency is through a simple example:

> Assume that I wish to lower my cholesterol level, and thus need to eat a salad for dinner. I have to decide whether to go to a steakhouse that has a great salad on its menu, or to go to a vegetarian restaurant which serves average quality salads. Normally, I would like to go to the steakhouse, since their salads are better. However, I am afraid that once I get there, I will not be able to resist the temptation. In other words, I know that once I get to the steakhouse, I will throw caution to the wind (or postpone my good-eating days by one) and have a steak instead of following through with my plan to eat a healthy salad. In this sense, I will be "dynamically inconsistent" if I go to the steakhouse with the intent to eat a salad, but end-up eating a steak instead. However, if left to my own devices, that is precisely what I will do: (i) I will justify going to the steakhouse by the fact that it serves a better salad than the vegetarian restaurant;

(ii) once there I will not eat a salad at all, and I would in fact be better off had I gone to the vegetarian restaurant that served a mediocre salad. The solution is one of two pre-commitment mechanisms: (1) go to the vegetarian restaurant so that you do not need to deal with the temptation of a steak on the menu; or (2) take your wife with you (or if unmarried, take a strong friend) to the steakhouse to ensure that you will not be able to order the steak.

The same logic can be applied to debt financing. In fact, credit card companies thrive exactly on that type of dynamic inconsistency. They offer you a credit line as you are finishing school. Therefore, as soon as you get a job, you will spend more than your salary to buy yourself some nice furniture, a good car, etc. Your plan is to spend less out of your future paychecks to pay back those debts. However, as time progresses, you start associating with people who dress better than you, so you start borrowing even more to buy some nice suits, or to spend more on eating out at the same restaurants, etc. Then, one step after another, you continue to violate your financial plans by borrowing more and more at each step. The solution, again is to put together a pre-commitment mechanism, such as the one imposed by asset-based Islamic finance.

Concluding remarks

We have thus dispensed with the overly-simplistic and false assertions regarding Islamic finance being "interest free," denying the "time value of money," etc. Instead, we relied on solid evidence from the classical sources of Islamic jurisprudence to show that there are two fundamental differences between the Islamic asset-based financing model and its conventional counterpart: (1) The Islamic model encourages marking assets to market, including the time value of an asset (value of its usufruct as measured by interest) when the time factor is relevant; and (2) Automatic collateralization that ties the financing to a given asset, thus imposing pre-commitment and discipline on the financial firms as well as their clients. I must end this article by saying that conventional financial institutions also aim to impose the same types of constraints. Indeed, the interest rate you would pay for a six-year car loan will be different from that you will pay for a 30-year mortgage rate, since the time value of money associated with those two assets (due to their riskiness, rate of depreciation, etc.) are different. Also, the credit rating according to which a conventional financial institution will decide whether or not to provide you with financing (or the rate at which to do so) will be a function of the amount of debt you currently hold, and your creditworthiness as suggested by your previous repayment history. This should not be surprising because the "marking to market" and "asset-based collateralization" objectives inherent in Islamic Law make for good business sense, and it is only natural that conventional banks will come to similar conclusions. The main difference is that Islamic Law, as elaborated by Islamic jurists over the centuries, gives us specific means of accomplishing those good business goals, in a manner that obeys Islamic Legal Texts (the *Quran* and the *Sunna*), and that cannot easily be altered to serve the interests of any individual or group.

Notes

* El-Gamal is the Chaired Professor of Islamic Economics, Finance and Management, and Professor of Economics and Statistics, at Rice University in Houston, TX.

1 Al-Nawawi, A. *Al-Majmu'* (Egypt: Matba'at Al-Imam, n.d.).

2 This argument ignores the fact that when the borrower fails to make a profit, the lender still demands payment of the interest in full, subject to an increase and compounding if there is a delay.

3 Al-Salus, A., *Al-Iqtisad Al-Islami wa Al-Qadaya Al-Fiqhiyyah Al-Mu'asirah* (Al-Duhah: Dar Al-Thaqafah, 1998), vol. 1, p. 29.

4 Yusuf-'Ali, A. *The Meaning of the Holy Qur'an* (Brentwood, MD: Amana Corp, 1991). Unless otherwise stated, all translations of the *Quran* in this chapter are from this edition of the translation of the meaning of the *Quran*.

5 Al-Tabari, *Tafsir Al-'Imam Al-Tabari* (Beirut: Dar Al-Kutub Al-'Ilmiyyah, 1992), vol. 2, pp. 109–10.

6 Ibid.

7 Al-Jaziri, A. *Al-Fiqh 'ala Al-Madhahib Al-'Arba'a* (Cairo: Dar 'Ihya' Al-Turath Al-'Arabi, 1986) and Al-Zuhayli, W. *Al-Fiqh Al-'Islami wa 'Adillatoh* (Damascus: Dar Al-Fikr), 1997.

8 Al-Mawdudi, A. *Al-Riba* (Beirut: Mawsu'at Al-Risalah, 1979) and Al-Sadr, M. *'Iqtisaduna* (Beirut: Dar Al-Ta'aruf, 1980).

9 Accessed at Encyclopedia Britannica website www.eb.com (http://search.eb.com/cgi-bin/dictionary?va=interest).

10 Al-Misri, R. *Bay Al-Taqsit: Tahlil Fiqhi wa Iqtisadi* (Damascus: Dar Al-Qalam, 1997), pp. 39–48.

11 Al-Mawdudi, op. cit., pp. 20–1 and Al-Sadr, op. cit., p. 639.

12 Sakhr, *Mawsu'at Al-Hadith Al-Sharif* 2nd edn (Cairo: GISCO, 1995). Author's translation.

13 Ibid. Author's translation.

14 Ibn Rushd, M. *Bidayat Al-Mujtahid wa Nihayat Al-Muqtasid* (Beirut: Dar Al-Ma'rifa, 1997), vol. 3, pp. 183–4.

15 Al-Zuhayli, op. cit., vol. 5, pp. 3724–5.

16 The same text which appears in (vol. 3, pp. 183–4) (bidayat), appears verbatim in (vol. 3, pp. 258–9 (footnote on *"al-farq al-tisuna wa al-mi'ah bayna qa'idat ma yadkhulhu Riba al-fadl wa bayna qa'idat ma la yadkhulhu riba al-fadl"*)) (R24). In fact stronger economic arguments for enlarging the scope of *Riba* were made elsewhere by Al-Hasan, and Ibn Jubayr, as reported in cite (ibid.) (R31), and rejected due to disagreement with the texts permitting trading in different quantities for different genuses. In this regard, Al-Hasan's reported opinion equates the reason for prohibiting *Riba* when trading in different quantities to trading items of different value, while Ibn Jubayr went as far as requiring equality of (marginal?) utilities (*manfa'ah*) of traded goods. Those arguments are indeed juristically stronger versions of the argument of Ibn Rushd on which this paper is based, but they share the same economic logic, as discussed in this chapter.

17 Ibn Rushd, op. cit., vol. 3, p. 184. Author's translation.

18 Sakhr, op. cit., Author's translation.

19 Al-Shawkani, *Nayl Al-'Awtar* (Egypt: Al-Matba'a Al-'Uthmaniyya Al-Misriyya, n.d.), Vol. 5, p. 164.

20 Lowenstein, G. and D. Prelec, "Anomalies in Inter-temporal Choice: Evidence and an Interpretation", *The Quarterly Journal of Economics*, 107(2) (1992), 573–97.

21 Thaler, R. "Some Empirical Evidence on Dynamic Inconsistency", *Economic Letters*, VIII, (1981), 201–7.

22 Ibid.

23 Tversky, A., P. Slovic, and D. Kahneman, "The Causes of Preference Reversals," *American Economic Reviews*, 80, (1990), 204–17.

8 What is *riba*?*

Abdulkader Thomas

Introduction

In the prior chapters, we have examined *riba* from numerous points of view: linguistic, the Abrahamic revealed tradition, *fiqh*, political, and economic. Each form of analysis points to complementary conclusions about *riba* and interest being very similar, particularly when one is extending a loan of money. The two most ancient perspectives presented in the translation of the entry for *riba* in *Lisan Al Arab* and the comparative religion perspective shared by Dr Cornell make clear that from the earliest times the increase paid on a loan of money has troubled the Abrahamic faiths to the extent that specialized words were selected to embody the fact that such gains are unacceptable when taken from one human by another. As such, the ban on interest was contemplated by most societies and is found in the Hammurabic codes, Roman law, even Buddhist meditations. In both the Torah and the *Quran*, the ban is formal, with the latter text elevating the ban to a universal tenant of the highest order when without equivocation, God forbids *riba* in the 275th verse of the second chapter of the *Quran*:

> Those who devour usury will not stand except as stands one whom the evil one by his touch hath driven to madness. That is because they say: "Trade is like riba," But God hath permitted trade and forbidden riba. Those who after receiving direction from their Lord, desist, shall be pardoned for the past; their case is for God [to judge]; But those who repeat (the offense) are companions of the fire: They will abide therein [for ever].

The immediately following verses[1] further emphasize this injunction with a threat of the most serious divine retribution for those who consume interest or *riba*.

The concept expanded

Curiously, we modern Muslims have chosen to limit the translation of *riba* to a one to one correspondence with the English word *interest*. Yet, the forbidden *riba* is so much more than *interest*, that it even borders on *shirk* or the association of a partner with God. Thus, the banning of *riba*, like Islam's re-establishment of pure monotheism, is the very essence of a revolution in financial affairs.

The *Quranic* quote mentioned earlier was the fourth and final revelation relating to *riba*. Three others preceded it. Each reinforces the fact that Islam is to seek a fundamental change in the socioeconomic order within the parameters of historical revelation. For instance, the first revelation was:

> That which you give as *riba* to increase the peoples' wealth increases not with God; but that which you give in charity, seeking the goodwill of God, multiplies manifold.
>
> (30:39)

As is consistent throughout the *Quran*, an alternative with a social benefit and an eternal reward is proposed. As with the *Lisan Al Arab* entry, there is a forbidden *riba*, which yields divine sanction. And, there is a permissible *riba*, which is the divine reward for being charitable during this lifetime. This first revelation makes this clear promise but neither defines the forbidden *riba* nor the causes. Here the *Quran* emphasizes that our orientation should be towards the community as a whole. One consideration of the duality of *riba* raised in the verse is that the forbidden *riba* tends to benefit the individual over society and naturally favors those with wealth over those in poverty.

The second revelation helps to define *riba* by setting it in distinction to the practice of the Jews in Madina and the apparently limited Biblical prohibition on interest found in the Book of Deuteronomy. In this case, the *Quran* reawakens the original revealed concept and restores its broadness, for the Jews ultimately chose to forbid interest among themselves but not in their relations with non-Jews:

> And for their taking *riba* even though it was forbidden for them, and their wrongful appropriation of other peoples' property, We have prepared for those among them who reject faith a grievous punishment.
>
> (4:161)

And, the third revelation places the use of *riba* in distinction to the practice of competing societies, a thought which seems to have evaded various Egyptian governments, described the Khalil in Chapters 4 and 5, which has associated modernization solely with the adoption of all Western civic and commercial practices including the use of interest. When the Muslims prepared for the Battle of Uhud, they wished to use their resources conventionally to earn *riba* and be better funded in preparation for war. But, the revelation came:

> O' believers, take not doubled and redoubled *riba* and fear God so that you may prosper. Fear the fire which has been prepared for those who reject faith, and obey God and the Prophet so that you may receive mercy.
>
> (3:130–132)

These descriptions from the *Quran* give a clear perspective that *riba* and interest are very similar, and that the nature of *riba* makes it one of the most serious detriments to the social order, preserving wealth and reducing effort for the wealth, but putting the poor at a greater and continuous risk than the rich in financial transactions. Islam seeks to give the poor the dignity and opportunity to lift themselves up.

The linguistic notion of *riba*

The root of the word or rbw^2, as described in *Lisan Al Arab*, entails the concepts of growing, or exceeding, or self-generated expansion. In one sense, the Arabs use a derivative of *rbw* to relate to nurturing or teaching. In these acts, we humans are *khulafaa* or stewards of God's creation. Allah, most High, implants knowledge or the elements of plant and animal growth. Through our stewardship children develop the responsibility of inherent knowledge; or plants and animals grow and become economically useful.

From this base, we may draw the analogy that *rbw* applied to commerce or money is, in fact, the attribution of self propelled or intrinsic value. This means that the mere passage of time causes money to gain value. This is unlike anything else created by God the Gracious, for He gives each creation its merits, and then some efforts must be expended to arrive at a greater value. To attribute intrinsic value to money is to declare that money does not require God in order to increase its value. This borders on the elevation of money beyond its place as a medium of exchange or unit of account. Hence, those who grant money an intrinsic value are perilously close to *shirk* or idolatry in their concept of money.

Riba in the *hadith* and *fiqh*

The *Quran* does not explicitly define *riba* as one type of transaction or another. But, Allah the Great does state the contrast that "... Allah has made trade permissible and forbidden *riba*" (*Quran*, 2:275). The efforts of the *fuqaha* or judicial scholars like Sh. Zuhaili and the examples of the *hadith* allow us to determine a clear idea of what is *riba*. In this segment, we will not cover the *hadith* that deal with the punishment for engaging in *riba* or other non-defined characteristics of *riba*.

The *fuqaha* divided *riba* into two categories. The first is *riba al jahiliya* or *riba an-nasiha*. Intriguingly, the door to permitting *riba* in Egypt was opened by the creation of a distinction between these two terms. Yet, a close analysis based on the classical juridical analysis as presented by Sh. Zuhaili shows that *riba* was common prior to the revelation of The *Quran* and has always been closely analogous to modern bank interest. In this first category, the lender does not commit to any business risk and asks for an increase in amounts lent based upon the mere passage of time.

The second category is *riba al-fadl*. This type of *riba* may entail keeping a counterparty out of the market or engaging an unwilling party in trade under duress. Some scholars argue that this form of *riba* has been prohibited to make *riba al-nasi'a* less possible.[3]

Riba al-fadl

Above all others, a number of *hadith* have generally assisted us to understand *riba*. Most of these deal explicitly with *riba al-fadl* and some are repetitive. The key examples are:

> * Following the conquest of Khaybar, the Muslim soldiers exchanged gold coins for gold bullion with the departing Jews. It appeared that some soldiers took advantage of the Jews, extracting more bullion for the minted gold than the price of gold by its weight merited. The Prophet, we ask God's peace and blessings for him, explicitly insisted that the exchange be weight for weight, saying, "Gold for gold, silver for silver, wheat for wheat, barley for barley, dates for dates, salt for salt must be of equivalent weight, hand to hand. He who gives or takes more incurs *riba* – the giver and the taker are equally [implicated]." This was repeated more than once on other occasions.
>
> (Bukhari and Muslim)

This is the single most important *hadith* relating to the question of *riba al-fadl*. Three critical elements are isolated in this *hadith*: duress, character of exchange, and timing of exchange. It is buttressed in the following *hadith*:

> * The Prophet, peace be upon him, on more than one occasion stated that exchanges should be "Do not sell gold for gold, unless equivalent in weight, and do not sell amount; do not sell gold or sliver that is not present at the moment of exchange for gold or silver that is present."
>
> (Bukhari)

Foremost, the situation at Khaybar raised the problem of some of the Muslim soldiers being unfair, and the Jews uncomplaining because the victorious Muslims were armed and the Jews feeling obliged to accept what they knew to be an unfair exchange. The Prophet, God's grace is asked for him, was unequivocal in his condemnation of the idea that a stronger party might oblige, by might, a weaker party's acceptance of a clearly unfair exchange.

Second, the nature of exchange related to the fact that the Muslims did not place any true premium on minted gold, and in their normal course of business they would not expect or give a premium for minted gold. In addition, they did not add any value to this gold by minting it or working it themselves. For the Muslims, minted gold and bullion were exactly the same. Even then, Islam requires one to value the result with a proper respect for the true market value of the component items, as well as the right to profit from craftsmanship as shown in the following *hadith*:

> On the day of Khaybar, Fadalh ibn Ubayd al-Ansari bought a necklace of gold and pearls for twelve dinars. On separating the two, he found that the gold itself was to be worth more than twelve dinars. So he mentioned this to the Prophet,

peace be upon him, who replied, "It [jewelry] must not be sold until the contents have been valued separately."

(Muslim)

The Arabs and their neighbors were in the practice of using a number of other commodities as media of exchange, hence the Prophet, peace be upon him, added silver, wheat, barley, and dates to his list of items requiring equal exchange. Later day Islamic jurists would add monetary commodities of the same genus to the list if they are used by the people in the place of money. An expansion of this concept is shown in a following *hadith* with explanation.

Third, the Prophet, peace be upon him, observed that in many cases of exchange, the Arabs would seek an increase by one party in the sum to be exchanged if that party were to delay the delivery of their share of the exchange. But, the difference of time neither added value to the commodities to be exchanged nor caused undue hardship to the party accepting the delayed delivery.

> * Abu Sa'id reported that Bilal, may God be pleased with him, brought to the Prophet, peace be upon him, some good quality dates whereupon the Prophet asked him where these were from. Bilal replied, "I had some inferior dates which I exchanged for these – two measures for one." The Prophet said, "Oh no, this is exactly *riba*. Do not do so, but when you wish to buy, sell the inferior dates against something [cash] and then buy the better dates with the price you receive."
>
> (Muslim and Bukhari)

In this *hadith*, a common form of debt settlement and exploitation among the pre-Islamic Arabs is ended. Dates were used as currency; qualitative differences were not used so much as denominations but as tools to extract more value from debtors or weaker parties. At the same time, dates were a commodity for which qualitative differences had a specific value to buyers. The Prophet's advice is to end the use of dates as currency and to require the monetization of debtor and other relations. This limits the capacity for exploitation of debtors, producers of ordinary qualities who must use the better quality as currency, and limits the valuation of the date to its edible commodity characteristics.

On this point, I differ respectfully from the classical scholars and jurists who argue as seen in Chapter 3 that the *riba* definitions have a specific derived meaning for foodstuff. Rather, it seems clear from a modern perspective that foodstuff have been included solely on account of the use as monetary instruments, a factor which could cause significant societal suffering in a time of famine.

> * The Prophet, peace be upon him, repeatedly forbids the sale of live for dead animals or livestock for butchered meat.

This *hadith* further expands the concept of *riba al-fadl* to an area of common abuse in barter economies and effectively pushes for the monetization of certain transactions to assure a fair and common standard of exchange. As a related concept, the following two *hadith* demonstrate that this abuse of the market may extend into a broader breakdown of market morality:

> * Anas ibn Malik reported that the Prophet, peace be upon him, said: "Deceiving an unknowing entrant into the market is *riba.*" (On the authority of Sunan al-Bayhaqi.) And,

> * Abdallah ibn Abi Awfa reported that the Prophet, peace be upon him, said, "One who serves as an agent to bid up the price in an auction is a cursed taker of *riba.*" (Cited by Ibn Hajar al-Asqalani in his commentary on al-Bukhari Suyuti, al-Jami' al-Saghir, under the word al-najish and Kanz al-Ummal, ibid. both on the authority of Tabarani's al-Kabir).

Each of these *hadith* describes *riba al-fadl*. The fundamental orientation is to assure that people make fair and open exchanges. This focus is particularly aimed at anything that might be both a currency and a commodity. The undisclosed or unequal trade of dissimilar groups of these commodities, as well as others, offers a clear opportunity for people to cheat or harm one another, even without intending to do so. The imposition of a medium, money, allows people to establish a known market value for commodities and facilitates fairer trade. The Prophet, peace be upon him, is unmistakably pointing towards the development of a monetary economy as a more fair economy than a barter or a mixed barter/monetary economy.

Some modern scholars argue that these four *hadith* describe the attribution of an *intrinsic* value to some forms of money that is not found in modern paper money. The *hadith* appear to prevent such commodities from being dealt with in a confusing manner when used as money. In fact, the third *hadith* recited previously reinforces direction to establish a monetary economy with distinct monetary instruments.

Overall, these *hadith* discuss *riba al-fadl* with a focus on assuring that one establishes clearly one's intention and use for an item: If one is dealing in gold, then is bullion the same as a minted coin for monetary purposes? If so, then to demand an increase is to demand *riba*.

With dates, once used as currency by the Arabs, should one trade two qualities at unequal weights, or should one find a common standard for valuing the dates: If one wishes to buy dates, let one do so. If one is seeking an advantageous trade of currencies, let one cease this type of trading, as described in the *hadith*, for fear of exploiting one's counterparty and harming the public good by undermining confidence in the currency.

Confidence in the currency is a fundamental base of an Islamic economy as an interest-free economy must be what is described by modern economists as a *sound money* economy. This means that an Islamic state should gear its economy to zero or low monetary inflation and that a currency ought to be stable. The risk of the *commoditization* of a currency is that trading unrelated to commerce and of a speculative nature may prove destabilizing to the productive sectors of the economy, as well as proving harmful to the livelihood and savings of the citizens.

Credit or delay *riba*

Another set of *hadith* deals with *riba al-nasi'a*: This is the form of *riba* that is most closely known in modern transactions. Again, a limited number of *hadith* help us to understand it.

> * As San'ani quoted Ibn Sireen as saying that Uay bin Kab was lent money by Umar bin Al Khattab, may God be pleased with him, who said, "Count it." It was worth ten thousand dirhams. Then Uay brought Umar a gift of dates which were well reputed. But, Umar returned the dates. So Uay said that he would return the money as "I have no need for anything which prevented you the enjoyment of eating my dates." Umar accepted stating, "*Riba* is committed by he who wishes to increase the payment because of delay."
>
> * Ibn Abbas reported that the Prophet, peace be upon him, said, "*Riba* is verily in deferred payment."
>
> (Ahmad and Muslim)

Based upon these two *hadith*, we may determine that most forms of interest and all forms of bank interest are *ribawi*, that is containing elements of *riba*, and, hence, forbidden to the Muslim. Interest, in its most common usage, is the concept of the *time value of money*, whereby the value of money ought to increase with the mere passage of time. This is precisely the point addressed in these *hadith*.

In modern parlance, the term *interest* has been broadened by various people and authorities in the West to include dividends from shares and rents. These usages, however, are neither consistent with the historical concept of interest in the West, nor with the object of this book and the *hadith* discussed herein. "There is no *riba* in hand-to-hand [spot] transactions" (Muslim). This *hadith* generally creates the distinction between the two forms of *riba* with spot transactions assuming both market governance and subject to the rules defining *riba al-fadl*.

Riba, in its own right, is more than interest and includes considerations relating to the fundamentals of social morality, such as the delivery of contractual obligations without fraud or deceit, or the delivery of similar commodities without a mutually agreed standard like a currency. These points were discussed under the concept of *riba al-fadl*.

A number of modern Muslim scholars contend that *riba* is only the doubling or quadrupling of principal in the event of a delayed payment. Indeed, such excesses occurred in pre-Islamic Arabian history and are part of the definition of *riba*. But, in the case of Umar, may God be pleased with him, in the first *hadith* reviewed earlier in this section, there was no offer or demand to double or quadruple: There was simply an offer for an increase related to the passage of time. Hence, the term *riba* clearly applies to the concept of *simple interest*.

The classical Muslim jurists appear to agree that an increased payment for delivery of a good today but to be paid over time is permitted. In this case, the buyer enjoys the utility of the good and may even make a profitable venture from its employment. The seller, however, is at risk that the buyer will not pay or will use and damage the good prior to being able to pay. This risk merits, like the buyer's utility, compensation. This approach to an increase also denies the time value of money concept inherent in the injunctions against *riba*. Nowhere in the *Quran* or *hadith* may one deduce that the mere passage of time merits any form of compensation when relating to the lending of money. But, the lending of goods or labor does accrue the right to compensation.

Moreover, those modern scholars who define *riba* simply as excessive interest ignore two factors. The first is the opinion of the classical jurists, an opinion which was not shaped in a vacuum. The second is that in modern times, consumption lending is a big business. The lender is neither the producer nor the seller in most cases. Whether or not one uses a loan for the stated purpose, and from the first moment of the loan, interest is due and payable. The lender claims a utility for his money only because time has passed. And, this is precisely the nature of *riba al-nasi'a*.

The *hadith* provide further protection, as with *riba al-fadl*, of public morality. It is not simply the overt, and ostensibly acceptable financial contract, which creates *ribawi* risks, it is also the harmless gift, or the exercise of graft. These are described in the following two *hadith*:

> * Anas ibn Malik reported that the Prophet, peace be upon him, said: "When one of you grants a loan and the borrower offers him a dish, he should not accept it; and if the borrower offers a ride on an animal, he should not ride, unless the two of them have been previously accustomed to exchanging such favors mutually."
>
> (Sunan al-Bayhaqi)

> * Anas ibn Malik also reported that the Prophet, peace be upon him, said, "If a man extends a loan to someone he should not accept a gift."
>
> (Bukhari's Tarikh and Ibn Taymiyyah's al-Muntaqa).

Finally, Muslims and Westerners have ignored the root meaning of the word *usury*, which was simply the Latin term for *interest*.[4]

The broader implications

The revolution inherent in the attack on *riba* is broad and has policy implications beyond the personal morality issue. Governments must engage in sound money policies and be anti-inflationary. They must seek sound exchange rates. Merchants must stand to specific and high standards of disclosure. Investors may not hedge their risks at the expense of others.

In Makka at the time of the Prophet, peace be upon him, this revolution meant that the Quraysh, the dominant merchant tribe of the time, had to change their habits and share their dominant financial role. In our modern Islamic world, whether in the Arabian east or in America, interest-free or *riba*-free finance pose the same challenge.

Yet, without many Islamic financial alternatives and with so few Muslim-populated states committed to Islamic ideals, what are we to do? Our *ulema* are divided. Although some agree that we must strive for the establishment of Islamic alternatives, few are willing to advise us about how to behave until the alternatives are in place.

If we do not take interest on our money in the bank, the bank will take it. The bank may then give it in charity to causes to which we object. To this some *ulema* have said that we should take the interest but give it to charity. Thus, it may not be used against us. Nonetheless, we may still be liable for some blame should the bank engage in the *haram*, and we may not consider our gift as *zakat* or *sadaqat*. In fact, modern jurists are developing the argument that such money is not ours, and as an act of stewardship, we donate it on behalf of the unknown owner or even on behalf of God as the ultimate owner of all things created.

Conclusion

Riba is part of a broader problem of belief and behavior. Refusing to combat *riba* is akin to disbelief. Conceding the argument that money has an intrinsic value is potentially a greater act of disbelief. The American, like most Western, financial and legal systems are not inimical to the Islamic approach. Thus, our resistance to taking up the steward's or *khalifa*'s mantle and solving the problem of *riba* is unmerited.

In the numerous *hadith* that deal with *riba*, we find guidance for constructing *riba*-free financial and commercial relationships. These *hadith* may be distilled to encourage us to consider the following points as definitions of *riba*-free financial transactions:

* Either a product or a service must be delivered.
* In order for a party to profit, it must commit to a true commercial or financial risk. In other words, there must be a bonafide transaction and one must be prepared to accept a loss as well as a profit.
* The parties must have a verbal or written contract that is clearly defined.
* The parties must deal in an open market, with fair information. No party should seek to deceive or defraud the other, even without the intention to harm.
* The profit must not be from the *haram*, businesses and actions that are explicitly for bidden in Islam.

These are simple tests for determining if one engages in *ribawi* contracts. As we have seen in the first four chapters, *riba* is clearly identifiable. Yet, as Chapter 5 demonstrates there is always someone who is willing to raise obstacles to understanding what is the forbidden *riba* and why we should not keep under its remit some commercial transactions. They do so ignoring the social ills raised by Dr Chapra in Chapter 6 and the divine wisdom pointed out by Dr El-Gamal in Chapter 7.

Notes

* This is adapted from an essay by the editor which originally appeared in *The Muslim Journal* and was previously modified for inclusion in *What is Permissible Now*.
1 This was the fourth of four revelations on the subject. It continues:

> God deprives interest of all blessing but blesses charity; He loves not the ungrateful sinner (276). Those who believe, perform good deeds, establish prayer and pay the

zakat, their reward is with their Lord; neither should they have any fear, nor shall they grieve (277). O'believers, fear God, and give up the interest that remains outstanding if you are believers (278). If you do not do so, then be sure of being at war with God and His Messenger. But, if you repent, you can have your principal. Neither should you commit injustice nor should you be subjected to it (279). If the debtor is in difficulty, let him have respite until it is easier, but if you forego out of charity, it is better for you if you realize (280). And fear the Day when you shall be returned to the Lord and every soul shall be paid in full what it has earned and no one shall be wronged (281).

2 Please see *Lisan Al-Arab* for the Arabic and Quranic definition of *riba*.
3 *Ibn al-Qayyim, Alam al-Muwaqqiin* (Cairo: Maktabah al-Kulliyyat al-Azhariyyah, 1968), vol. 2, pp. 154–5. This reference was originally taken from *Towards a Just Monetary System*.
4 The Latin word *usury* means simple interest. In modern English it is now means exorbitant interest, with no definition was what is too high. The Oxford English Dictionary (Oxford: Oxford University Press, 1971), vol. 1 A–O, p. 394.

Appendix

The challenges in Pakistan*

M. Akram Khan and Abdulkader Thomas

Introduction

Through three constitutions, as well as the pre-constitutional Objectives Resolution of 1949, Pakistan has sought to eliminate *riba* from its economy. This has brought vociferous debate between members of Pakistan's religious scholars and its industrial and landed elites. One would have thought that the November 23, 1999 *Sharia'a* Appellate Bench of the Supreme Court of Pakistan announcement of a historical judgment, disposing off a number of appeals against the Federal *Sharia'a* Court Judgment on *Riba* of November 1991 would have brought the matter to its end. The Appellate Court endorsed the judgment of the Federal *Sharia'a* Court and declared that all types of interest fall in the purview of the *Quranic* prohibition of *Riba*. At the same time, the Appellate Court gave a deadline of June 30, 2001 to the government of Pakistan for enforcing a law to prohibit all transactions involving interest and also to introduce an alternative system of Islamic finance.[1] The government expressed its intention to comply with the court's order. Despite what appeared to be the necessary preparatory work, interest remains entrenched in the economy well after the June 30, 2001 deadline.

What are the concerns

Subsequent to the 1999 ruling, government officials have worried about whether or not it is possible to achieve a smooth transition to an Islamic financial system. The government set up a commission for the transformation of the economy on Islamic lines. Reportedly, the commission has submitted its interim report. Besides, a number of subcommittees in the Ministries of law, religious affairs, and finance have made their contributions to the development of an alternative system based on Islamic principles. At present, a high-powered Task Force headed by the Minister for Finance is fine-tuning the proposal that may be put in practice from July 2001.

The government's permanent *Commission for the Islamization of the Economy* has a primary mandate to study how to eliminate interest from the economy and published its recommendations in 1991. But, the Commission has suffered limitations. All of its members including the chairman are working full-time jobs. For example, the chairman is the Minister for Religious Affairs, which is a large ministry within the federal government. Similarly, other members are busy in their respective jobs and attend the meetings of the Commission on request. Thus, the mechanism to bring such an enormous change is at best a part-time institution. Of course, the Commission has a secretariat, but it provides secretarial support and is not responsible for any actual policy formulation. Thus, moving from published recommendations to implementation has been a significant challenge to the Commission.

The elimination of interest from the economy is not wholly a legal process. Even when a law was passed to abolish it, interest would not wither away. Economic compulsions would sustain it, even though as a black-market phenomenon. The abolition of interest requires economic conditions that would make interest redundant, meaning that it would not be in the self-interest of the people to deal in interest. Interest-based transactions should be more unattractive when compared to equity-based transactions. Such a market-based solution requires political will. Despite the existence of the Commission and the decisions of the *Sharia'a* courts, the government has not, since the time of Zia ul Haq, made any clear and unequivocal statement of its intentions of introducing and supporting the process of Islamization of the economy and elimination of interest.

The debate on *riba* and interest

Since the establishment of Pakistan as a Muslim homeland in 1947, as a result of partition of the Indian subcontinent, the *ulema* has raised a demand for transforming Pakistan into a modern Islamic state. Naturally, such a demand would present the most awkward situation in a country where the financial institutions were being run on the basis of interest. Those members of society who most benefited from the existing interest-based infrastructure, westernized secular elites and many feudal landowners, resisted any change in the financial system. Nonetheless, the popular demand was that since interest was prohibited by the *Sharia'a*, the financial institutions should be reformed and based on some interest-free basis.

The early thinking was quite rudimentary and those who raised this slogan were not quite sure about the alternative basis of interest. However, they invoked two types of response. First, a sizeable number of people in Pakistan and other Islamic countries accepted their position and started thinking and suggesting alternative models of interest-free banks (as they were called in those days).

The second response came from the western-educated modernist elite. They feared that the demand for creating an Islamic order may take society back to the seventh century. The latter group had the vision of making progress and keeping with the latest trends in the West. At the same time, they had a sincere affiliation with Islam's broader vision of life. They adopted a different route in discussing the prohibition of *riba*. They argued that the *Quran* prohibited *riba*, which most probably, related to usury on consumption loans taken by the poor and the indigent. The main plank of their argument was that this type of *riba* should, of course, be prohibited as had been done in the developed countries. However, the interest on commercial loans should remain intact, as it was neither unjust nor usurious. Instead, it helped in the development of trade and industry. This line of argument was led by such eminent scholars as Fazalur Rahman, Jafar Shah Phulwarwi, and Abdullah Yusuf Ali, in Pakistan (like Muhammad Abduh and Rashid Rida in Egypt). While these scholars were arguing their case on these lines, scholars of the more conservative view continued with their intellectual effort.

The strength of the feudal landowners and their frequent allies in government, the western-oriented elite, meant that the Government of Pakistan made no efforts to accelerate the adoption of Islamic economic principles through the government of Zulfiqar Ali Bhutto. This resistance had parallels that played out in the 1975 formation of the Islamic Development Bank (IDB). This multi-state body was meant to be variously a development bank and a central bank to the Islamic states like the Bank for International Settlements, but it was also intended to operate on a basis other than interest. During the IDB's formative debates, proponents of interest worked to assure that the IDB would not be effective in promoting interest-free banking.

Just as the IDB enjoyed considerable support from Pakistan, so did the First International Conference on Islamic Economics in Makka in 1976. This meeting of several hundred Muslim scholars and economists unequivocally declared that interest and *riba* were one and the same. This latter development was an important underpinning to the first steps that were to be taken when Pakistan came under the leadership of the late military ruler, Zia ul Haq. In 1980, the Council of Islamic Ideology issued its report seeking the elimination of *riba*. This was followed the next year by a formal mandate which was given to implement interest-free banking on the basis of profit-and-loss sharing. Then, on July 1, 1985, a decree was made that all Pakistan Rupee transactions were to be interest free, but foreign banks would be exempted. To many, this exemption was evidence of the opposition of the international bankers and Pakistan's trade partners. With such strong objections from key financial supporters of the impoverished state, the primary beneficiaries of trade and international transfers would and did fail to support the implementation of interest-free banking. Surprisingly, the various efforts to Islamicize the economy in the 1980s did not include the government sector and its domestic and international debt issuances.[2] Following General Zia's death, Benazir Bhutto came to power in 1989, and the movement for an Islamic economy stalled.

After successfully arguing that interest and *riba* are the same, the religious lobby adopted a legal course of action. They approached the Federal *Sharia'a* Court of Pakistan[3] requesting it to issue an injunction against interest and to oblige the government of Pakistan for restructuring the entire financial system of the country on some alternative basis. At the same time, the Council of Islamic Ideology undertook a detailed exercise in studying all laws of Pakistan, clause by clause, and pointed out the sections or parts that should be deleted or modified, because they contained some reference to interest. The government of Nawaz Sharif, knuckling under the pressure of the religious lobby, appointed a committee headed by Raja Zafarul Haq for proposing changes in the financial system of the country. The main plank of that committee's report (although not made public) was that the government should pass a law prohibiting interest. In fact, the committee also proposed a draft of the law in its report. Nonetheless, the government was reluctant to adopt the report's recommendations and filed an appeal in the Appellate Bench of the Supreme Court of Pakistan in November 1991 to stay an order of the *Sharia'a* Court's judgment on the prohibition of *riba*.

Following the landmark November 23, 1999 decision, a second commission was formed – the Commission to Transform the Financial System. This was to report back to the public in October 2000 and again in May 2001 with a final report in August 2001. Although constructive proposals were made, no concrete steps were taken to formally implement the interest-free banking system. Faced with a June 2001 deadline and significant pressure from the religious lobby, the Musharraf government has shown limited interest and may lack, given the current international political situation, capacity to implement the recommendations of the Commission.

Conclusion

The problem in Pakistan is the inverse of Egypt. Instead of strong objections by the government and manipulation of the *Sharia'a* scholars as in Egypt, Pakistan has seen ineffective implementation by the government in the face of strong opposition from the moneyed classes. As noted by many analysts, there have been procedural gestures without any adoption of the spirit of *riba*-free finance in the case of Pakistan.[4] Without political resolve, enhanced public support (especially among the moneyed classes), and better knowledge sharing and a legal framework, many proponents of interest-free banking in Pakistan fear that the system will not be transformed.[5] Better still, the real challenge for Pakistan and other countries is to adopt such economic policies and treading on such economic path that would gradually make interest unnecessary without legally making it so.

Notes

* This Appendix is adapted from two articles by Mr Khan in the Renaissance Magazine *Is the Elimination of Riba from the Economy a Legal Issue?* and *Elimination of Interest: A Proposed Strategy* (December 2001 and January 2002) and one in New Horizons July 1995, and supplemental research by Mr Thomas and special thanks to Professor Shujaat Ali Khan for comments on the historical context in Pakistan.

1 Khan, Waqar Masood, *Transition to a Riba Free Economy* (Islamabad: the International Institute of Islamic Thought, 2002), pp. 72 and 74. The Court struck down some, but not all laws governing interest, leaving a number of matters open to further interpretation.

2 Ibid., p. 46.

3 Ibid., p. 71. According to Waqar Masood Khan, the *Sharia'a* courts have limited competence to examine provisions of the constitution, which protects federal borrowing powers.

4 Khan, Rakhsana and Suleman Aziz Lodhi, *Impediments in Interest Free Banking in Pakistan* presented at the Conference on Islamic Wealth Creation at Durham University, July 2003.

5 Ibid.

Bibliography

Abu Yusuf, Yaqub ibn Ibrahim (d. 182/798), *Kitab al-Kharaj* (Cairo: al-Matbaah al-Salafiyyah, 2nd edn, 1352 AH).

Ahmad, Ziauddin, Khan, M. Fahim and Iqbal, Munawar (eds), "The Qur'anic Theory of Riba," *Islamic Quarterly* (London) (January/June 1978), pp. 3–14.

——, *Money and Banking in Islam* (Jeddah: International Center for Research in Islamic Economics, King Abdul Aziz University, 1983).

Al-Ahram, Cairo, September 8, 1989, pp. 1, 13.

——, Cairo, September 21, 1989, pp. 1, 7.

——, Cairo, September 22, 1989, pp. 13.

——, Cairo, September 27, 1989, p. 7.

——, Cairo, September 28, 1989, pp. 5, 7.

——, Cairo, September 29, 1989, p. 13.

——, Cairo, October 1, 1989, p. 7.

——, Cairo, October 3, 1989, pp. 7, 9.

——, Cairo, October 6, 1989, p. 13.

——, Cairo, October 25, 1989, p. 7.

——, Cairo, November 2, 1989, p. 7.

——, Cairo, November 9, 1989, p. 7.

Ali, Yusuf, a., *The Meaning of the Holy Qur'an* (Brentwood, MD: Amana Corp., various).

Altman, I., "Islamic Legislation in Egypt in the 1970's," *African and Asian Studies*, 13 (1979), pp. 209–12.

Anderson, J.N.D., "The Sharia'a and Civil Law (The Debt Owed by the New Civil Codes of Egypt and Syria to the Sharia'a)," *Islamic Quarterly*, 1(29) (1954), p. 85.

——, *Islamic Law in the Modern World* (New York: New York University Press, 1959).

——, *Law Reform in the Muslim World* (London: Athalone Press, 1976).

Ibn Aws, Shaddad, *Kitab al-Sayd wa al-Dhaba'ih, Bab al-amr bi Ihsan*, vol. 3, *Sahih Muslim* (n.p.).

Badawi, I.Z., "Nazariyyat al-Riba al-Muharram," *Majallat al-Oanun wal Iqtisad* (Cairo, 1939), pp. 387–446, 533–66.

——, *Nazariyyat al-Riba al-Muharram* (Cairo: Al-Majles al-A'la li-Ri'yat al-Funun, 1964).

Ballantyne, W.M., *Commercial Law in the Arab Middle East: The Gulf States* (London: Lloyds of London Press, 1986).

——, "The Second Coulson Memorial Lecture: Back to the Sharia'a," *Arab Law Quarterly*, 3(4) (November 1988), pp. 317–28.

Bank for International Settlements, Press Release of October 19, 1998.

——, *Annual Reports*.

Baron, Salo W., "The Economic Views of Maimonides," in Salo W. Baron (ed.), *Essays On Maimonides* (New York: Columbia University Press, 1941).

Al-Bayhaqi, *Sayyidah A'ishah in Shuab al-Iman*, vol. 4 (n.p.).

Bigsten, Arne, "Poverty, Inequality and Development," in Norman Gemmell (ed.), *Surveys in Development Economics* (Oxford: Blackwell, 1987).

Bokare, M.G., *Hindu-Economics: Eternal Economic Order* (New Delhi: Janaki Prakashan, 1993).

Chapra, M. Umer, *Towards a Just Monetary System* (Leicester: The Islamic Foundation, 1985).

——, "Islam and the International Debt Problem," *Journal of Islamic Studies* (July 1992a), pp. 214–32.

——, *Islam and the Economic Challenge* (Leicester: The Islamic Foundation, 1992b).

——, *Islam and Economic Development* (Leicester: The Islamic Foundation, 1993).

——, "Monetary Management in an Islamic Economy," *Islamic Economic Studies*, 3 (Jeddah: IRTI/IDB) (December 1996), pp. 1–34.

——, *Future of Economics: An Islamic Perspective* (Leicester: The Islamic Foundation, 2000), pp. 5–20.

——, "Why has Islam Prohibited Interest?" *Review of Islamic Economics*, 9 (May, 2000).

Christ, Carl, "On Fiscal and Monetary Policies and the Government Budget Restraint," *American Economic Review*, 69 (1979), pp. 526–38.

Cohen, Abraham (ed.), *The Soncino Chumash* (London: The Soncino Press, 1956).

Coulson, Noel, J., *Conflicts and Tensions in Islamic Jurisprudence* (Chicago, IL: University of Chicago Press, 1969).

——, *Commercial Law in the Gulf States* (London: Graham & Trotman, 1984).

Crockett, Andrew, "Address at the 24th International Management Symposium in St. Galen on June 1, 1994," *BIS Review* (June 22, 1994).

Ibn Daqiq al-'Id, *al-Ilman bi ahadlth al-ahkamn* (Damascus: Dar Al-Fikr, n.d.).

Delorenzo, Yusuf, *Shariah Boards and Modern Islamic Finance: From the Jurisprudence of Revival and Recovery to the Jurisprudence of Transformation and Adaptation* presented at the conference of the Islamic Financial Services Board at London, May 2004.

Al-Durr al-mukhtar, vol. 4 (n.p.).

The Economist, July 12, 1997, p. 42.

Edge, Ian D., "Comparative Commercial Law of Egypt and the Arabian Gulf," *Cleveland State Law Review*, 34 (1985–86), pp. 129–44.

Encyclopedia Judaica, vol. 16 (Jerusalem: The Macmillan Company, 1906).

Fatawa al-Imam Muhammad Rashid Rida, vol. 11 (Beirut: Dar al-Kitab al-jadid, 1970).

Al-Furuq, Al-Qarafi, vol. 3 (n.p.).

El-Gamal, M., "The Survival of Islamic Banking: A Micro-Evolutionary Perspective," *Islamic Economic Studies*, 5 (1,2) (1998), pp. 1–19.

El-Gamal, M. (tr.) and Wahba Al-Zuhayli, *Financial Transactions in Islamic Jurisprudence* (Damascus: Dar Al Fikr, 2003).

Al-Garida al-Rasmiyya (Egypt), vol. 20, May 16, 1985, pp. 992–1000.

——, vol. 25, June 20, 1987, pp. 2071–5.

Ghiyat al Muntaha, vol. 2 (n.p.).

Gilchrist, J., *The Church and Economic Activity in the Middle Ages* (London: Macmillan and Co., 1969).

Government of Pakistan, *Economic Survey, 1997–98*.

Greenspan, Alan, *Federal Reserve Bulletin* (October 1998), p. 1046.

Habachy, Saba, "Supreme Constitutional Court (Egypt) – Sharia'a and Riba: Decision in Case No. 20 of Judicial Year No.1," *Arab Law Quarterly*, 1(1) (November 1985), pp. 100–7.

——, "Commentary on the Decision of the Supreme Court of Egypt Given on May 4 1985 Concerning the Legitimacy of Interest and the Constitutionality of Article 226 of the New Egyptian Civil Code of 1948," *Arab Law Quarterly*, 1(2) (February 1986), pp. 239–41.

Haq, Mahbubul, Inge Kaul, and Isabelle Grunberg (eds), *The Tobin Tax: Coping with Financial Volatility* (Oxford: Oxford University Press, 1996).

Hashiyat al-Dasuqi, vol. 3 (n.p.).

Hashiyat al-Qalyabi wa 'umayra, vol. 2 (n.p.).

Hashiyat al-Sharqawi, vol. 2 (n.p.).

Al-Hattab, *Mawahib Al-Jalil* (n.p.).

Al-Haythami, *Majma' Al-Zawa'id* (Egypt: Maktabat Al-Qudsi, n.d.).

Ibn Hazm, *Al-Muhalla bi-l'athar* (Egypt: Matba'at Al-Imam, n.d.).

Hicks, John, "Limited Liability: The Pros and Cons," in Tony Orhnial (ed.), *Limited Liability and the Corporation* (London: Croom Helm, 1982).

Hill, Enid, *Mahkamah, Studies in the Egyptian Legal System* (London: Ithaca, 1979).

——, "Al Sanhuri and Islamic Law: the Place and Significance of Islamic Law in the Life and Work of 'Abd al-Razzaq Ahmad al-Sanhuri' Egyptian Jurist and Scholar 1895–1971," *Arab Law Quarterly*, 3(1) (February 1988), pp. 33–64, and 3(2) (May 1988), pp. 182–218.

Ibn Al-Humam, *Fath Al-Qadir, Sharh Al-Hidaya* (Cairo: Mataba'at Mustafa Muhammad, n.d.).

International Monetary Fund, *Government Finance Statistics, 1998*.

——, *World Economic Outlook*, May 1995 and May 1998.

——, *International Financial Statistics, 1998 Yearbook*, and also monthly issues.

——, *International Financial Statistics*, CD-ROM and November 1998.

Iqbal, Munawar (ed.), *Distributive Justice and Need Fulfilment in an Islamic Economy* (Leicester: The Islamic Foundation, 1988).

Jami' al-'Usul, vol. 1 (n.p.).

Al-Jaziri, A., *Al-Fiqh 'ala Al-Madhahib Al-'Arba'a* (Cairo: Dar 'Ihya' Al-Turath Al-'Arabi, 1986).

Johns, C.H.W., John Dow, W.H. Bennett, and J. Abelson, "Usury," *Encyclopedia of Religion and Ethics*, vol. 12 (New York: Charles Scribner's Sons, n.d.), pp. 548–58.

Jones, Alexander (ed.), *The Jerusalem Bible* (New York: Bantam Double Dell Publishing Group, Inc., 1968).

Ibn Juzayy, *Al-Qawanin Al-Fiqhiyyah* (Fes: Matba 'at Al-Nahdah, n.d.).

Kahneman, D. and A. Tversky, "Prospect Theory: An Analysis of Decision under Risk," *Econometrica* 47(2) (1979), pp. 263–92.

Karsten, Ingo, "Islam and Financial Intermediation," IMF *Staff Papers* (March 1982), pp. 108–42.

Al-Kasani, *Bada'l Al-Sana'i* (n.p.).

Kathir, Ibn, *Tafsir*, vol. 1 (n.p.).

Ibn Khaldun, Abd al-Rahman, *Muqaddimah* (Cairo: Al-Maktabah al-Tijariyah al-Kubra, n.d.).

Khan, M.S.A., "Mohammedan Laws Against Usury and How They Are Evaded," *Journal of Comparative Legislation, 3rd series*, 11 (November 1929), pp. 23–4.

——, *Elimination of Interest: A Proposed Strategy* (London: New Horizons, July 1995), accessed online on December 28, 2004.

——, *Is the Elimination of Riba from the Economy a Legal Issue?* (Renaissance Magazine, December 2001 and January 2002) (London: New Horizons, July 1995), accessed online on December 28, 2004.

Khan, Rakhsana and Suleman Aziz Lodhi, *Impediments in Interest Free Banking in Pakistan* presented at the Conference on Islamic Wealth Creation at Durham University, July 2003.

Khan, Waqar Masood, *Transition to a Riba Free Economy* (Islamabad: The International Institute of Islamic Thought, 2002).

Al-Khatib Al-Shirbini, *Mughni Al-Muhtaj* (Egypt: Matba'at Al-Babi Al-Halabi, n.d.).

Kocherlakota, Narayana R., "The Equity Puzzle: It's Still a Puzzle," *The Journal of Economic Literature* (March 1996), pp. 42–71.

Lowenstein, G., "Frames of Mind in Inter-temporal Choice," *Management Science*, XXXIV (1988), pp. 200–14.

Lowenstein, G. and D. Prelec, "Anomalies in Inter-temporal Choice: Evidence and an Interpretation," *The Quarterly Journal of Economics*, 107(2) (1992), pp. 573–97.

Madbatat Maglis al-Sha'b, Session 70 (1982), pp. 32–41.

Mallat, Chibli (ed.), *Islamic Law and Finance* (London: Graham & Trotman, 1988).

Al-Manar, "Asilah wa Fatawa," December 5, 1903, vol. 6, p. 717.

—— , "Sanduq al-Tawfir fi Idarat al-Barid," March 18, 1904, vol. 7, pp. 28–9.

—— , "Ayat al-Riba," May 24, 1906, vol. 9, pp. 332–56.

—— , "Ribh Sunduq al-Tawfir," February 22, 1917, vol. 19, pp. 527–8.

Mankiw, Gregory, David Romer, and David Weil, "A Contribution to the Empirics of Economic Growth," *Quarterly Journal of Economics* (May 1992), pp. 407–37.

Mawardi, Abu al-Hasan Ali, al- (d. 450/1058), *Adab al-Dunya wa al-Din*, Al-Saqqa, Mustafa, (ed.) (Cairo: Mustafa al-Babi al-Halabi, 1955).

Al-Mawdudi, A., *Al-Riba* (Beirut: Mawsu'at Al-Risalah, 1979).

Mayer, Ann Elizabeth, "The Regulation of Interest Charges and Risk Contracts: Some Problems of Recent Libyan Legislation," *International and Comparative Law Quarterly*, 28 (October 1979), pp. 541–59.

Melitz, Jacques and Donald Winch (eds), *Religious Thought and Economic Society* (Durham, NC: Duke University Press, 1978).

Al-Misri, R., *Bay Al-Taqsit: Tahlil Fiqhi wa Iqtisadi* (Damascus: Dar Al-Qalam, 1997).

Moore, P., *Islamic Finance: a Partnership for Growth* (London: Euromoney and Abrar Group International, 1997).

Morgan Guaranty Trust Company of New York, *World Financial Markets* (New York: Morgan Guaranty Trust Company of New York, January 1987).

Muhammad, Mustafa, ed., *Al-Muwafaqat of Shatibi*, vol. 4 (n.p.).

Mukarram, Imam Abi Fadl Jamaluddin Muhammad bin, *Lisan Al Arab* (Beirut: Dar Saadr, n.d.), p. 304.

Mukhtasar al-tahawi (n.p.).

Al Muntaqa 'ala al-Muwatta, vol. 4 (n.p.).

Nasb Al Raya, vol. 4 (n.p.).

Al-Nawawi, A., *Al-Majmu'* (Egypt: Matba'at Al-Imam, n.d.).

Nelson, Benjamin, *The Idea of Usury* (Chicago, IL: University of Chicago Press, 1969).

Neusner, Jacob (tr.), *The Mishnah: A New Translation* (New Haven, CT and London: Yale University Press, 1989).

Noonan, John, T. Jr, *The Scholastic Analysis of Usury* (Cambridge, MA: Harvard University Press, 1957).

October (Egypt), December 24, 1989.

Organization for Economic Cooperation and Development, *Economic Outlook*, December 1991 and June 1998.

The Oxford English Dictionary, vol. 1 A–O (Oxford: Oxford University Press, 1971), p. 394.

Peters, Rudolph, "Divine Law or Man-Made Law? Egypt and the Application of Sharia'a," *Arab Law Quarterly*, 3(3) (August 1988), pp. 232–53.

Plender, John, "Western Crony Capitalism," *Financial Times* (3–4 October 1998).

Poterba, James, M. (ed.), *Public Policies and Household Saving* (Chicago, IL: University of Chicago Press, 1994).

Presley, J.R. and J.G. Sessions, "Islamic Economics: the Emergence of a New Paradigm," *The Economic Journal* (May 1994), pp. 584–96.

Al-Qalyubi, *Sharh Al-Jalal Al-Muhalla Lelmenhaj* (Egypt: Matba'at Subih, n.d.).

Al-Qarafi, *Al-Furuq* (Beirut: Alam Al-Kutub, n.d.).

Al-Qawanin (n.p.).

Ibn al-Qayyim, *Alam al-Muwaqqiin*, vol. 2 (Cairo: Maktabah al-Kulliyyat al-Azhariyyah, 1968).

——, *Al-Qiyas* (n.p.).

Ibn Qudamah, *Al-Mughni* (Beirut: Dar Al-Kutub Al-Ilmiyyah, n.d.).

Qureshi, Anwar Iqbal., *Islam and the Theory of Interest* (Lahore: Ashraf, 1974).

Radd al-Muhtar, vol. 4 (n.p.).

Rahman, Fazlur., "Riba and Interest," *Islamic Studies* (Karachi) 3(1) (March 1961), 1–43.

Al-Ramli, *Nihayat Al-Muhtaj* (Egypt: Al-Matba'at Al-Bhiyyah, n.d.).

"The Risk Business," *The Economist* (October 17, 1998), pp. 21–2.

Ibn Rushd, M., *Bidayat Al-Mujtahid wa Nihayat Al-Muqtasid* (Beirut: Dar Al-Ma'rifa, 1997).

Ibn Rushd Al-Qurtubi, *Al-Muqaddimat Al-Mumahhidat* (Beirut: Matba'at Al-Sa'adah, n.d.).

Al-Sadr, M., *'Iqtisaduna* (Beirut: Dar Al-Ta'aruf, 1980).

Sahih Muslim, Kitab al-Birr wa al-Silah wa al-Adab, Bab Tahrim al-Zulm, vol. 4 (1955), p. 1996:56.

Sakhr, *Mawsu'at Al-Hadith Al-Sharif* (Cairo: GISCO, 2nd edn, 1995).

Saleh, Nabil, A., *Unlawful Gain and Legitimate Profit in Islamic Law* (Cambridge: Cambridge University Press, 1986).

Al-Salus, A., *Al-Iqtisad Al-Islami wa Al-Qadaya Al-Fiqhiyyah Al-Mu'asirah* (Al-Duhah: Dar Al-Thaqafah, 1998).

Al-Sana'ani, *Subul Al-Salam* (n.p.).

Al-Sanhuri, Abd Al-Razzaq Ahmad., *Masadir Al-Haqq fil-Fiqh al-Islami*, 6 parts in 2 volumes, Part 3 (Egypt: n.d.).

Al-Sarakshi, *Al-Mabsut* (Beirut: Matba'at Al Sa'adah, 1st edn, n.d.).

Schacht, Joseph, "Islamic Law in Contemporary States," *American Journal of Comparative Law*, 8 (Spring 1959), pp. 133–47.

——, "Riba," *First Encyclopaedia of Islam* (Leiden: E.J. Brill, 1987).

Searth, Wan, "Bond Financed Fiscal Policy and the Problem of Instrument Instability," *Journal of Macroeconomics* (1979), pp. 107–17.

Sharia'a Courts' Ordinance (*La'ihat al-Mahakirn al-Shar'iyya*).

Al-Sharif, Muhammad Abd al-Ghaffar, Dr, *The Shariah Supervision of Islamic Banks*, paper presented at the First Conference of Shariah Supervisory Boards for Islamic Financial Institutions, organized by AAOIFI in Bahrain, October, 2001.

Al-Shawkani, *Nayl Al-'Awtar* (Egypt: Al-Matba'a Al-'Uthmaniyya Al-Misriyya, n.d.).

Al-Shirazi, Abu Ishaq, *Al-Muhadhdhab* (Egypt: matba'at Al-Babi Al-Halabi, n.d.).

Siegel, Jeremy, J. and Richard H. Thaler, "Anomalies: The Equity Premium Puzzle," *Journal of Economic Perspectives* (Winter 1997), pp. 191–200.

State Bank of Pakistan, *State Bank Bulletin*.

Subki, ed., *Takmilat al-Majmu'*, vol. 10 (n.p.).

Suhaibani, M.I., *Athar al-Zakat ala Tashghil al-Mawarid al-Iqtisadiyyah* [Effect of *Zakat* on the Employment of Economic Resources] (Riyadh: al-Ubaykan, 1990).

Al-Suyuti, *Tanwir Al-Hawalik, Sharh Muwatta Malik* (Cairo: Matba'at Al-Halabi, n.d.).

Al-Tabari, *Tafsir Al-'Imam Al-Tabari* (Beirut: Dar Al-Kutub Al-'Ilmiyyah, 1992).

Takhriq al-furu' 'ala al-usul (n.p.).

Al-Talkhis al-habir (n.p.).

Ibn Taymiyyah (d. 728/1327), *Majmu Fatawa Shaykh al-Islam Ahmad ibn Taymiyyah*, Abd al-Rahman al-Asimi (ed.) (Riyadh: Matabi al-Riyadh, 1st edn, 1381–83/1961–63).

——, *Al-Hisbah fi al-Islam*, Abd al-Aziz Rabah (ed.) (Damascus: Maktabah Dar al-Bayan, 1967). In English: Mukhtar Holland and Ibn Taymiyyah (tr.), *Public Duties in Islam: The Institution of the Hisba* (Leicester: The Islamic Foundation, 1982).

——, *Minhaj al-Sunnah al-Nabawiyyah*, M. Rashad Salim (ed.) (Riyadh: Imam Muhammad Islamic University, 1986).

Thaler, R., "Some Empirical Evidence on Dynamic Inconsistency," *Economic Letters*, VIII (1981), pp. 201–7.

Thomas, Abdulkader and Nathif J. Adam, *Islamic Bonds: Your Guide to Issuing, Structuring and Investing in Sukuk* (London: Euromoney Books, 2004).

Thomas, Abdulkader and Virginia Morris, *Guide to Understanding Islamic Home Finance* (New York: Lightbulb Press, 2002).

Thurow, Lester, *Zero-Sum Society* (New York: Basic Books, 1980).

Tversky, A., P. Slovic, and D. Kahneman, "The Causes of Preference Reversals," *American Economic Reviews*, 80 (1990), pp. 204–17.

Al Umm, vol. 3 (n.p.).

Viner, Jacob, *Religious Thought and Economic Society*, Jacques Melitz and Donald Winch (eds) (Durham, NC: Duke University Press), p. 35.

World Bank, *Policy and Research Bulletin*, April–June, 1998.

Zarqa, F., *al-Madkhal al-Fiqhi* (n.p.).

Zarqa, M. Anas, "Capital Allocation, Efficiency and Growth in an Interest-Free Islamic Economy," *Journal of Economics and Administration* (Jeddah, Saudi Arabia) (November 1982), pp. 43–55.

Al-Zayla'i, Al-Hafiz, *Nasb Al-Rayah fi Takhrij ahadith al-hidayah* (n.p.).

Zipperstein, Edward, *Business Ethics in Jewish Law* (New York: Ktav Publishing House Inc., 1983).

Zuhayli, Wahba, *Al-Fiqh al-Islami wa Adillatuhu*, vol. 4 (Damascus: Dar Al-Fikr, 1st edn, 1404/1984).

——, *Al-Fiqh Al-Islami wa Adillatuhu* (Damascus: Dar Al-Fikr, 1997).

Index